Girls
Without Limits

Second Edition

D1558921

Dedication

Patricia F. R. Cunningham II, PhD, aka "Dr. Patty"

1979–2017

You were a warrior for equity and justice and worked tirelessly on behalf of the forgotten and marginalized. Thank you for supporting me, inspiring me, and continually reminding me that service is indeed the rent we pay for living. I promise to continue your legacy. I miss you.

Girls
Without Limits

Helping Girls Succeed in Relationships, Academics, Careers, and Life

Second Edition

Lisa Hinkelman

FOR INFORMATION:

Corwin
A SAGE Company
2455 Teller Road
Thousand Oaks, California 91320
(800) 233-9936
www.corwin.com

SAGE Publications Ltd.
1 Oliver's Yard
55 City Road
London, EC1Y 1SP
United Kingdom

SAGE Publications India Pvt. Ltd.
B 1/I 1 Mohan Cooperative Industrial Area
Mathura Road, New Delhi 110 044
India

SAGE Publications Asia-Pacific Pte. Ltd.
18 Cross Street #10-10/11/12
China Square Central
Singapore 048423

Publisher: Jessica Allan
Senior Content Development
   Editor: Lucas Schleicher
Associate Content Development
   Editor: Mia Rodriguez, Sharon Wu
Production Editor: Megha Negi
Copy Editor: Shamila Swamy, QuADS
   Prepress Pvt. Ltd
Typesetter: Hurix Digital
Proofreader: Jeff Bryant
Indexer: Integra
Cover Designer: Janet Kiesel
Marketing Manager: Maura Sullivan

Printed in the United States of America

Library of Congress Cataloging-in-Publication Data

Names: Hinkelman, Lisa, author.

Title: Girls without limits : helping girls succeed in relationships, academics, careers, and life / Lisa Hinkelman.

Description: Second edition. | Thousand Oaks, California : Corwin Press, [2021] | Includes bibliographical references and index.

Identifiers: LCCN 2020035590 | ISBN 9781071807507 (paperback) | ISBN 9781071807521 (epub) | ISBN 9781071807538 (epub) | ISBN 9781071807545 (ebook)

Subjects: LCSH: Girls–Psychology. | Self-esteem in adolescence. | Self-confidence. | Interpersonal relations. | Interpersonal communication. | Parenting.

Classification: LCC HQ777 .H56 2021 | DDC 305.23082–dc23

LC record available at https://lccn.loc.gov/2020035590

This book is printed on acid-free paper.

24 25 26 27 28   14 13 12 11 10 9

Table of Contents

Preface

What's New in the Second Edition

As I reflected on the world of girls since the original publication of *Girls Without Limits* in 2013, I needed to take a step back to consider what is *actually* different and what has remained the same. While there is much that has changed through the years—the #MeToo movement has brought issues of sexual harassment to the forefront, female athletes and women's sports teams have become household names, the first all-female crew of astronauts took to the skies, and women have been elected to political office at the highest rates in history—there are still so many challenges that persist for girls. These challenges aren't simply social or political challenges; they are interpersonal, relationship, and confidence challenges that represent the core of girls' experiences. Girls continue to struggle with self-esteem and body image, and they often have tumultuous relationships with other girls. They still have trouble being assertive, speaking their mind, and demonstrating leadership. Despite the fact that there have been gains in girls' access to new opportunities and an increased awareness of issues of equity and representation, many of the long-standing issues that have historically affected girls and women persist. I know this not simply from being an observer of society but from rigorously researching the experiences of girls.

I have been actively working with and researching girls in several different capacities. I spent 8 years as a professor of counselor education at The Ohio State University, 19 years as a licensed professional counselor, and 9 years as the founder/CEO of Ruling Our Experiences, Inc. (ROX), a national nonprofit focused on girls. My research team and I have surveyed and interviewed thousands of girls of different backgrounds, ethnicities, socioeconomic statuses, and ages. We have talked with girls who are incarcerated, girls who are homeless, those who live in middle-class homes, and those who live in mansions. We learned from girls who are in two-parent families, foster care, single-parent families, or divorced families, and those who live with their grandparents. We spent time listening to girls in high-needs urban schools, middle-class suburban schools, elite independent schools, and low-income rural schools. Girls in public, parochial, private, and charter schools participated in our research and shared their thoughts, feelings, and opinions with us. We provided them with a safe place to talk and share, and we did not pass judgment. We just listened.

Since the first edition of *Girls Without Limits*, I and my research team designed and deployed the country's largest survey of its kind with nearly 11,000 diverse girls. This survey, called The Girls Index™, was designed to help us better understand the lived experiences, opinions, and behaviors of girls in grades 5 through 12. We asked nearly 80 questions that focused on the relevant and timely issues affecting girls, such as relationships, social media, body image, leadership, academics, sports, and careers. We partnered with schools across the country to survey girls through online and paper-pencil assessments and also held dozens of focus group discussions and individual interviews. You will see the findings from these surveys and hear the girls' opinions throughout each chapter. It was important to me that the voices and stories that are represented in this book are based on much more than just my own experiences and interactions with girls and are representative of girls' experiences across the country.

What we learned is that there are vast differences among girls in regard to their experiences, thoughts, and opinions. Girls' knowledge of various topics is based on the environment in which they are raised. Depending on what they have been exposed to, girls' perceptions of the opportunities available to them can vary greatly. But the one thing that continued to amaze me as I learned from more and more girls was that the fundamental issues that are facing girls are *much* more universal than different. While girls can have extremely different experiences based on their socioeconomic status, race and ethnicity, family composition, or ability, I have found that the experience of girlhood, while unique for every girl, looks amazingly similar for girls across the country. Despite the vast differences among girls, the commonalities and shared experiences strongly outweigh the differences. Negotiating friendships and fitting in, experiencing insecurity about one's body, managing dating relationships and sexual pressure, and dealing with the social, emotional, and cognitive changes of adolescence seem to be universal issues for most American teen girls. Girls are under pressure and are at risk for negative outcomes simply because they are female. Girls are more likely than boys to dislike their body, go on a diet, feel pressure to look sexy, experience sexual violence, have low self-esteem, experience depression, or attempt suicide.

The statistics from The Girls Index™, which are shared throughout this book, are the summary findings from the research. The survey respondents included predominantly public school (88%) students who attend suburban (58%), urban (18%), and rural (24%) schools. Girls from elementary (22%), middle (37%), and high (41%) school participated, and girls from diverse socioeconomic backgrounds (high poverty, 29%; medium poverty, 27%; and low poverty, 38%) shared their experiences. The participants were 57.5% Caucasian, 12.1% Black/African American, 9.4% Hispanic/Latina, 4.7% Multiracial, 3.8% Asian, 1.4% Hawaiian Native/Pacific Islander, and 0.9% Native American/American Indian (10.2% did not answer). The full research report, as well as additional companion reports and data analyses, can be downloaded at www.rulingourexperiences.org/the-girls-index-report or bit.ly/TheGirlsIndexReport.

In addition to the inclusion of this new data source, this book also addresses one of the biggest changes of the past decade—the rapid proliferation of technology and social media. This innovation has massively changed the landscape of how girls build and sustain relationships, communicate with others, make sense of their environment, and develop their own identity and sense of self. Where technology and social media were previously secondary to in-person communications, these modalities are now the primary modes of connection and as such require different education, approaches, and considerations. Determining how best to help girls navigate their digital world while simultaneously keeping them safe is one of the consistent questions that I receive from adults who desperately want to know how to implement limitations and protections that insulate girls from the damaging effects of technology; yet they often struggle to know precisely what to do.

In this edition of the book I have expanded the information on technology and social media, as I do believe it is critical for girls' safety and development. However, I caution the reader to ensure that they do not view social media as the cause of all of the challenges that girls are facing. The actual issues that girls are grappling with—friendships, relationships, body image, sexual harassment, and pressure—are not new; rather, they have only been exacerbated by social media. So you will find that in this book I focus on actual ways to relate to girls, to start hard conversations, and to teach girls the *actual* skills that they need to interface better with ever-changing technologies, rather than simply focus on technology as the sole cause of distress.

Despite all of these challenges that are discussed in this book, I know that girls are strong and resilient. They consistently exceed the limited expectations that are placed on them by society and media, and they continue to amaze and inspire me. I also know that girls are better able to fully realize their potential when they have caring adults in their lives who nurture, challenge, encourage, and support them.

My goal in writing this book is to give a voice to girls who often feel that their thoughts and opinions are unheard and devalued. I want girls to know that what they think, feel, and believe matters. I want to know what are the big things going on in their lives that adults don't understand. What do they dream about? What fills them with insecurity? And ultimately, what can we do to help them? I want to provide adults with a glimpse into the lives of girls, as described by the girls themselves, and offer concrete strategies for how adults can better understand, communicate with, and motivate the girls in their lives.

I recognize that this book does not address the unique issues that face every girl. As a researcher who works primarily in public schools, there are legal and ethical limitations to the types of questions I can ask students. The Protection of Pupil Rights Amendment ensures privacy protection for students, and even though our surveys were anonymous, we were still not permitted to question girls on topics such as sexual orientation and gender identity, religion or spirituality, specific developmental or learning issues, country of origin, trauma or abuse history, or mental health status of the student or her family. While this can limit the specificity of the information I share, the sample size of our research population (10,678) ensures, with 99% confidence, that our findings are representative of how we would expect *most* girls in the United States to respond. More than anything this book offers a perspective on the shared experiences of girls and the ways in which, because of their gender, all girls can experience limitations and decreased expectations in life.

Our role as caring adults in the lives of girls is to understand these challenges and equip girls with the skills to effectively navigate their adolescent years and construct a life that is full of purpose, meaning, pride, and fulfillment. We want girls to perceive their options as infinite and their abilities as expandable, and we each have a role in helping girls construct a life without limits.

Acknowledgments

It is not until you sit down to write an acknowledgments section that you fully realize that your accomplishments have very little to do with you and everything to do with the people who surround you. While I love research and writing, the ideas that swirl around in my head would never make it to paper if I did not have a team of amazing humans who help me distill my thoughts, curate my musings, challenge my preconceived ideas, and provide me with opportunities to actually sit at my computer and write.

I am lucky enough to have a husband and partner in this life who gives me the space and freedom to explore my passions, immerse myself in my work, and pursue some pretty crazy ideas, all while ensuring that I never take myself too seriously and that I have a ton of fun along the way. Bob, thanks for making sure that I finished my dissertation instead of playing women's professional football and for having me think twice about joining that roller derby team. More than 20 years into this adventure, and it is only getting started.

My brother, Rev. Richard Hinkelman, has been one of my steadfast champions and supporters. He is the most selfless person I have ever met (sometimes to a fault) and is committed to creating a world that is caring, equitable, and just. His life journey is an inspiring tale of overcoming obstacles and dealing with discrimination and ostracization, all while persevering to achieve his true calling. As a pastor who leads a fully inclusive and affirming church, Richard helps me think hard about issues of social justice, inclusion, equity, and genuine care for others. We have deep and challenging conversations and continually help each other grow. I am proud to be his sister and grateful for our close, fun, and amazingly supportive relationship.

I am lucky to have amazing parents, Hink and Joan, who instilled in me an early sense that girls can do and be anything they want. I was a rough-and-tumble, athletic girl with a tendency to be messy and loud. Never placing undue limits on me, they gave me the chance to explore my passions, interests, and whims, whether or not they were something that "girls should do." From them I learned the value of *really* hard work, of not spending much time in front of a TV, and of caring for others above myself. Their ongoing prayers and support have sustained me, and it is my sincere hope that little girls everywhere have the opportunity to grow up with parents who give their daughters the gift of confidence and a sense of limitlessness that my parents gave me.

There are three very special women who have passed on from this life who have been some of the most significant influences in my life and my work—my grandma Irene, my professor and mentor Dr. Susan Sears, and my friend and colleague Dr. Patty Cunningham. From them I learned the importance of hard work and tenacity, of standing up for yourself and what you believe in, and of righteous resistance to the status quo. These women taught me to never give up on my dreams, to care deeply and authentically for others, and to ensure that my life is one of service to others. Each inspired me in different ways to focus my life's work around serving girls and women, while they simultaneously challenged me to become a better version of myself.

I am also lucky enough to have amazing women in my life who sustain and support me and who are the steady and constant forces in my life that I know will stand with me through the highs and lows. Lauren Hancock and Deb Schipper are my friends and colleagues who have helped me make many of my dreams, including this book, a reality. From reading versions of chapters and providing insights and feedback to being on hand for a cocktail and a reality check, to kicking me in the butt to meet my deadlines, these women are honest, loyal, hilarious, and one of a kind.

So many others have helped this project in large and small ways. From offering a writing retreat to providing substantive and practical feedback on my ideas, to keeping me sane and entertained, I am richly blessed by friends and colleagues who help sustain me. A heartfelt and sincere thanks to Jessica Allen, Maureen Casamassimo, Mary Cusick, Tammy Roberts Myers, Dr. Tina Pierce, and Dr. Sibyl West. I have also been blessed to work with a wonderful team of women who are collectively making the world safer for girls, and I am honored to work alongside them. Crystal Hill, Dorothy Martindale, Martinique Ridley, Lauren Morosky, Nancy Willis, and Rachel Zufall are deeply committed to creating generations of confident girls who control their own relationships, experiences, decisions, and future, and I love working with them every day at the ROX World Headquarters.

To all the graduate students, school counselors, educators, and ROX facilitators who I have had the opportunity to work with over the past decade, you have given of your time and tremendous talent to positively affect the lives of girls in your community and throughout the nation. Because of you thousands of girls will have different opportunities, different perspectives, and a chance to live a life that is free from limits and restrictive expectations. You have delivered programming, assisted with data collection, and have been the amazing role models that young girls need in their lives. I am grateful for your ongoing commitment to girls and your willingness to make a substantial and sustainable impact in the life of each girl you work with. You give me hope for the future.

A final thank you to all the parents, teachers, counselors, administrators, and especially girls who have taken the time to talk with me over the past several years about their thoughts, opinions, and experiences. Without you none of this work would have been possible. I have been amazed at the willingness of people to share their personal experiences with me and have been honored to hear your stories and thoughts. It is my hope that by sharing their stories with you, you are able to not only understand the challenges that girls face but also recognize the strength, potential, and promise in today's generation of girls. These girls are our future; let's help them succeed!

About the Author

Dr. Lisa Hinkelman is an educator, counselor, researcher, and author who has spent nearly 15 years researching girls and educating counselors both as a professor at The Ohio State University and as the founder and CEO of ROX (www.rulingourexperiences.org). ROX is a national nonprofit that provides evidence-based empowerment programming for girls, professional development for counselors and educators, and research on the critical issues affecting girls. ROX is focused on creating generations of confident girls who control their own relationships, experiences, decisions, and future.

Dr. Hinkelman has spent years working with girls, parents, and educators in both educational and counseling settings and has been aggressively researching the experiences of diverse girls as the principal investigator and author of the groundbreaking publication *The Girls' Index: New Insights Into the Complex World of Today's Girls* (2017). The Girls Index™ reveals the findings from a survey conducted with nearly 11,000 girls across the country and includes the girls' thoughts, behaviors, and beliefs in regard to confidence, body image, relationships, school, social media, careers, and leadership. She consults regularly for schools, organizations, and agencies on the critical issues affecting girls, stress and pressure, social media, sexual harassment and violence prevention, and other social, emotional, safety, and mental health issues faced by students and schools.

Dr. Hinkelman is a graduate of Chatham College in Pittsburgh, Pennsylvania, where she earned her degrees in psychology and education. She additionally earned her MA and PhD in counselor education from The Ohio State University. She can be reached at 614-488-8080 or lisahinkelman@rulingourexperiences.com.

What's Really Going on for Girls, and How Can We Help Them?

1

I don't think that adults have any idea what our lives are really like. They think they know what is going on, but they don't really. When I think about the big things going on for girls my age, I think the first thing is girl drama. It is constant and never ending. Girls just look for ways to create drama and will make stuff up when everything is fine. Girls talk behind each other's backs and try to get certain girls to not like other girls. You just have to make sure that you are in with the "right" girls so you don't get caught up in the middle of it all.

—Laci, seventh grade

The drama of girlhood. Is it a reality made up by girls who have too much time on their hands, or is it a necessary rite of passage that all girls experience? Do the issues that we see in the media greatly influence how girls see themselves, or have we overplayed the importance of social media and popular culture in the lives of girls? What do girls like about being a girl? What frustrates girls about the adults in their lives? What are the big issues that girls are dealing with, and what keeps them awake at night? And perhaps most important, how can we best support these young women?

These are the questions that I set out to answer more than a decade ago when I began to research girls. I wanted to talk to girls and hear their perspectives and their realities, in their own words. I wanted to give a voice to girls who feel that sometimes their thoughts and opinions are overlooked. More than anything, I wanted to determine how we can best support, encourage, and empower girls to be in control of their own relationships, experiences, decisions, and future so that they are able to achieve their full potential.

Since that time I have continued to immerse myself into the world of girls, both as a researcher and as the leader of a girl-serving nonprofit organization where I work with more than 5,000 girls and 3,000 adults each year. The statistics and stories in this book are current, relevant, and informed by thousands of girls and the adults who educate, parent, mentor, coach, and care for girls.

As I talked to the teachers, counselors, and parents, I learned that most adults are eager to help girls but they often don't know where to begin. They recognize that girls' lives are challenging but realize that they have difficulty relating and connecting to girls. The goal in this book is to give adults who work with and care about girls key insights into the lives of girls and provide strategies for building strong relationships and working more effectively with girls.

In asking girls about the big things going on in their lives, lots of different topics emerged. Even among girls who live in close-knit families, attend high-performing schools, and are involved in multiple extracurricular activities, they still report struggling with friendships, dating relationships, and body image concerns. They talked about pressure, issues in their families and their relationships with their parents, difficulty in friendships and dating relationships, tremendous pressures around weight and body image, and major concerns surrounding self-esteem and how they feel about themselves. They talked about puberty, academics, getting their driver's license, and dealing with depression and suicidal thoughts. Girls talked about politics, sexual harassment, racial equity, and sexual orientation. But overwhelmingly, the issues that girls talked about the most about were clustered around a handful of topic areas, including friendships, relationships, drama, dating, weight and body image, and pressure.

A consistent theme was that adults don't *really* understand what they are going through, so girls have difficulty openly sharing their issues and concerns with the adults in their lives.

In talking with adults many felt at a loss as to how they could develop more effective relationships with girls. Teachers reported frustration with girls "dumbing themselves down" around boys, counselors struggled with how to address the girl drama and bullying plaguing their schools, and parents felt anxiety regarding how they could best help their daughters deal with the increased pressures and challenges of middle school and high school.

What became increasingly obvious was that adults are hungry for information, strategies, and activities that they can use to connect with the girls in their lives. They want to find ways to help girls become the best they can be and experience rich, fulfilling, and productive lives. When asked what girls need to be successful, overwhelmingly, teachers, administrators, counselors, and parents identified "confidence" as most important. Interestingly, when the same question is posed to girls, their response is also "confidence." It is clear that both girls and adults recognize that confidence is a key variable in girls' lives; however, both struggle with how to actually cultivate confidence.

Arguably, how a person feels about themself can affect nearly every decision that they make. Our level of self-confidence and self-concept influences our decisions and can help determine the choices that we make in many facets of our lives, including our relationships, academic pursuits, and careers. For example, if I am in an unhealthy dating relationship and I lack self-confidence, I may stay in the relationship because I am afraid to leave and I don't think that I could do any better. If I lack confidence around my academic abilities, I may opt to take a general math course instead of trigonometry because I fear that I might not succeed. If I lack self-esteem, I may feel that I am not smart enough to be successful in my dream career, so I will compromise and pursue something less risky or less prestigious. How different would our decisions be if we moved through the world with confidence in ourselves and our abilities!

In an attempt to begin to more fully understand girls' realities, I led a research team through a first-of-its-kind, large-scale national survey called The Girls' Index™ (Hinkelman, 2017). The Girls' Index™ was designed to develop a deeper understanding of the thoughts, experiences, perceptions, beliefs, behaviors, and attitudes of girls throughout the United States. This national effort sought data from a large representative sample of girls about their thoughts, experiences, and perceptions on key issues, such as confidence, body image, friendships, pressure, leadership, career aspirations, school, academics, technology, and social media.

These data showed that girls' confidence declines sharply between fifth and ninth grade. In fact, the percentage of girls who would describe themselves as confident declines more than 25% throughout the middle school years, from 86% to 60%. By ninth grade confidence is at its lowest point, and then it levels off for the next three years. Girls reported that confidence does not return to pre–middle school levels for the remainder of high school.

The decline in confidence coincides with the onset of puberty changes in girls. Girls often report that they do not feel confident in themselves or comfortable with their changing bodies and can become withdrawn and unsure of themselves. Have you ever seen a rowdy group of fourth- or fifth-grade girls who are loud and laughing without a care in the world and then when they hit seventh grade, they become insecure and consumed with their looks, their social media profile, and their potential dating partners? I recently had a ninth-grade girl tell me that the last time she felt confident and happy with her body was when she was in fourth grade.

During the childhood and adolescent years girls bodies and brains are changing rapidly, and they are simultaneously inundated with negative messages about, and unrealistic images of, females. As girls begin to develop an understanding of themselves and their environment, they are influenced by the messages that they receive from others. They can internalize these often negative and limiting messages, which contribute to poor self-concept, dissatisfaction with their bodies, lowered expectations about their academic and career opportunities, increased acceptance of violence in relationships, and long-term self-esteem issues.

Despite these developmental and psychosocial challenges, we also know that girls are brave, courageous, and resilient. They have the potential to make tough decisions, chart their personal goals, and control their own experiences. Girls can rise above the negative messages and influences that they are exposed to and construct a confident and strong sense of self. Our role is to help instill a sense of confidence and capability in girls, so that they know that they have the right to a happy and fulfilling life and they also have the support and skills to actually construct a life that they love.

How Can We Help Girls?

> I don't understand these girls!

> I have no idea how to talk to my daughter; she just rolls her eyes every time I say something.

> Girls today are way different from how they were when I was a teenager; I just don't even know where to start.

These comments from educators, parents, and other adults illustrate that girls who were once open, communicative, and easy to understand as children or tweens have become confusing strangers, and adults feel paralyzed as to how to forge a new, or repair an existing, relationship with a girl.

While we might not always understand what is going on in girls' lives and we may have difficulty comprehending the way they think and reason, there are many things that we can do to communicate care and concern to the girls in our lives. While the remainder of this book will delineate specific issues and topics that affect girls' lives, there are some general recommendations that can help us effectively make connections with, communicate with, and help the girls in our lives.

Those of us who work with youth know that despite our best efforts, we are unable to control what is happening in girls' lives outside of our interactions with them. Educators know that girls may come to you with histories of abuse, a violent home life, and a lack of supportive and caring adults. They may not have a bed to sleep in, food for breakfast, or clean clothes when they come to school. While we can at times feel frustrated and helpless, with a desire to fix the situation, our role in these situations is to determine where we can add positive and prosocial elements to these girls' lives. Research tells us that the more deficits, challenges, or barriers that girls have, the more positive supports we need to add to their lives (Bernard, 1993). We believe that our positive intervention can outweigh the impact of the negative factors in their lives.

We do this by communicating our care, our passion, and our genuine concern for the development and well-being of girls. We want to help girls identify and find their dreams. We want to help girls find their own happiness and be able to articulate what that looks like for them. What excites them? What fuels their passion? What do they care about? And how can we help them construct their lives to be fulfilling, passionate, and purposeful?

There are some simple and concrete things that adults can do to connect with, care for, motivate, and support the girls in their lives.

#1: Be Aware

Be aware of what is going on in the lives of girls by paying attention to the things that they care about. Whether it is popular culture, music, news related to girls, media attention around girls and women, or the pressures that girls face, attempting to be relevant and knowledgeable can be helpful in creating an effective bond with the girls in your life. Start conversations about the issues affecting girls in the media, share news articles about the accomplishments of girls throughout the world, bring up interesting topics, and solicit girls' opinions. Girls report feeling that adults don't get them and don't understand what is happening in their lives. They feel that adults are far removed from the actual challenges that they face and that it's nearly impossible for adults to truly understand what it is like to be a girl today.

Maintaining an awareness of the things girls care about can mean paying attention to the relevant and contemporary issues facing girls—for example, recognizing how the media and culture inform and influence girls: Who are the best new actors, the musicians on the stickers on their computers or water bottles, the latest Netflix series or YouTube star? This does not mean that we overemphasize the importance of media and popular culture, but rather, we demonstrate to girls that we care about what is going on in their lives and, at least in some small way, have an understanding of what is "cool" and relevant. Of course, we don't have to actually *agree* that anyone or anything is cool, but we need to know what or who the girls think is cool.

You might make a habit of tuning in to popular reality shows while cleaning the house, scrolling through Instagram in your free time, and listening to different types of music while driving your car. Does this mean that you are into reality TV, Instagram models, or hip-hop music? Not necessarily. It just means that you are trying to stay connected to what girls are exposed to on a daily basis.

Assess your own knowledge of contemporary girl culture:

1. Who are the top musicians or bands that your girls are into?
2. What is the current "must see" movie or streaming series for teen girls?
3. What is the social media platform, app, or network of choice for girls?
4. What books are girls reading?
5. What would girls say they like to do in their spare time?
6. What social issues are girls paying attention to?

While it is important to attempt to understand the realities of girls' lives, it is equally important to maintain an appropriate relationship with the girls in your life. And that brings us to our second strategy.

#2: Be the Adult

A caring adult does not take on the role of a friend or a peer. Often, we see adults who work with girls seeking to be a friend to the girls rather than maintaining an appropriate adult-teen relationship. This is one instance where the attempt to be knowledgeable and relevant can go too far. As adults we are not the contemporaries of the girls in our lives, and we do not want to send confusing messages to them.

A middle school principal shared a story about one of her seventh-grade student's mothers who was very intent on being the "cool mom." She wanted to be the mom that all the other girls would come to and with whom they could gossip about other kids. This particular mother was overinvolved in the girls' lives and took great pride in being the person that the other girls could share their secrets with. She followed all of their social media accounts and worked a little too hard to stay in the know about their lives.

Where the situation went from mildly uncomfortable to slightly more inappropriate was when the mom would get upset if she wasn't invited to be part of the girls' conversations when they had sleepovers at her house. She admitted to hiding on the staircase and listening in on the girls' discussions because she felt left out when the girls retreated to the basement game room for private conversations. When her own daughter turned to the school counselor to share her concerns and talk about her problems, the mother became very distressed and angry with the school counselor. Mom was frustrated and upset that her daughter did not want to tell her the things that were bothering her but would rather seek out the listening ear of another caring adult in her daughter's life. Instead of getting angry about this situation, the mom should have been thrilled that her daughter had strong and caring relationships with other responsible adults who were willing to listen to and support her daughter.

There is a fine line between being relevant and understanding and trying to relive your teen years through your kids or students. We must ensure that we maintain a healthy balance of relevance coupled with appropriate boundaries. We don't want to make things confusing for girls by requiring them to discern what the relationship boundaries should be. So while it is important that we stay informed and connected, it is probably less important and would even be embarrassing for the girls if we blurred the boundaries between adult and peer.

#3: Start the Conversation

One of the most important ways that we can help girls is to be the one to start the conversation—any conversation—and then work to maintain open lines of communication. Sometimes, however, starting a conversation can be difficult, particularly if it has been a challenge for us in the past. Communication can ultimately dictate the success or failure of any relationship, and often a hallmark of the adolescent years is a decrease in effective communication between adults and teens.

Our goal in communicating with girls is to make them feel that what they have to share with us is valuable and important and that they are the most important person in our lives at any given time. We start the conversation by inviting girls to share with us what is going on in their lives and then really listening to what they have to say. If we only try to have meaningful conversations when there is something serious to discuss—like "the talk"—our communication skills are likely to be a little rusty. Additionally, girls are less likely to be open to a meaningful dialogue. But if we regularly try to engage in open, nonjudgmental conversations about all sorts of things, we are laying the groundwork for a reciprocal, communicative, and lasting relationship.

We demonstrate our interest, care, and concern by genuinely seeking to understand the other person's reality. It always feels good when another person truly wants to understand how we feel, what our experience has been, and how we make sense of a situation, without seeking to impose their own beliefs or advice onto the situation. This type of listening is listening to *understand*, not listening to *respond*. When we are truly seeking to understand someone else's experiences, thoughts, and feelings, we invite the disclosure from their own space, without seeking to impose our beliefs or our judgment on them. When we do this, other people feel safe and comfortable in the relationship. They know that they won't be judged, and they know that their feelings won't be deemed silly or inappropriate.

Here are some ways to start an open conversation that allows the girl to decide what to talk about:

- Tell me about yourself.
- Share with me something you're especially proud of.
- Tell me more about that.
- I don't know a lot about that. . . . It would be great if you could explain it to me.

- I saw _____ on TV last night. What do you think of him/her/it?

- Wow, that situation seems pretty tough. Tell me how you are dealing with it.

- What do you think about _____?

Great conversation starters are open-ended and can't easily be answered with a "yes" or "no" response. As you can see, different situations call for different types of communication, but creating a safe and open space for dialogue must be an intentional activity on our part. Sometimes this means that we have to monitor our own language, tone of voice, and communication patterns and then intentionally reframe our responses.

#4: Reframe the Response

Our communication style can sometimes unintentionally raise defenses and shut down the dialogue. To open up the lines of conversation requires an effort on our part that I call *reframing the response*. When we reframe our responses, we pay attention to what we might *normally* say to girls in a particular situation, and we catch ourselves and reframe what we *actually* say. Sometimes our initial responses can sound judgmental or patronizing and can serve to stifle the conversation. If our responses are not perceived as judgmental but rather as an attempt to understand, how much more productive would our communication actually be!

When we reframe our response, we must first monitor our own communication style. How often do we say things that others could perceive as snippy, judgmental, or paternalistic? Instead of saying, "Do you seriously think you are going to wear that outfit out of this house?" it is wiser to suggest, "Honey, I am not sure if that outfit is the best choice for this event. Let's think about this together." Despite what we may actually be thinking, when we control our nonverbal messages (i.e., the expressions on our face, what we do with our eyes, if we look angry, surprised, disgusted, etc.) as well as our verbal messages (i.e., the tone and content of what actually comes out of our mouths), our chances of increasing communication and maintaining a more open dialogue are much improved.

For example, if you say to a teen who may have recently made a poor decision, "Now tell me, did you think that that was a good idea?" you can fairly easily guess what the response will be. Asking a question in this way only serves to suppress the conversation and probably completely shut it down. If we instead say, "Share with me a bit about what you were thinking and what was going on for you when this happened," we might get a very different response. Obviously our inflection and tone of voice matter when we communicate, but the actual words that we say matter as well. Consider the following examples.

Example #1:

- *Option 1:* "Did you see Billie Eilish on the awards show last night? She is so dark and weird. I don't get how people think she has any talent at all. What do you think about her?"
- *Option 2:* "What did you think about Billie Eilish's performance on the awards show last night?"

Example #2:

- *Option 1:* "Your teacher told me that you haven't been turning in your homework, and I would like an explanation right now."
- *Option 2:* "I'm wondering if you have been having some trouble with your math homework. Your teacher shared some concerns with me, and I wanted to check in with you."

Which statements do you think would encourage a girl to open up to you, help her believe that her opinions matter, and make her feel that you are a safe person to talk with about her problems?

#5: Communicate Care and Concern

One of the most important things we can do in the lives of girls is to communicate that we care and that we are concerned. Research tells us that there is perhaps no stronger predictor of success in a child's life than the legitimate and genuine care and concern of even one adult (Bernard, 1993). Care and support are the building blocks of resiliency, but for some girls it may be difficult to identify even one adult who cares deeply for them.

When you think back on your adolescent years, who was the person, or persons, who cared deeply for you? Who held high expectations for you and tried to ensure that you were successful? Who was the person you could rely on who would never let you down?

Some girls can identify a long list of caring adults in their life, but other girls have difficulty coming up with even one name. Obviously, you are reading this book because you care about girls and have young ladies in your life. You know the person you pictured when you were posed the aforementioned questions. I believe that our goal is for girls to picture us when they are asked those very same questions.

How You Can Show That You Care

Pay attention to the things that are important to her, and follow up accordingly. This could mean asking how her softball tournament went over the weekend, how her family is adjusting to having a new baby in the house, or how the visit with her grandparents over the holidays went. This shows that you listen and pay attention—that you care.

Look for opportunities to connect her to positive people and activities. Girls flourish when they have meaningful and positive connections in their lives. Unfortunately, we are observing a generation of teens who are becoming more socially isolated and who see their main sources of socialization and entertainment as connecting with peers online and via social media. Getting girls involved with people and activities that will build them up, challenge them, support them, and encourage them is key in building resilient girls. Some ideas include the following: youth groups, sports teams, volunteer opportunities, neighborhood cleanups, mission or service trips, book clubs, science camps, art classes, hiking and nature camps, martial arts, ice skating, scrapbooking events, and music lessons. National organizations where girls can connect with other girls as well as with caring adults may include Girl Scouts, Big Brothers/Big Sisters, Black

Girls Code, Girls Who Code, Boys and Girls Clubs, Girls Inc., Girls on the Run, Ruling Our Experiences, Inc. (ROX), Girls' Leadership, and the YWCA. Research the local organizations or activities in your community that offer programming and opportunities for girls.

Spend time rather than money. I work with a 13-year-old girl, Natalie, who is having trouble getting along with her parents. They are constantly bickering, and both the teen and the parents are frustrated. Taking a solution-focused approach, I asked Natalie to share with me what is happening when she and her mom are getting along. What are the things that she is doing, and what are the things that her mom is doing? Natalie said, "When she buys me stuff, we get along." Later, when I talked to Natalie's mom about the same topic, she agreed that she often bought things for Natalie because she was constantly looking for what would make her daughter happy and encourage her daughter to be nice to her. Unfortunately, this strategy backfired because Natalie has begun to associate her mother's affection with shopping and buying new things, and as Natalie gets older, mom is continually trying to buy bigger and more expensive things to show her daughter her love. Thus, Natalie is getting spoiled, and the mom-daughter relationship is not improving. Building a relationship around shared interests and quality time together creates meaningful and sustainable bonds, whereas basing interactions on more superficial factors can equate to fewer authentic exchanges.

#6: Set Goals, and Expect Success

It is possible to be caring and supportive while also holding high expectations for girls. We want girls to be successful. We want them to have success in their relationships, friendships, academic pursuits, and career decision-making. We want girls to envision a successful life for themselves and hold themselves to high expectations of performance and achievement.

As discussed previously, and will be discussed later in this book, there can be situations where girls perceive the expectations that parents and others place on them as unrealistic and stressful. When this occurs, girls can internalize their desire to please others and become stressed out and perfectionistic. Having high expectations and holding girls to achieving their expectations can be an important goal as well as a delicate balance. We want girls to believe in themselves but also know that we believe in them. Holding high expectations for girls communicates to them that we believe that they are capable of achieving at a high level and that we will support them in getting there.

We can support girls in achieving their dreams by helping them set goals. Goal setting is a very purposeful and concrete activity, and when done correctly, it can make even the largest task feel manageable. For nearly every topic addressed in this book, the activity of setting goals can be incorporated. I have used the following exercise to address academic performance, career development, healthy behavior, and physical activity, and I have even used it with two people to identify ways to make improvements in their relationship.

Too often, we set goals that are vague, unrealistic, and unattainable. For goals to be appropriately motivating, they need to be specific, but they also must be *both* challenging and realistic. A common strategy for goal setting is using the SMART goal framework. While you may see various iterations of the acronym, SMART goals are as follows:

Specific: Identify what it is precisely that you want to accomplish. A goal has a much greater chance of being achieved if it is specific and well articulated rather than vague or general.

Measurable: Determine how you will measure progress on the goal, and use a concrete metric to monitor your progress. This will help you celebrate small successes and will keep you on track.

Attainable: Goals should be appropriately challenging but also attainable. Goals that are too easy to achieve tend to not require much motivation or focus—we can easily get bored. Conversely, goals that are far out of reach can seem unwieldy, and we can become easily frustrated and can give up.

Relevant: Goals must be based on the actual realities of your life and should take into consideration the environment, climate, and the "givens" of a situation. They should be meaningful and significant and make a difference in *your* life. If a goal does not feel relevant to the person (but rather is a goal that someone else is setting for them), there is little motivation to achieve. I, personally, have to see the goal as important and relevant to my life if I am going to work hard to achieve it!

Time sensitive: Include a timeline when setting a goal because it can help ensure that the task will get completed. This can mean that a student has nine weeks to improve her grade in science or that she will learn how to play a challenging arrangement on the piano in time for the recital that is two months away. Goals can have relatively short timelines (a few weeks) or long timelines (over the course of years). Working against a deadline can keep us engaged and motivated.

There are many ways to use a goal-setting activity such as this. Having girls think about goals that are important to them and then helping them translate their ideas into SMART goals is an initial step. Next, it is important to help girls identify the activities and supports that will help them achieve their goals. What will they have to do to make progress on their goals? What are the behaviors they will have to engage in, and what are the resources and supports they will need to achieve their goals?

Example:
- *General goal:* I will improve my physical fitness.
- *SMART goal:* I will work out at the gym three days a week for the next six months. I will do cardiovascular exercises two days a week and strength training one day a week.

To set the SMART goal above, I need to have access to a gym that has cardio and weight training equipment. I need to have transportation to the gym, and I need to be able to fit three days a week into my schedule. Considering the realities of the situation can help us set goals that are realistic and achievable.

#7: Encourage Risk Taking

Encouraging risk taking does not mean encouraging girls to engage in risky behavior; rather, it means encouraging girls to push themselves beyond their own perceptions of their capabilities. Risk taking allows girls the opportunity to see themselves as being able to achieve more than they thought possible. We want to instill in girls the sense that if they try something new, they may fail or they may develop an entire new set of competencies and skills. Examples include trying out for the school play, running for student government, standing up to a bully, taking an Advanced Placement course, or joining a sports team. Risk taking means putting oneself in a situation where success is not a sure thing. While it can be difficult and painful to watch those we love struggle at certain things, we are helping them prepare for life's ups and downs. We recognize our need to keep our girls protected and well insulated from the dangers of the world; however, when we help instill a strong sense of self in a girl, she is more apt to "stick her neck out" and try something that she may have been less inclined to try if she had lower self-confidence.

We want girls to know that the only regret we don't want them to have is the regret of not having done something because they feared failure. Girls need to know how to experience both success and failure and be prepared to effectively and graciously manage both. Encourage them to get out there and try something new—and be there to support them regardless of the outcome!

#8: Don't Just Set Limits; Teach Skills

We know that girls will have to deal with pressures, negative influences, and difficult situations. They will find themselves in predicaments that will require them to trust their instincts and make good decisions. Our hope is that when girls are in such situations they have the wherewithal to make the right decision. We have an opportunity to help prepare girls by teaching them the actual skills they will need to use in tough situations.

Too often, our desire is to keep girls protected by imposing strict rules and limits for their behavior. No social media until you are 15, no mixed gender parties, no riding in cars with friends, no dating until you are 16, no listening to certain types of music, and no going to concerts. While rules, limits, and consequences are critically important, limiting girls' access to information and experiences can backfire when they have to handle a difficult challenge. Parents often say, "We've talked about right and wrong, and my hope is that when she finds herself in that situation she will know what to do." This can certainly be true. Family values and norms can be deeply embedded in children and can serve as a moral compass that can help influence behavior. However, what can be equally powerful is for girls to actually have the experience of learning *how* to handle a situation and practice actually *doing so*. Taking a situation from hypothetical to reality helps build the necessary skills and competencies to manage the circumstance.

We must balance our need to shelter and protect girls with the realization that they are eventually going to have to function on their own in this world. While our tendency is to protect them and to want to handle challenges for them, we do girls a greater service by helping them develop the skills for themselves. This could mean helping them learn how to approach a teacher who may have scored their exam incorrectly, tell a dating partner that they do not want to go any further sexually, or refuse to ride in a car with someone who has been drinking. Letting girls know that these are dilemmas that they are likely to face and providing them the space to explore and practice their potential responses can increase their ability to do the right thing in the actual situation.

A Future Full of Promise

This book is not designed to illuminate all the things that are wrong in girls' lives. It has not been written to say, "Look how bad everything is for girls." Conversely, the future for girls is bright. They have more opportunities than they've ever had to be successful, take risks, chart new paths, and live vast, varied, and fulfilling lives. They can play competitive and professional sports and go to college, medical school, law school, or graduate school. They can have unique and interesting careers, achieve business and political success, and give birth to and raise children and have a family. Girls are special, unique, and full of possibility. They have the opportunity to take a stand, set new records, and pave the way for an entire generation of girls to follow.

The approach in this book is to look at the areas of a girl's life where she is likely to be limited by her gender. What are the topics, concepts, and issues that can affect girls in negative or restrictive ways? We want girls to love being girls, but we also want them to have access to the broadest range of opportunities and possibilities. We want to prepare them for the rewards and challenges that they will face, and we want to equip them with the skills that they will need to negotiate their growing up years.

Girls have all the potential in the world, but they need adults in their lives who will guide them, protect them, nurture them, and challenge them. They need people who will have honest conversations with them and prepare them for the often difficult challenges that they will face. They need caring adults who recognize the pressures that they face, understand the realities of their lives, and work to ensure an equitable and just future for all girls. It is my hope that you also believe this and that is why you are reading this book.

Streaks, Likes, Followers, and Friends 2

The Impact of Social Media in Girls' Lives

Without a doubt the element of girls' lives that has changed most markedly in the past 10 years has been the proliferation of social media. In the past several years we have seen the profound ways in which social media can influence the political climate, galvanize social movements, and create rapid, viral awareness of new issues. We have also observed the ways in which individual social media use has a profound impact on girls, their relationships, their mental health, and their perceptions of themselves and their abilities—both online and IRL (in real life)!

Have you ever been with a group of teen girls all sitting side by side one another staring at their respective cell phones? It is easy to wonder why they wanted to be together since they aren't even speaking to one another. But unless one is looking for a collective group eye roll, they shouldn't attempt to be funny with a quip like "Hey girls, are you all texting each other?" Because it is at this point that the girls may actually start texting each other—maybe even with a comment about how out of touch the adult seems to be.

The reality is that most adults *are* out of touch with the social media landscape of teens today. Even if we consider ourselves tech-savvy, are active on social media ourselves, and have all of the latest tech gadgets, the way we understand and use technology is fundamentally different from that of today's generation of girls. The majority of adults who are currently raising or educating school-age children did not have cell phones, and definitely not smartphones, when they were in middle school or high school. Many remember getting their first phone in high school, college, or young adulthood, and they chuckle at the thought of the giant, gray, brick-size phone with an antenna and a green screen that was their induction into the technological era.

Today, the majority of U.S. girls have smartphones by the age of 10 and begin engaging with social media between the ages of 10 and 11. Overall, 95% of teens have access to a smartphone, and 45% report that they are online "almost constantly" (Anderson & Jiang, 2018). Even if girls don't have smartphones, they are quite adept at using technology as many have been using an iPod, iPad, or tablet since they were toddlers. When these devices are connected to Wi-Fi, they essentially have all of the features of a smartphone at their fingertips: cameras, messaging, Wi-Fi calling, video chatting, interactive app usage, location tracking, and social media access, to name a few. The only additional feature that an actual smartphone provides is the ability to access all of these amenities when a Wi-Fi connection is not available.

Social Media Use Among Girls

By the time girls are in high school they report spending up to six hours per day using social media and eight or more hours per day engaged with all types of technology (Hinkelman, 2017). Social media has become a primary tool for communication and connection among youth and adults alike, and it is often the place where people get their family updates, school information, news, recipes, jokes, entertainment—the list goes on. The majority of all social media users report checking their social media sites at least once per day, with high school girls checking on average 8 to 10 times per day.

There is variability in the ways adults and teens report using social media. When adults are asked, most of them report the desire to stay connected to family members who live out of town, to stay in touch with friends from high school or college, and to stay abreast of news, current events, and issues that are of interest to them. Girls report using social media to stay connected, to know what is going on with their friends, to communicate with their friends, and to follow their interests. They talk about the importance of being active on social media so that they aren't "left out." In my interviews with girls I hear statements like these:

> Sometimes I just post random stuff so that I stay part of the conversation. It's like if you aren't posting, then you are basically invisible—you aren't in the room. It doesn't matter that much what I actually post, just that I have put something out there.
>
> —Lizzie, 15

> Posting or commenting on other people's posts keeps you part of the group. So you go through and "like" or comment on everyone else's posts so they know that you've seen them. Even if you don't actually like the post, you need to basically acknowledge that you saw it. So everything that my group of friends posts, I "like" when I see it. Sometimes friends will actually send a text and tell me, "Hey, I just posted something. I need you to go on Instagram and 'like' it."
>
> —Madison, 17

> There is a lot of pressure to post certain kinds of things on social media because everyone wants to present themselves in a certain way. You want to be cool but not like you are trying too hard. You want to look pretty but not like you've spent a ton of time trying to look a certain way. It's supposed to look effortless, but really it takes so much time.
>
> —Chantel, 14

Girls maintain their activity on social media so that they stay part of the conversation and aren't forgotten by their peers. It is as though each post is a little reminder that is saying, "Hey, I am still here! Don't forget about me!" And while social media is the new tool for communication and connection in our society, the way it is used among teens, young adults, celebrities, influencers, and politicians is now not just for connection but also for status. How many friends or followers do you have? How many likes did you get on your post? Who liked your post? Through my research I have learned that there is a distinct difference between whether my mom liked my post and whether my crush liked it.

Trying to Understand and Stay Connected

When I conduct workshops focused on technology and social media with parents and educators, I am continually asked the question "How do I get them to put their phones away?" or "How can I convince her that social media is not real life?" Adults are continually frustrated by both the amount of time and the psychological investment that girls place around social media. It is as though there are competing realities: the in-person, synchronous, in-the-moment conversations and connections that are happening in real time and the online, asynchronous communications and engagements that are a constant, unending narrative and continuous feedback loop shaping the decisions and behaviors of our teens. Both have a substantial role in shaping youth behavior; however, increasingly, the immediate nature of communication via social media can shift opinions, perceptions, and behavior in marked ways.

Many adults who work with or parent girls have a hard time understanding the importance that girls place on their social media persona and presence. While it is true that adults may also invest a great deal of time into curating their own online profile, in general, there is a significant disconnect between the way teens and adults use and understand social media. Much of this disconnect is based on the fact that today's parents of school-age kids did not grow up with social media. They did not live in a state of constant connectedness where there was an ongoing and incessant feedback loop. Their earliest memories around friends and dating did not center on decoding texts and emojis or scanning posts for clues about interest or attraction.

The generation of adults who are currently parenting and educating girls can still remember a time *before* that first cell phone. When calls had to be made from a home phone or (gasp!) from a pay phone. A time when dates and plans to see one another were made in person or on the landline, when maps or printed directions were required to find out how to get to new places. A time when going to a coffee shop meant ordering what you wanted to drink and then actually standing there and waiting for it. This generation made relationships the "old-fashioned way." They spent time with people because they had common interests. They had long conversations about ideals, views, and perspectives.

Doesn't this all sound so very nostalgic—those simpler, easier times before technology took over our lives? If any part of that last paragraph sounded cozy and familiar to you, you may sometimes wish that things still operated that way. Because most of us have a tendency to think that the way that we did things was the "right" way. That our communication, our relationships, our hobbies, and our interactions with friends took place in the way these types of things *should* take place. This approach worked for us, so to us it is "normal" and perhaps even what we see as ideal.

However, the adult generation has also established a new normal. We are the generation that did not grow up with all of the technology, but we have brought it into our lives so voraciously that it is now an extension of ourselves. We synch our phones, our cars, our thermostats, our security cameras, our music, and our watches. We rarely find ourselves more than a few feet from our cell phone, and we instantly panic if we temporarily lose track of that magical device. In short, we have quickly assimilated to this new normal, but at times we still long for the "before."

Girls today don't have the "before." They are not able to make a comparison between life before and after technology because, if they were born any time after 2000, they have never known life without the sophistication that the digital boom has afforded. They were born into a hyperconnected society where life and relationships move at a rapid pace, where the flow of information is constant, where communication is steady and robust, and where the feedback they receive from others is often unsolicited and incessant. Disengaging from this means that they miss out, that they aren't included, or that they fall behind. Girls are developing relationships in entirely different ways from how most of the adults in their lives forged relationships. Group texts, interest groups, video chats, and interactive apps have replaced passing notes, sleepovers, long phone conversations, and football Friday night hangouts. The new normal is that girls are available, accessible, and immediately responsive.

"I feel like she is totally overreacting!"

> I just don't understand why she is constantly connected to that phone. It is literally like an extension of her body, and she freaks out if she can't check it constantly. Lately, she has been complaining a lot about a specific group of girls that are the "popular" girls. My daughter has been trying to be a part of that group since we moved to this school district, and she has had moments where she has been included but many more where she has been excluded. I watch her follow the every move of these girls on social media, and it is crushing to watch her completely deflate when she realizes that she wasn't invited to the party or the sleepover. I tell her to put the phone away and quit caring so much about what these girls say, think, and do. She screams at me that I have "no idea" what she is going through and storms out of the room in tears.
>
> —Danielle, mom of a 12-year-old girl

Responding to this situation is complicated and emotional. On the one hand, it is so hard to watch our girl try so hard to connect and still be excluded and hurt by her peers. But on the other, it is frustrating to realize how much value she places on the opinions of a group of 12-year-olds. It is hard to know how to respond to something for which we may have a limited frame of reference, and using the line "I know how you feel" can be wholly inadequate and inaccurate. We actually don't know how she feels at this precise moment, so we shouldn't tell her that we know or try to convince her that we know. We can't diminish the emotions that she is having; instead, we should ask her how she feels. We should allow her to be the expert on her life in this precise moment and invite her to let us in to understand it. She may be feeling embarrassed, excluded, angry, sad, annoyed, or any combination of these. The intensity of her emotions might be amplified by the fact that she perceives that everyone else knew that she was excluded as well because—different from what it may have been for us—everything is on blast online for everyone to see.

For today's girls social media is an inextricable part of their relationships. They are using their online connections as a social barometer, gauging their popularity, relationships, and at times perceived value based on the feedback that they receive from others. Where we once thought of the lunch table as the place where social hierarchies evidenced themselves, we now see group chats and number of followers as the visible indicators of who is "in" and who is "out." A group chat can start with six or seven members, and then without warning, one girl can be left off from the conversation—intentionally or unintentionally—and the conversation proceeds without her. Plans are made, parties are discussed, and she is initially oblivious to the fact that she has been excluded. Only later, when she sees the posts from the party that she wasn't invited to, does she realize what has happened.

As a group of eighth-grade girls who attend a small private school explained to me,

> Our teachers have this rule that if you have a group chat, everyone in the class has to be on the chat. But that makes no sense because you aren't close friends with everyone. You are going to have people that you are closer with than others— that's just the reality. They don't understand that sometimes you just want to talk to your closest friends and that should be fine.

I can certainly understand their perspective, because it is true. None of us are friends with everyone equally. We have relationships that are stronger than others and individuals who we connect with in more meaningful ways than with others. Hopefully, we have learned how to savvily navigate our relationships to avoid overt exclusion and hurt feelings and how to nurture the relationships that are the most satisfying and sustaining for us. We might not always do it right, but years of experience has taught us how to (hopefully) not mess it up all the time.

We have to help girls navigate both their individual and their group relationships in open and communicative ways. Unfortunately, this can become more complicated when the primary form of communication is through electronic communications and social media.

Cues are missed, body language is absent, and the nuances of face-to-face interactions are conspicuously missing. For these reasons we are often biased against communication via technology.

Do You Have Tech Biases?

Did you have a smart phone in middle school? Did you have the opportunity to text a friend and get an immediate response? Did you know everything that every one of your peers was doing in real time? These are some questions to assess your own biases as they relate to engagement with technology. Rate the degree to which you agree or disagree with the following statements:

1 = *Strongly disagree*, 2 = *Disagree*, 3 = *Agree*, 4 = *Strongly agree*

1. I think relationships are best formed in person rather than online.

2. Communication is most authentic when it is face-to-face.

3. I first met my closest friends in person, not via technology.

4. Talking with someone versus texting or emailing is always the better way to communicate.

5. Girls put too much value on what people think of them online.

6. Digital life is not real life and shouldn't be given as much attention or importance.

7. If people would just put their phones down more often, the world would be a better place.

If you find yourself strongly agreeing with these statements or have noticed that you have made similar statements to girls, you likely carry some biases regarding the value of social media and technology. If you made these same statements to girls, how do you think they might respond? Likely, you will identify at least a few areas where there is a clear disconnect between your perceptions and theirs.

This disconnect can contribute to frustration, misunderstanding, and a lack of open communication between girls and adults. As Nikki, an eighth grader, explained, "Basically, anyone who is like, over 35, doesn't understand social media. They don't really get it, and they don't think it matters." When girls hear from adults that they "spend too much time on their phones," "shouldn't care about what people online think about them," "let social media dictate their emotions," or "are wasting their time online," it causes girls to be less open with adults about their digital lives.

Let's think about this for a moment. If I am into something that I know you think is stupid or a waste of time—Star Wars, cat videos, board games, Netflix marathons—I will likely make a conscious decision to ensure that I *never* talk to you about that thing. I will go out of my way to not bring it up with you because I want to avoid your indifference, judgment, or ridicule. I feel as though you don't get me and you aren't even making an attempt, so why should I bother trying? This is often what girls experience when it comes to communicating with adults about what is happening for them—both good and bad—online. We don't get it, we don't make serious attempts to understand, and we think it is useless and a waste of time. Girls know this too, so sometimes they just stop trying.

"I think social media is a stupid waste of time. I just don't get it."

> I think Snapchat is the devil. It is literally the worst thing that has ever been invented, and I told my 11 year-old daughter she is not allowed to have it on her phone until she is 13. She is allowed to have Instagram as long as I am following her and I can see what she is posting. But absolutely no Snapchat; it is entirely too dangerous, and quite frankly it is stupid. My 13 year-old daughter is on it and is obsessed with her Snapchat streak. When our family was going on vacation and I told her that we would not have internet access for a few days, she literally started crying and told me that I was ruining her life because her 300+ day streak would be ruined. This is literally one of the dumbest conversations we've ever had, and I am at a complete loss at what I should do here.
>
> —Nate, dad of an 11-year old and a 13-year old girl

If you are wondering what a Snapchat streak is (don't worry you are not alone!), it is when two people send at least one photo to each other within a 24-hour period of time. If you and I are in a Snapchat streak, I snap you a photo—of anything. It can be a photo of my foot or the floor. Then you snap me a photo back. Once again, of anything at all. We keep this going every day without fail, and we earn virtual trophies along the way as we lengthen our streak.

This might not capture our interest, but for many girls this streak is an indicator of a robust friendship. The fact that this other person is thinking about me every day and that we have committed to this personal connection is a tangible demonstration of our friendship. It is akin to the modern-day note passing in the hallway. Missing a day on the Snapchat streak means that we have to start over—literally on day 1. It means that the past 300 days that we were "on fire" simply goes away as though it never existed.

If we approach our conversations with this girl from our position that this is a complete waste of time—"This is so stupid! I don't understand why you spend so much time on this"—or that she is ridiculous for having this reaction to the situation—"If she is your true friend, it shouldn't matter if the streak ends"—it is likely that she will quickly learn that this is one of the topics that she can't openly discuss with you. Later, if she finds herself in a sticky situation on Snapchat—maybe she is observing bullying or perhaps she is receiving unsolicited photos that make her uncomfortable—she'll remember that you think Snapchat is "stupid," and she'll work to figure it out on her own. Because in her mind figuring it out on her own is easier than hearing you say, "I told you so."

Impact of Social Media

Researchers have a difficult time reaching a consensus on the impact of social media in the lives of teens—in part, because the research is relatively new and also because to measure the relative impact of social media use *exclusively* while removing the impact of all other variables is actually quite difficult. To understand both the positive and the negative impacts of social media, we have to look at the correlations between specific behaviors and societal trends to come to a conclusion.

Contrary to the negative light in which social media is often presented, girls report that there is a great deal about social media that they like. They like knowing what's going on with their friends, they like feeling connected to their peers, and they like being part of something bigger than themselves. According to the Pew Research Center's survey of 784 teens, nearly 8 in 10 reported that social media makes them feel more connected to their friends, and nearly 70% reported that it helps them interact with a more diverse group of people and contributes to their feeling that they will have people to support them through tough times. Teens generally rate their social media use with more positive than negative feelings—they feel more included, more confident, more authentic, and more outgoing than they do without social media (Anderson & Jiang, 2018).

Despite these overwhelmingly positive feelings, there is clear evidence emerging on the negative mental health impacts of social media. Between 2009 and 2015 there was a 33% increase in adolescents exhibiting high levels of depressive symptoms, with 31% more dying by suicide. This increase was found to be nearly entirely driven by females (Twenge et al., 2018). In trying to isolate the causes of these increases, Dr. Jean Twenge and her research team took a deep look into teens' activities, both screen time and non–screen time related. She found that adolescents who spent more time on activities that involved some type of screen (phone, tablet, computer, TV, etc.) were significantly more likely to have higher depressive symptoms than those who spent less time.

The Girls' Index™ research had similar findings. The amount of time that girls spend engaged with electronic devices was correlated with increased reports of sadness and depression. Among the nearly 11,000 girls from fifth to twelfth grade who completed the survey, we found that the girls who spent the most time—eight or more hours a day—engaged with technology were five times more likely to report sadness and depression six or seven days per week. This group was also the least likely to report having supportive friendships, participating in extracurricular activities, or enjoying coming to school. Twenge (2018) found that among girls exclusively, more social media specifically was correlated with increased depressive symptoms. It is important to be cautious in the interpretation of these findings because the data do not tell us specifically that social media use causes depression but, rather, that there is a relationship that exists between the two. The question that remains is whether or not girls already had increased levels of sadness and depression and so they use social media more often or they spend extensive amounts of time using social media and, as a result, develop increased levels of depression?

When researchers look at the variables that are connected to decreases in depressive symptoms, they find that more social interaction, consuming print media versus digital media, and participating in sports and exercise all contribute to lower levels of depression. While the initial temptation may be to simply limit the time that girls spend on social media, the fix is not quite that easy. A girl's engagement in lots of other positive activities is also critical to her overall well-being and mental health. We have to focus on decreasing the time she spends on social media while we simultaneously increase her interest and engagement in many other activities: sports, clubs, workshops, reading, exploring, camping, traveling, crafting, and creating.

Social Media and Safety

We are really strict in our house about technology and social media use. Our kids didn't get phones until they were 13, and they were forbidden from using any social media until they were 15. Then they were allowed to use it, but ONLY if we were friends and I could monitor what they and their friends are posting. The kids know that we track their whereabouts on our phones, and we also monitor the content of their text messages and social media posts. Basically, I get a copy of every keystroke, photo, post, etc. that they make. When they were younger, I would sign into the iPad while they were in their rooms texting and I would sit in the living room and read the conversations they were having in real time. When we talk about what they send to others and what they post online, I reiterate that everything is permanent and that the choices that they make today will impact their lives forever. Making a stupid decision now will keep them from getting into college or getting a job later. I make sure that they know that if they even think about sending or receiving a nude photo they can be on the sex offender registry for the next 30 years.

—Amber, parent of 15-year-old and 17-year-old daughters

At first glance this seems like a pretty involved and sophisticated parent, right? A parent who is diligent with strict parameters and consistent monitoring in an attempt to keep their child safe. She is definitely *not* one of the 61% of parents who rarely or never monitor their child's use of social media (Hinkelman, 2017).

Parents, and the world of internet safety tools, are trying desperately to keep up with the rapidly advancing technology that kids can access. Unfortunately, the way we understand and use technology is changing faster than ever. It often feels that as soon as we get a handle on the latest app or trend, it becomes quickly outdated and replaced by a faster, more sophisticated, more intuitive option.

While Amber is putting forth great effort in her attempt to keep her girls safe, there are some critical issues that are important to note and discuss:

1. *They can only have social media if we are connected, so I can monitor what they are posting and seeing.* This may be the most common strategy that parents implement when initially introducing their kids to social media, and while it is a laudable effort, it may prove to be a bit short-sighted as we all have the ability to control who sees what content within our feed.

   Regardless, if you are "friends" with or "following" another person on social media, they have the easy ability to control what you can see from what they post. From limiting your access to specific posts to ensuring you can't see their full friend list, privacy settings and viewing controls allow for customized experiences for each user. Making a post that "everyone, except Mom" can see is a real thing, as is making a post that only 10 of my closest pals can see.

   Often, when girls experience high levels of parent monitoring, they create an alternate social media profile.

On Instagram, the fake profile is called a "finsta," or fake insta. The finsta is where they post all of the "authentic" and "real" content—basically a place for the stuff they don't want their parents to see. Girls describe this alternate profile as the platform where they are their true selves and they can "look normal" or "be silly" without being judged, whereas their "regular" page has to be perfect. Ironically, the curated, beautiful life that they work so hard to construct is the one that they knowingly identify as fake, while the finsta is considered the more authentic profile.

Adequately monitoring the activity of an avid user of social media can turn into a full time job, particularly as girls make more social connections, friends and followers. When girls have 500+ connections, it can be hard to monitor all of the interactions, direct messages, group chats and posts that all of their friends make. And when social media "handles" (i.e. the username that someone uses instead of their real name) don't reveal a person's identity, girls may unknowingly accept friend requests and connections from acquaintances they have met just one time or even strangers who are trolling for connections. While girls report wanting to keep what they post private, specifically from parents and teachers, over 40% report accepting friend requests from people that they don't know (Hinkelman, 2017).

2. *They know I track their whereabouts and their activity with monitoring apps and programs.* Parents today have the ability to track their child's location (or at least the location of the child's phone). They can know if their teen is driving faster than the speed limit, can receive a report on each text message and email that they sent on a particular day, can monitor their social networks for signs of depression or suicidality, and can be alerted if potentially risqué photos have been sent or received.

One of the most obvious challenges here is that the software and apps used for these purposes can be easy for kids to simply uninstall or figure out how to work around. I've heard many of the strategies: "I just leave my phone in my locker or at my friend's house, and it looks like that is where I am" or "My mom monitors my iMessages through the iCloud, so we just use WhatsApp instead" or "Sometimes I just shut my phone off and tell my parents that the battery died."

This is not to say that keeping track of kids is useless or a waste of time. Rather, it is not a fail-proof approach to keeping kids safe. Kids today are savvy and curious. Many see the parental limits, surveillance, and tracking as a challenge for them to work around, and they uninstall or circumvent the monitoring devices. Of particular concern is when the parental monitoring takes place without the knowledge of the teen. When they invariably discover the situation, it can do little more than create increased distrust, angst, and consternation in the relationship.

3. *I tell her everything is permanent and that the decisions that she makes now will have life-long consequences.* There is some truth to this statement, but it is also an intense scare tactic. Much like the "scared straight" programs of the 1970s and 1980s that were designed to whip kids into shape so that they never do drugs or become juvenile delinquents; these approaches don't often resonate with adolescents who are often living in the moment. Developmentally, adolescents tend to perceive their experiences and emotions as completely unique and see themselves as relatively invincible. Teens routinely engage in risk-taking and sensation-seeking behaviors, often without regard for the consequences.

If you work in schools or are parenting tween or teen girls, it's likely that you've been exposed to programs that focus on digital footprints, digital dangers, digital citizenship, or privacy and etiquette online. These programs and workshops often provide good information on what kids might be getting into online and include insights into the latest trends and usage patterns. However, where many of these workshops fall short is that they focus primarily on all of the horrors and the things that could potentially go wrong, rather than helping students build the actual skills and competencies they need to navigate their digital world. There is no all-or-nothing mentality when it comes to helping girls stay safe on social media. There must be a hybrid approach that combines expectations, monitoring, and limit setting alongside skill building and open communication.

What Can We Do?

Acknowledge the importance that connection to technology and social media engagement play in girls' lives and relationships. When girls are spending up to eight hours or more a day using technology and social media, we have to recognize that this investment of time is also a prioritization of their peer relationships and connection to others. Developmentally appropriate for this age, teen girls often define themselves and construct their identity based on their relationships with others. They are consistently navigating and negotiating their interactions, and the presence of technology has amplified the value, importance, and longevity of these interactions. Their phone is their perceived connection to the world, and for some, it can be completely devastating if taken away. Rather than minimize the value or importance of technology and social media, we need to acknowledge its importance while also seeking opportunities to amplify other relevant forms of care and connection.

Stay informed about the technology and social media landscape, even if you are not using it yourself. If technology and social media aren't your thing, don't worry; you don't have to turn into a Silicon Valley tech guru in order to be relevant to today's girls. However, you do have to at least try to stay educated and informed so that you can share a common language and understanding of a very important priority in her life. Take time to learn about the most common apps that teens are using, the YouTube stars that they are into, and the interests/groups they are following. As you learn, use this knowledge to foster open communication and to create points of connection so that she'll share more openly with you because she sees that you "get it."

Work with your girls to set reasonable time limits and shared expec-tations regarding technology and social media use. Girls get really frustrated when adults simply try to impose random and arbitrary rules, particularly surrounding their technology use. While there is clear evidence that time engaged with social media can have negative implications, simply restricting its use does not adequately address the concerns. We know that it is not simply less time using the tech-nology that matters; it is also ensuring that there is more time for engagement with other healthy and prosocial activities. Help girls examine not only the amount of time that they spend using social media and technology but also how they use these tools. When we recognize that not all social media engagement is negative and detri-mental, we can begin to identify its healthy and supportive aspects. From communicating with peers who they don't spend much time with to connecting with others who share similar hobbies or inter-ests, girls' online interactions have the potential to provide support, reduce isolation, and increase engagement.

For most of us, it is easier to feel motivated to do something when we have a say in the process or some agency in the decision. Instead of simply stating, "I have read some new research and have decided you can now spend a total of two hours per day on your phone," you might start a conversation with her about what she thinks is a rea-sonable amount of time and how she came to that conclusion. You might use the "screen time" function on her phone to understand how much time she is currently spending using her device and how, specifically, she is spending that time (social media, school work, YouTube, messaging, etc.).

Implementing limits is much easier if this conversation happens as soon as a new technology is introduced to a girl—for example, when she gets her first phone. It is much more difficult, but not impossible, to backtrack into an agreement after the fact, but your negotiating skills will need to be much stronger!

Instead of reinforcing scare tactics, focus on teaching the actual skills girls need to navigate their electronic world. The skills that girls need to effectively and safely navigate social media are nearly identical to the skills that they need to navigate tough situations in real life.

If I can teach a girl to use her voice to decline an unwanted back rub while she is standing at her school locker, I can also help her use her voice to refuse to send a risqué photo of herself to a peer who solicits the image. If she can appropriately and confidently stand up to bullying or disrespect in person, then teaching her how to do that via technology should be relatively straightforward. The assertiveness and the refusal skills that she would utilize are the exact same set of skills—they are just being applied in different environments.

It is important to consider whether your girl has the skills to stand up for herself, share her opinion, appropriately disagree with someone, and set boundaries. If you rarely observe her speaking her mind or enforcing a boundary, it is likely that she struggles with these skills or perhaps doesn't have opportunities to practice and hone them. Help her find her voice in low-risk environments and situations, so that when she finds herself in higher-stakes scenarios, she knows what to do and how to react. As she becomes more adept at these strategies, she can more readily apply them in a variety of settings.

Unfortunately, when it comes to technology, we often fail to recognize that there are lots of skills that girls need to develop and practice to be effective digital citizens and to be safe consumers of digital content. By teaching girls how to effectively communicate with others, set appropriate boundaries, refuse certain activities, and know when to engage an adult in the conversation, we are helping them develop the competencies they need to navigate their lives and relationships more effectively.

Being a Girl Today Is Hard 3

Gender Roles, Body Image, and Confidence

There really is this expectation of what girls are supposed to look like. We are supposed to have long hair and be skinny but also be curvy and have perfect skin and eyebrows. Our makeup is supposed to be just right. It can't be too much or look like we tried too hard, but there are literally a million YouTube videos on how to perfectly put on makeup. It's like we are supposed to be sexy at the same time we are supposed to be cool, and if it looks like we are working too hard at any of it, then people think you are fake. Guys don't have it this hard.

—Izzy, 15

A Pink Box or a Blue Box?

For years I have talked in academic and educational settings about the early expectations surrounding gender that are put in place by society. That from the time a baby is born, there are expectations in place that are based exclusively on the baby's physical sex. From the moment the announcement is made "It's a girl!" we already have expectations on what the baby should wear and what colors are most appropriate for a little baby girl or boy.

Research studies have observed people's reactions toward babies who are wrapped in a pink blanket or a blue blanket. How would people respond to the baby based entirely on the color of the blanket? Would they do or say anything different if the baby was in pink or in blue? When they saw a baby wrapped in a pink blanket, they overwhelmingly commented on the baby's delicate features and physical beauty. When the same baby was wrapped in a blue blanket, people commented about how strong or strapping the baby was. If the baby was wrapped in yellow or green, most people thought twice about what they should say. What was the appropriate reaction now? They didn't want to say or do anything wrong or make an incorrect guess as to the baby's sex. If a baby is not wearing one of the assigned colors, we may be initially unsure of the sex of the child. Have you ever seen a baby who was not dressed in clothing that was gender congruent and felt confused as to what the sex of the baby was, what you should say to the parents, or how you should comment on the child?

We now see that this phenomenon begins well before the child is even born. Over the past several years the concept of the *gender reveal* party has been introduced. The gender reveal is generally a gathering of friends and family—often filmed for posting on social media—with an extravagant announcement accompanied by a pink or blue surprise that can explode out of a firework or emerge from a cake. We can now begin to adopt the pink or blue box stereotypes months in advance of a baby's arrival.

I had the opportunity to experience this first hand as I recently made my way through my first pregnancy. Having been a student of psychology, education, and gender studies for many years, I thought I was prepared for the onslaught of inquiries about the gender of the baby I was carrying, who was still many months from being born. After hearing the initial news, "We are having a baby!" nearly 100% of the time the announcement was followed by the question "Do you know what you are having?" Unfortunately, the response "A human baby" does little to satisfy the most curious inquisitors.

I realized very quickly that there is a real discomfort when the sex of the baby is not known. Friends and family may be at a loss as to what color gifts to buy and may begrudgingly choose grey, yellow, and green items as they await the chance to really splurge once they know for certain whether the baby is male or female. A family member shared that she just stood in the middle of the baby store looking around because, while she wanted to send a gift in advance of the birth, she was stuck because she didn't know whether to look in the boys section or the girls section. When a salesperson noticed her lack of direction in the store and asked her if she needed help, she said, "Well I don't know if it is a boy or a girl, so I don't know where to look."

Ever the social scientist, I wanted to investigate this theory myself prior to the baby's birth just to see what the reactions of others might be. While my husband and I decided not to find out the sex of the baby in advance, we were very aware that everyone else was keenly interested in this data point. After a doctor's appointment early in the pregnancy, the scheduler asked us on the way out, "Do you know what you are having?" and I replied, "I'm not sure, but I think it's a girl." She immediately responded, "Ohhhh! You are going to be buying all the bows and tutus!! How fun!" My husband and I silently gagged, and once we got out of the office to the elevator, I said, "See I told you! This is what people do!"

I, of course, had to try this again to see what the response would be when I tried out the alternate, "I think it's a boy." This was met with responses such as "You are so lucky! Boys are so much easier than girls" and "I bet your husband is so happy to be having a boy to play sports with" and (my favorite) "I bet that feels like a big relief for you since you are the 'girl expert'." Ouch!

Early Expectations for Boys and Girls

The early expectations that we have for boys and girls go well beyond color schemes and can influence the way we define and accept feminine and masculine gender for girls and boys, men and women. Early in life we begin to place value on certain traits or specific characteristics that we associate with boys or girls, and we may unconsciously impose rules or limits based on what is generally considered acceptable for either gender. How do these early impressions or expectations translate into our ongoing thoughts about what is right for boys and girls?

Carol Gilligan, a prominent Harvard psychologist who has studied the development of girls, believes that girls construct their identities and their understanding of their gender based on how other people respond to them (Gilligan, 1982). Girls develop thoughts, feelings, and behaviors based on the messages they receive from others regarding what it means to be a girl. For example, children generally learn at a very young age that girls, but not boys, wear dresses. They also learn that girls play with dolls and boys play with trucks. Boys don't cry. Girls don't fight. Girls do the dishes, and boys take out the garbage. The interactions that we have with children can help shape their understanding of what it means to be a boy or girl and can influence what they perceive to be "appropriate behavior" for their gender.

This early learning can affect and influence our decision-making later in life because our earliest experiences shape how we see ourselves in the world. Girls often learn how to be more feminine, while boys learn that showing emotions is equated with weakness. Girls understand that caretaking and nurturing are valued, and boys learn that toughness and masculinity are keys to acceptance.

Early expectations extend further than social and emotional development and can influence other decisions that we make as well. From who we date to the careers we choose, to the hobbies we pursue, so many of our day-to-day activities can often be categorized based on whether they are typically done by men or women.

⭐ ACTIVITY: WHO DOES WHAT?

Consider the following common tasks, chores, and activities. As you read through the list, can you easily assign an "expected gender" to the task? Are there items that jump out in your mind as things that, in general, girls/women do and things that, in general, boys/men do?

- Takes out the garbage
- Goes golfing
- Cooks dinner
- Hosts a dinner party

- Cleans the house
- Drinks beer
- Cuts the grass
- Drinks wine
- Plants the flowers
- Buys new shoes
- Washes the car
- Plays video games
- Does the laundry
- Watches documentaries
- Organizes the carpool
- Reads fashion blogs
- Buys the groceries
- Follows NFL football
- Irons the clothes
- Plays baseball
- Cleans the garage
- Tap dances
- Feeds the baby
- Goes to the PTA meetings
- Writes the thank-you notes
- Goes to the spa
- Bakes the birthday cakes
- Vacuums the carpet
- Pays the bills
- Changes the diapers
- Drives on a date

As you completed the above activity, did you find that many of the tasks are stereotypically assigned to a specific gender? Some are a bit more obvious than others, but of course, *all* are activities that both men and women can and do engage in. Did you notice whether or not *you* participate in more of the gender-typical or gender-atypical activities? It can sometimes be difficult to step outside the expected roles. Think about stay-at-home parents, for example. It is not all unusual for a mother to be a stay-at-home parent; however, it continues to be much less frequent that a father is the stay-at-home parent.

A colleague recently said to me,

> I started to think more about what my daughters were learning by observing me and my behavior as it relates to some of these gender roles. While I think that my husband and I really share the parenting load, I am for sure the one who coordinates childcare, makes the doctor's appointments and ensures everyone has food and clean clothes. I was never really bothered by this. Then one day my daughter asked me, "Momma, why does Daddy always drive the car when we are all together, but you only drive the car when he is not here?" Her observation totally rocked me! I have no idea why that is the case. I am a good driver and enjoy driving. But she is right; I am always the passenger if my husband is there.

Just as it can be difficult for adults to cross the lines of typical gender expectations, it can be difficult for both boys and girls to do this as well. Both worry that they will be judged or ridiculed in some way because they are different. Janya, a sixth-grade girl said,

> I think that everyone expects girls to play with dolls and makeup and do super-girly stuff. I like doing girly things sometimes, but I would rather play outside with my older brothers. I am really good at sports, but sometimes I feel like people tell me I should be quieter and act more "like a lady." I guess I am a tomboy.

Clearly, Janya is dealing with the pressure that she feels from others to be or act in a certain way. She knows what she likes and what she is good at but also recognizes that some of the things she enjoys do not necessarily fit in with what she has learned girls are supposed to do or be.

While girls now have more options than ever before to explore their interests and skills, they still recognize that there are expectations that people put on them based on their gender. I've talked to many parents, teachers, and counselors who say that they treat both boys and girls the same and tell them both that they can be and do anything they want. They see increased equality surrounding the things that girls can do, such as get good grades, play sports, and go to college.

Shouldn't We Just Do Away With Gender?

I recently was speaking to a group of educators about the differences that exist between the way boys and girls experience the world, and I was specifically highlighting some of the social and interpersonal challenges that disproportionately affect girls. One of the participants raised the question "Shouldn't we be doing away with gender?" I found the question intriguing, and I asked her to expand on her thought. What did she mean by "doing away with gender"? She shared that she felt like there is increasing pressure to avoid conversations about gender because the topic is becoming taboo or political. She went on to explain that forcing students to identify as a particular gender can result in backlash from students or parents, so it seemed better to simply avoid the whole topic. She posited that we should be treating all students the same regardless of gender, so perhaps it was time to move on from these binary categories.

I left this conversation feeling challenged and curious. As I later reflected on this exchange, I realized that the general premise behind this approach makes sense. While biological sex is a binary category of male or female, gender is a bit more complicated as it is the expression of one's identity. As gender norms evolve and become more fluid, do the discrete categories continue to have merit or value? If we treated all people the same, by giving them the same opportunities and access, would we achieve equality? As ideal as this concept sounds, it is impossible to discount the social and historical context that affects this discussion. Boys and girls have historically been treated differently because of their gender, with girls generally having fewer options and opportunities and more restrictions placed on them. The ensuing impact of this differential treatment is still present today. We know that girls continue to be at risk for negative outcomes simply because they are girls. Girls are more likely to have issues with confidence and self-esteem, experience sexual violence, or be diagnosed with a mental health disorder. We also know that girls are less likely to lead a Fortune 500 company, coach a sports team, or oversee a school district. So if we were to approach our work with all students from a "gender-free" perspective and strive to systematically and uniformly deliver services in an attempt to achieve social and educational equality, we would be failing to account for the inequity that is already present. Boys and girls are not starting at the same place, and their experiences throughout life exacerbate the differences in the opportunities offered to them.

As we approach these conversations, we have to think not just about equality but also about equity. *Equality* means that everyone gets the same thing. For example, if I am a basketball coach and I issue all of my players the exact same-size uniform, I am technically promoting equality. Thus, regardless of the height, weight, or build of the player, the players get the same uniform. In doing so I ensure that no one can complain about differential or preferential treatment. That is equality. *Equity,* on the other hand, means that I take the time to make certain that each player receives the specific size that they need for their unique body. I ensure that they get precisely what is required for them to do their best and flourish in that specific environment.

When we approach our work with girls, we must recognize that there continue to be differences, as well as barriers, that exist for girls and women that require unique and tailored supports to ensure that they have the opportunity and the resources to overcome some of the most difficult challenges that they will encounter.

A second part of this discussion that is important to consider is how individuals define and describe their own identity. Terms such as *gender fluid, gender nonconforming, gender free, gender nonbinary,* and many others are making their way into more mainstream discourse. Pushing back against traditional gender stereotypes, these terms of identification allow an individual to more holistically and inclusively define and describe their gender identity in ways that have not been previously available. The question is not how we "do away with gender"; rather, how do we create inclusive and inviting spaces for *all* students, regardless of their sexual orientation or gender identity or expression? Rather than simply determine that the categories are irrelevant, shouldn't we be working diligently to expand the rigidity of the categorization itself? We should be pushing to make those pink and blue boxes bigger and more inclusive and we should also have other "boxes" where all students can find acceptance as they create, shape, name, and own their unique identities. Understanding and celebrating different identities means that there is a place for all, not that all must fit into a particular category. This is equity.

Forming an Identity and Developing Confidence

Self-discovery and identity formation are critical developmental milestones of the adolescent years. As discussed earlier, girls are utilizing the feedback that they receive from others to construct their identity and sense of self. They are also consuming vast amounts of media, particularly social media, which contributes to their developing self-perception and, more often than not, judging themselves harshly when they compare themselves with what they see in the media.

As girls go through puberty, their sexuality becomes more salient (Salomon & Brown, 2019), and their perception of their physical appearance becomes a barometer for their self-esteem. The world continues to elevate the outward characteristics of girls over their internal traits and strengths. This prioritization is not lost on girls. They discuss the pressures they feel to look a certain way, have specific styles or brands of clothes, and possess ideal body characteristics. Girls also go to great lengths to achieve a specific look. Skin, hair, nails, eyebrows, breasts, legs, eyelashes, lips, stomach, eyes, nose, butt, and teeth are all body parts that girls report wanting to change. They tan their skin, straighten their hair, augment their eyelashes, whiten their teeth, sculpt their eyebrows, pad their bras, and starve their bodies in an attempt to achieve what they see as ideal beauty. We can clearly see in the media that girls are exposed to images of women that are overtly sexual, often very thin or unnaturally curvaceous with unrealistic and surgically enhanced proportions. In turn, one of the biggest struggles that girls experience is pressure to look a certain way. This "certain way" varies somewhat based on environment, culture, and ethnicity, but overwhelmingly girls report experiencing the pressures of the mainstream media on a daily basis. Many know what it feels like to spend hours of time each day thinking about their appearance, their body size and shape, and what they will wear.

Early exposure to many of these beauty ideals can be harmful to girls. Girls who are exposed to media images that promote a thin-as-ideal body actually have increased dissatisfaction with their own body. Additionally, girls who spend the most time on social media are also more likely to want to change their appearance (Hinkelman, 2017). The longer they are exposed to these kinds of images or messages, the more dissatisfied they become and the more likely they are to report being on a diet. This was found to be the case even among girls who were already thin, with a low body mass index, as well as with very young girls (Knobloch-Westerwick & Crane, 2012).

One of the most important predictors of self-esteem in girls is their own thoughts about their appearance and body weight. Girls' perception of their appearance affects their self-esteem more than girls' self-esteem affects their perception of their appearance. This means that the way girls *think* they look has more to do with how they *feel* about themselves than almost anything else. Young women report that their body weight is the aspect of their life with which they are most dissatisfied (Kutob et al., 2010), meaning that girls become more consumed with how they look than with who they are or what they do. They come to learn that their value in our society comes more from their outward appearance than from their work ethic or accomplishments.

In my survey research with nearly 11,000 girls in The Girls' Index™ (Hinkelman, 2017), I sought to further understand the concepts that contribute to girls' identity development and what is correlated to their ratings of their own confidence. During the period when girls' confidence drops the most precipitously, between fifth and ninth grade, their desire to change their appearance increases at nearly the same rate (see Figure 3.1), and the more time they spend on social media, the lower the levels of confidence they report and the less satisfied they are with their appearance.

Social media is the ultimate looking glass for teens and adults alike. It is the place where we put something out there—a post, a video, a photo—and then we wait for the responses, judgment, or affirmations that come from others. The feedback that we receive can affect our emotional state positively or negatively and can also influence our future behaviors. Girls are especially vulnerable to this feedback

Figure 3.1 Decline in Girls' Confidence Versus Girls' Desire to Change Their Appearance

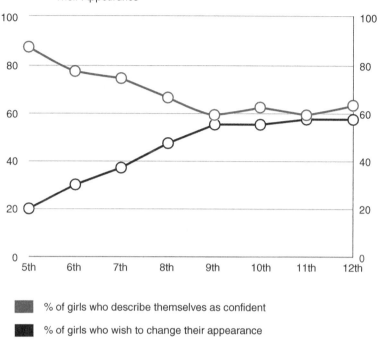

% of girls who describe themselves as confident

% of girls who wish to change their appearance

Source: The Girls' Index, 2017.

loop. As one tenth-grade girl explained to me, "I will take like 100 selfies to try to get a good one, and sometimes even then I don't get a good one. But then, once I have one that is ok, I can crop it and filter it and make it look really good." She went on to explain to me that instead of simply posting the photo once she got it to the place where she was satisfied, she would save it for posting later that evening because around 9 p.m. "everyone would be on" and the photo wouldn't "get lost in the feed."

I learned that after making a post there is a critical period of time in which to accumulate "likes" from your followers. For this particular post she referenced 100 likes within the first 10 to 15 minutes—after which the photo would be removed and perhaps recycled for a later post. I learned that it is not just the number of likes that are received or the timing of the likes; it is also the quality of the likes that matter. There is a significant difference between whether your mom likes your post and whether your crush likes your post. (Sorry mom!)

☆ ACTIVITY: CRITICALLY ANALYZE THE MEDIA, AND DISRUPT THE FEED

The images of girls throughout the media are often overtly sexual, airbrushed, cropped, and resized. The skin of Black women is often lightened, and complexions of models are edited to look as though they have no pores and flawless skin. Even supermodels and Instagram influencers do not look the same in real life as they do in advertising. Girls often see these images and feel that this skinny, curvaceous, pretty, sexy ideal is what they should look like and is the image that they should emulate.

We want girls to develop a critical eye when it comes to media consumption, to possess the ability to recognize the difference between a "real" body and a digitally enhanced body, and to be cautious about judging their own bodies against these unrealistic images.

Unfortunately, the comparisons that we make on social media don't stop at beauty and body image. We often compare other aspects of ourselves—our relationships, possessions, vacations, employment, hobbies, and so on. Taking an opportunity to intentionally analyze the content that we are consistently viewing can help us become more aware of the effect it has on us. If you find through this social media audit that the content that you or your girls are consuming is having more of a negative than a positive impact, you can make some proactive choices to adjust the type of content that is being regularly consumed.

This approach is a little tricky because it is unlikely that you will find great success in telling girls that they should simply "unfollow" a bunch of people, artists, or interest groups that they have been following. The following are some questions to consider:

1. Which three people/ideas/concepts do you follow that generally make you feel annoyed/frustrated/uncomfortable/inadequate? Every time you see a post from this person, your blood pressure rises, or each time you watch a diet tip from the amazingly and unrealistically fit Instagram model, your spirits instantly sink. Pick

the three that consistently irritate you, and hide or unfollow them for a couple of weeks. You don't have to commit to unfollowing them forever, but take a break from the constant annoyance, and note how much, if at all, you miss it. This might not be that much of a stretch as 44% of teens report that they sometimes unfriend or unfollow people on social media (Anderson & Jiang, 2018), and 78% of the time they unfollow people who are "creating too much drama."

2. What are some cool things your girl is interested in that she may not already be following on social media? Is she a softball player perhaps following NCAA Softball, USA Softball, or ESPNw? If she's into theater, perhaps Broadway Spotlight will provide some interesting insights. Maybe coding is her jam, and Girls Who Code or Black Girls Code would be cool sites for her to follow. The idea here is not that she is only consuming content that is always inspiring, uplifting, and intellectually enriching (although wouldn't that be great?) but that there is positive content that is disrupting the constant narrative of neutral or even negative content.

3. What would it be like to completely stay off social media for a period of time? In the same way that we limit other seemingly toxic things in our lives—like carbs, alcohol, and sugar—a social media detox can offer us a break from all of the comparisons and the exhaustion that we sometimes experience. When girls actually had a break from social media, even for one day, they reported higher levels of happiness (Twenge et al., 2018); when they had a break for more than a week, their happiness levels soared (after they had gone through their initial "withdrawal" period).

Many summer camps are now "tech-free," and kids have to check in their phones when they arrive at the camp. I recently talked to both a girl who attended one of these camps and a parent who sent her daughter to a camp. Both reported an initial reticence about the camp. The mother was concerned that her daughter wouldn't have immediate access to her if she needed something. The girl was initially resistant to attending the camp because her

(Continued)

(Continued)

friends refused to attend due to the "no-tech" rule, but then after the first few days passed, she came to embrace the experience. She said that it was different because "none of the kids there had phones, so it wasn't like you were the only one"; if she was one of the only people there who didn't have access to technology, she would have felt markedly different. And the mom? She was comforted by the fact that the camp sent the parents a summary email each day and there were designated times when their kids could contact them for a specific period of time.

Other Contributions to Body Insecurity

While social media can play a significant role in how we feel about ourselves and our bodies, the messages that we receive from parents, teachers, and peers are also critically important. I saw this first hand with Meghan, a young woman who struggles with issues around body image. She shared with me that at least half of the thoughts that she has on a daily basis revolve around her weight, her eating, and her appearance. She, at age 21, says that she feels better and more confident when she is thinner and that she will avoid going places or meeting up with friends if she feels like she has gained weight or does not look "presentable."

I was interested in learning when her thoughts and negative feelings about her body began. She told me that when she was in second grade, she went on her first diet. Her mother was on Weight Watchers, as were all her mother's friends. She said she remembers them all being over for lunch one day, and all they talked about was food, diets, exercise, and fitting into a bikini in the summer. Meghan said that day she went to her room and looked at her own body in the mirror. She said she never wore a bikini before and thought that she needed to be slimmer to do that. She began to notice that she was not as small as the other girls in her grade and made the decision to start a diet. She said ever since second grade she has been on some type of diet or eating plan and was constantly trying to lose weight. More than 10 years later, and well within a healthy weight range,

Meghan is still dealing with feelings of inadequacy, low self-esteem, and negative body image. She says,

> I also remember when I was in elementary school, my dad came up to me and kind of pinched my stomach and made a comment about my weight. I don't really think he was trying to be mean, but that experience has stuck with me for all of these years. I can still feel the exact feelings that I felt on that day when that happened. My dad is my best friend but also my biggest critic. When I slip up with my eating, he is the first person who will comment on it.

As we can see from Meghan's situation, our issues with food and eating do not disappear when we become adults. Many of the insecurities and pressures that we had as young girls continue for us well into our adulthood. When I talk to parents and teachers about some of these issues, I always bring up the infamous office potluck. Lots of schools and offices have potluck lunches or birthday lunches where everyone is responsible for bringing something to contribute. Rarely can we observe an entire lunch without hearing multiple comments about diet, weight, what we can or should eat, and what is off limits. "Oh, those brownies look so delicious, but I just shouldn't" or "I am cheating today and going to have to do some extra time at the gym tomorrow" or "As soon as this diet is over, I can't wait to eat some pizza!"

Regardless of the actual comments, it is rare that you can have a room of women together with food without there being negative and self-deprecating dialogue.

⭐ ACTIVITY: OBSERVE THE POTLUCK AND THE DIETERS

Many of us will be at lunch or dinner at some point in the future with a group of friends or colleagues. Pay attention to who in the group is more likely to talk about food, calories, diets, fat, exercise, or guilt. Do more men or women obsess about their eating? Who is on a diet in the group, and how do you know that?

While girls are watching these subtle, or more indirect, comments that we make around food, eating, body size, and shape, they are also profoundly affected by our more direct comments and behaviors. Girls all around us are paying attention to our own relationship with food. They watch what we eat, how we talk about food, and how we talk about our own bodies. The role that we, as adults, have in shaping girls' attitudes about their own bodies cannot be overstated. We can see from Meghan's story that her early interactions with her mother and father around her body and eating have stuck with her as an adult and significantly affect how she thinks about herself today.

The comments that Meghan experienced and observed were obviously damaging, but they were much less overt and direct than what some girls experience from their parents. One parent proudly shared a story about how she was dealing with Zoe, her "chubby, six-year-old daughter." The mother, a middle school vice principal in an affluent suburb, was complaining about her daughter's overeating and recent weight gain. She shared that on a recent shopping trip to the mall she planned to "nip that problem in the bud." The mother stated, "I marched Zoe right down to the Lane Bryant store and told her that if she keeps it up, this will be the only store where she would be able to buy clothes."

In the same way that Meghan clearly remembers what it felt like when her father pinched her stomach, I imagine six-year-old Zoe will have a destructive memory of her experience. It is hard to believe that an adult would proudly share this story, but it reiterates the fact that just because we grow up and become adults does not mean we figure out how to address complicated issues and internal insecurities. Zoe will face pressures around her looks and body size from the media and from society and will also have to endure the negative pressures and feedback from her mother. Unfortunately, she is a girl who will be a prime candidate for developing an eating disorder when she hits her teenage years.

As we think about cultivating body confidence in girls, we must think about the active and passive messages they are receiving and the potential impact of each. Comments from a parent can sting differently than a scrolling advertisement on social media. Ongoing consumption of content that encourages and celebrates diversity in shape, figure, fitness, weight, ability, dress, and all things appearance related can help encourage acceptance of a healthier body and appearance, which is much less limiting for girls. Perhaps one of the first elements of this acceptance would be to encourage girls to have a strong and healthy body rather than a skinny or sexy one.

How I Think I Look = How I Feel About Myself

This seems to be the case for Meghan, discussed above, who told me that she estimates that about 80% of how she feels about herself is related to how she feels about her body and whether she feels skinny or pretty. She said the other 20% is connected to her other characteristics, such as who she is as a friend, whether she is kind, and her relationships with her family.

If the number one thing that influences and affects girls' self-esteem is the perceptions they hold of their bodies and the thoughts they have about their own physical attractiveness, then girls are viewing their appearance as their major sense of worth. When physical beauty and external traits and characteristics are constantly reinforced as important for girls at the expense of other traits, skills, and characteristics, we are—perhaps subconsciously—telling girls that their value comes largely from their outward appearance.

Is this too far-fetched? Probably not. In our research with girls we have seen that they place extreme emphasis on outward appearance and especially on being sexy and attractive. Girls talk about the importance of being "tall and skinny, with big boobs and nice hair," and why wouldn't they? This is the consistent image that they receive from the mainstream media on what is attractive, beautiful, feminine, and sexy.

With body image so tightly connected to self-esteem, how can we change the way girls feel about and experience their own bodies? We have to find ways to direct the messages that girls receive surrounding body image and ideal bodies. This is not accomplished by simply telling girls that all body shapes and sizes are beautiful. We must make concentrated efforts to assist girls in learning how to base their self-esteem on personal attributes other than body weight and shape.

Girls have so many positive qualities that are not associated with looks; however, these qualities are rarely emphasized. In much the same way that the baby in the pink blanket receives comments and compliments about being pretty or delicate, adolescent girls also receive many more compliments about their appearance than about their other qualities or their abilities. We need to help girls focus on their positive qualities, traits, and characteristics that are not related to body image. When girls are able to do this, their perceptions of their body changes, and they experience less body dissatisfaction. Girls who can identify the things that they do well and the positive characteristics that they possess tend to rely less on weight and body shape to determine their self-esteem (Armitage, 2012). Simply stated, when girls recognize that they are good at things other than being attractive, they experience higher levels of self-esteem.

☆☆ ACTIVITY: STRENGTH BOMBARDMENT

Sometimes it is difficult for girls to identify their own positive traits. Having a group of girls participate in an activity called "strength bombardment" gives them the opportunity to identify the traits and characteristics of their peers that they admire and allows girls to hear positive comments from an entire group of their peers.

This activity should be used with a group of girls who already know one another. The group sits in a circle, and one person at a time takes a turn sitting in the middle of the circle. The person who is in the middle should not speak; rather, she should just listen to the comments made by each person in the circle. Each person in the circle takes a turn sharing a positive comment or compliment about the person who is in the middle of the circle, but the comment cannot be related to looks, beauty, clothes, or any external factor. Compliments and comments must be related to character, kindness, behavior, or work ethic—internal qualities.

After each girl around the circle shares a comment about the girl in the middle, the girl in the middle should say thank you and return to her seat in the circle. She shouldn't argue with the compliments or try to discount the feedback from her peers. The next group member then can make her way to the center of the circle, and the process is repeated until all of the girls have participated.

What Can We Do?

Encourage girls to identify their strengths and talents. We are all good at different things, but sometimes it is difficult to truly identify what those things actually are. Girls have a very difficult time believing that they are good at many things, and as they get older, their ability to identify their strengths becomes further compromised. Girls in elementary school have a much easier time identifying the things they are good at than girls in high school. Ask girls to make a list of the things they do well, and help them think broadly about all of their skills, talents, and interests. Creativity, empathy, compassion, tenacity, and athleticism are all traits and characteristics that girls may not readily identify in themselves, but these descriptors represent more of who they are as individuals than any of the physical attributes they possess.

Pay attention to how you think about and reinforce traditional expectations around masculinity and femininity. Do you have long-standing beliefs about what boys and girls are supposed to do or supposed to be good at? Do girls who do not fit into a traditional mold get treated differently? When we reinforce traditional ideals for girls, we limit them and their options. We must encourage strength, determination, and competence in girls. Teachers can ensure that room tasks are evenly divided between girls and boys and that every time there is a physical task to be completed a boy is not automatically chosen for the job. Similarly, boys can be selected for domestic or caretaking room tasks, demonstrating that these chores are not inherently masculine or feminine.

Expand girls' exposure to and experience in diverse life skills. Life skills are not skills for boys or skills for girls. Girls need to know how to jump a car battery, shovel snow, hard-boil an egg, stand up for themselves, iron a shirt, throw a baseball, and cut the grass. Boys need to learn these things as well. These are not activities that one sex can inherently do better, but they are skills that we tend to see become assigned to either boys or girls. To make it through life most successfully and with the highest levels of competence, girls and boys need to develop skills in all areas, not just the areas that have been typically associated with their gender.

Emphasize and compliment internal rather than external traits. As a society, we easily notice and compliment the external characteristics of others. How often do we hear someone saying, "You look great! Have you lost weight?" or "Your hair looks great!" or "I love that outfit" and "You must have been in the sun: your skin is glowing." It is much easier to comment on these factors; however, in doing so we reinforce the value placed on external factors and/or looks. The following chart provides examples of external versus internal traits:

External	Internal
Body shape	Competence
Weight/body size	Persistence
Clothes	Courage
Hair	Performance
Skin tone	Character

Pay attention to the way you talk about your own body, about other women's bodies, and about food. Girls who have women in their lives who diet and constantly talk about food, calories, and body size are far more likely to develop issues around their own bodies at a very early age. Does she overhear you criticizing how you look in a particular outfit? Do your comments about the appearance of other women uplift and encourage or demean and degrade? I have a friend who is the mother of two daughters; she shared with me that the only "*F* word" that is banned in her house is "fat."

Finally, pay attention to what you say about food and calorie consumption in front of girls. Girls are watching us when we comment on how everything looks so delicious but we "shouldn't," "couldn't," or "mustn't" have dessert. Pay attention next time you are at an office meal or potluck, and see how many people comment on their food selections. Also, notice if your visceral reaction is to participate in this dialogue as well.

Host a "no fat talk" day/week/month, and make your home or office a "no fat talk" zone. "Fat talk" is the way we consciously or unconsciously give ourselves negative messages about our bodies. Often these passing remarks are so pervasive that we barely even notice them unless they are brought into our awareness. When we are aware, the opportunity exists to point out the ways in which our self-focused and self-deprecating thoughts are pervasively centered on how unfit or fat we are. Several groups, including the Eating Concerns Advisors and the national sorority Tri Delta, have sponsored and publicized events focused on limiting the negative messages we give ourselves about our bodies. An undertaking such as this actually is a harder concept to pull off than you might think. Try it with a friend first, and see how often you talk about weight, body shape, eating, calories, and so on within a specific period of time. Then expand this to your home or your office, and ensure that each person has responsibility for calling out the "fat talk" behaviors of others by saying things like "We don't fat talk here" or "In this office we celebrate all body shapes and sizes."

Emphasize strong, healthy bodies rather than thin bodies, and point out unrealistic images of girls and women in the media. Skinny does not necessarily equal healthy, and overweight does not always equate to body negativity. The way an individual experiences her body is unique, often changing, and generally unpredictable. We may look at another person's figure and think to ourselves, "If I looked like her, I would strut around in a bikini all day." Or we might judge another person's appearance by saying, "I can't believe she is wearing that. She doesn't have the body to pull off that outfit."

The media has a focus on lean or femininely muscular body shapes for women. It is only recently that softer, fuller, and more curvaceous body types are being celebrated in mainstream media, but still these images continue to be in the minority. When you see billboards, advertisements, social media feeds, music videos, and television commercials, ask girls to identify the bodies that look strong and healthy. What do they notice about the differences between the various body types? Help them adopt an acceptance of body diversity in others and in themselves.

Mean Girls 4

Dealing With Drama and Relationships

I don't even understand how it happened. We were all best friends one day, and then it seemed like overnight everything changed. I don't even know what I did. But somehow, my friend—I guess I should call her my ex-friend—got it in her mind that I was talking to her boyfriend or something, and then the next day at school the entire group ignored me. They conveniently didn't have an extra seat for me at the lunch table, and then at volleyball practice they would not even make eye contact with me. When I walked into the locker room, everyone just stopped talking and stared at me. Then that same night, on Instagram, they were posting all of these messages about how "true friends don't steal each other's boyfriends" and "that it is good to know who in life you can really trust and who you can't" and "Be careful, you can be surprised when you learn that the people who you thought were your friends are really backstabbing whores"—yes, they called me a backstabbing whore, and I didn't even do anything! I can't even figure out where this all came from, who started it, or how to make it stop. It just feels like it is out of control, and there is nothing I can do. I hate all of this drama!

—Morgan, eleventh grade

Girl Drama

In my research survey called The Girls' Index™ (Hinkelman, 2017), I had the opportunity to ask nearly 11,000 girls the same question, "What are the big things going on for girls your age?" Girls from fifth through twelfth grade responded by writing in all sorts of responses, from academics to popularity, to weight and body image, to family issues and sports. Overwhelmingly, there was one word that occurred more frequently than any other word in the survey, and that was the word *drama*.

When I combed the data for what girls actually meant by the word *drama*, I saw responses like "girls being mean to each other," "spreading rumors and gossip," "getting into arguments," "ignoring or excluding other girls," and "fighting over friends and boyfriends." *Drama* is the word that girls use to describe the frustrations of their social lives, the difficulties they have navigating relationships, and the challenges they face communicating effectively with their friends. So really what girls mean when they talk about drama is actually *conflict* in their relationships.

Teachers, counselors, and parents describe "drama" similarly. They say, "It's girls excluding each other from parties and social events," "girls fighting over boyfriends or making fun of other girls' clothes," "girls just being downright mean to one another; I don't get it why these girls are so cruel," and finally "I think it is just girls being girls."

Seventy-six percent of girls say that most girls are in competition with one another; 41% of girls say they do not trust other girls.

As girls get to late elementary school, issues with friendships and relationships with other girls have increased importance, and by middle school nearly 80% of girls say that friendship and girl drama are big issues facing girls their age. Often the aggressive behavior that happens between girls is overlooked as simply "Girls being girls." There is a pervasive expectation that girls are "catty," "will stab you in the back," and lack authenticity in relationships. As Tiana, a seventh-grade girl, stated, "I think people expect girls to compete with each other. They like to see a cat fight."

Competition between and among girls is very real. Three out of four girls believe that most girls are in competition with one another, and more than 40% say that they don't trust other girls. When I ask girls what they are competing for, there is a wide variety of responses, from grades, looks, and popularity to sports, attention, and boys. Adults question, "Why are these girls so mean? Why don't they care about anyone else's feelings? When do they grow out of this horrible stage? Is this aggression and meanness just a part of girlhood?"

While these are all legitimate questions, the real questions that we want to answer is "What is going on in the lives of girls that makes their social aggression so pervasive? How are they learning to communicate with one another and handle conflict? And is there anything that we can do to change it?"

Boys and girls both go through a period of time when they navigate and negotiate friendships and relationships, but there seem to be big differences in how they approach these processes and how they approach conflict. Girls tend to have more difficulty than boys in directly addressing conflict and they tend to use different strategies when managing tumultuous situations or relationships. As one teacher said, "Guys will get in a fight one day and then be cool with each other the next day. Girls hang on to this stuff for years. It is almost like they enjoy the drama."

What Is Relational Aggression?

Relational aggression is girl bullying. It is the way in which girls use their relationships with one another to be mean, manipulative, exclusionary, and hostile (Crick & Grotpeter, 2005; Grotpeter & Crick, 1996). While bullying in schools has received much attention in recent years and many schools and concerned communities are doing more to address this important topic, few have figured out how to address the more covert bullying that often takes place between and among girls. Many states have adopted legislation that requires schools to develop and implement policies that address bullying and cyberbullying, and some of girls' relationally aggressive behavior falls into these categories. However, the type of bullying that is most common between and among girls—relational bullying and aggression—can be overlooked because there are rarely physical acts of intimidation (Young et al., 2006). When aggression is relational, it does not necessarily assume the power differential as defined in traditional bullying—picture the big kid stealing the smaller kid's lunch money. Relational aggression is a type of aggression that occurs through the relationships that we have with one another. Individuals who use relational aggression often know one another, have (or have had) close friendships or relationships with one another, and may be in the same social circles.

Relational aggression includes "sarcastic verbal comments, speaking to another in a cold or hostile tone of voice, ignoring, staring, gossiping, spreading rumors, 'mean' facial expressions, and exclusion, all acts aimed to damage the target's social status or self-esteem" (Remillard & Lamb, 2005, p. 221). In other words, relationally aggressive relationships are based on intimacy, and the relationship is used as a tool to manipulate. Overtly aggressive relationships are based on a desire to act aggressively toward, intimidate, or control another person. Relational aggression is much less obvious but can often be much more damaging.

Girls use acquaintances, friendships, and even dating relationships as fodder for aggression in a different way from what boys do. Though both boys and girls can be aggressive, we tend to see more overt and physical aggression in boys and more relational and manipulative aggression exhibited by girls. When I met Sadie, a tenth grader, and heard her story, I became increasingly aware that relational aggression is intense and can truly affect any girl regardless of her ethnicity, social status, income, or intelligence level. Sadie lives in an affluent community with her caring and involved parents. She is an honor roll student and an athlete and has been generally well liked by her peers. She has an older sister and a younger brother. She is attractive, intelligent, and very social:

> I'm in the school musical and am totally consumed with that right now, so I haven't been hanging out with my "usual group" of friends as much as I normally do. There is this group of girls, and we have been friends for the entire year. We hang out after school and on the weekends together—I

thought everything was cool. Then one of the guys that one of my friends liked started messaging me. I thought he was really cute, and they weren't dating or anything, so I didn't think it was a big deal if I just messaged him back and started talking to him. We hung out one time at the varsity basketball game, and apparently it was a really big deal to my so-called friends. Before I even got to school the next day, there were Instagram postings, Snaps, and group messages going around saying stuff like "Sadie is a dirty slut" and "Watch out, or Sadie will have sex with your boyfriend" and "Sadie does 'such-and-so' to boys in the bathroom," and there were even worse ones if you can believe that. It was like in a matter of hours the entire school was talking about me, and none of it was true! It's been a couple of months, and nothing has been the same. I mean, all you can really do is tell people that the rumors aren't true, but once people get something in their mind, it is really hard to change it. I can't stand school right now. . . . I mean, I really hate going there.

Unfortunately, Sadie's experience is not at all unique. Girls, parents, and teachers give similar examples of how they see girls gossip, spread rumors, and be mean to one another in very intense and intentional ways. With the proliferation of technology and the use of social media as the primary tool of communication, bullying and relational aggression now take place at any moment of the day or night—not merely during school hours. Students who once were able to retreat from a hostile school environment during the evenings or weekend are now susceptible to victimization 24 hours a day, seven days a week. As one teacher said to me, "We spend all day Monday dealing with what happened on social media over the weekend. We essentially lose a day of learning."

Social Media and Girls' Relationships

Technology has added a new dimension to girls' lives. While there are tremendous benefits from the technological advances that we have achieved, there is a very dark and dangerous side to technology as well. The ability to monitor, stalk, spread rumors, and defame others has become easier and more anonymous through the use of the internet. From creating fake profiles to posting embarrassing or manipulated photos, social media has become a very easy medium for rumors to fly, mistakes to be exploited, and relationships to be tested.

Cyberbullying, or the "willful and repeated harm inflicted through the use of computers, cell phones, and other electronic devices" (Patchin & Hinduja, 2012), has risen among teens over the past several years and is a prevalent form of relational aggression among girls. With the vast majority of U.S. teens having access to the internet and to smartphones, the use of technology to bully others has reached new heights. Teens have developed a preference for technology over face-to-face communication and interaction (D'Antona et al., 2010), and more than 82% of teens have reported that someone has said something mean or hurtful about them online. What was once a post on the bathroom wall where a handful of others could see it has become a post that hundreds or potentially thousands of "friends" can see. In fact, the more time that girls spend using social media, the less likely they are to have supportive friends to talk to about serious issues and the more likely they are to say that they don't trust other girls (Figure 4.1; Hinkelman, 2017).

This type of indirect aggression is consistent with the ways in which girls bully one another, and the instantaneous nature of virtual communication means that rumors, gossip, pictures, and videos can go

Figure 4.1 Hours Spent on Social Media and Mistrust of Other Girls

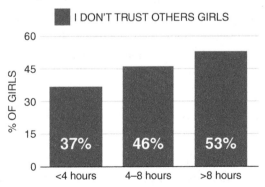

Source: The Girls' Index, 2017.

"viral" in a matter of seconds. An embarrassing moment caught on film is now shared with the entire school almost as quickly as it happens. Social media is now the stage on which girls' relationships are configured, and the activities and intimacies that would typically occur privately between friends are now on display for others to observe, comment on, and judge.

Cyberbullying differs from traditional bullying in that the victim may not know who the bully is or why they have been targeted. The virtual exchange also limits the ability to read visual cues and see the immediate impact of the communication. When we can't see the other person's reaction, we may fail to realize the depth to which our comments or actions may have hurt them. Girls will say and do things online that they would not say or do face-to-face. They can be cruel, sarcastic, and ruthless. Girls can take on different personas, manipulate their environments, and ostracize their peers.

Is This Just Girls Being Girls?

It is probably safe to say that most people have engaged in some of the relationally aggressive behaviors discussed. Gossiping or ignoring somebody are probably things many of us have done at one time or another. But we must recognize behavior that is normal and developmental and behavior that is damaging and used to manipulate or ruin someone's reputation.

The research that I conducted with girls revealed a difference between their definition of bullying behavior and their perception of their own experience in girl bullying. Specifically, girls were first asked if they had ever participated in girl bullying. In the survey a little over 35% of the girls reported that they have engaged in girl bullying. Next, the girls were asked to respond to a series of behaviors and indicate whether or not they had participated in specific behaviors that are considered examples of girl bullying or relational aggression (i.e., teasing, excluding someone, spreading a rumor, lying about another girl, etc.). The results were markedly different. More than 70% of the girls reported engaging in teasing or name calling; 53% stated that they had intentionally excluded someone from a social event. This tells us that the prevalence of actual relational aggression is extensive; however, girls do not define their own behavior as girl bullying.

It seems that the traditional definition of bullying, which is often perceived as physical aggression, such as pushing and shoving, does not necessarily resonate with girls. When they think of bullying, they are thinking of being pushed in the hall or someone stealing their lunch money. Girls are not necessarily defining the more subtle and relational bullying behaviors as actual bullying. So when they are engaging in more relational types of aggression, they do not always see these behaviors as participation in bullying.

This became extremely evident to me as I was working with a group of eighth-grade girls at an urban charter school. I had been asked to come to the school to work with a group of 12 girls who were deemed to be problematic—the queen bees: the socialites, the bullies, the manipulators, and in some cases the leaders. These were the girls who were creating the most distress for the entire grade and perhaps the entire school.

When I got to the school and met the girls, I realized that the queen bees are not always the queen bees when they are in a group of all queen bees! At different times, in different environments, and around different groups of people, we tend to experience one another and ourselves differently. In some cases where we have more power, social capital, or privilege, we can use or exploit that differently than if we are in a situation where we perceive ourselves to have less power or authority. This also applies to girls in situations where they are with new or different groups of girls. There is a period of time when they seek to establish their social order or hierarchy. I watched as the girls negotiated their roles, attempted to exert their control over the group, and tried to determine who belonged where.

As we moved through the activities for the day and engaged the girls in a variety of activities related to building trust, increasing communication, and having a positive impact on the school climate, I quickly realized that these girls had very little awareness that they were, in fact, part of the problem. They actually went as far as to say that there is "no bullying that really happens at our school." When I asked what they meant by that, the girls said, "Well, I mean, sometimes people will shove you in the hall or try to fight. But in general, I don't think that we have a lot of bullying happening at our school."

I next asked the girls about the way the girls treat one another. I asked them if they see girls who spread rumors, exclude other girls from activities, and gossip about other girls in the school. At this point they laughed and said that this sort of behavior happens all the time at their school! But that this was just how girls were; it wasn't really girls being bullies—just girls being girls. I wondered at what point social exclusion, rumor, and gossip spreading had become an accepted part of girls being girls.

⭑⭑ ACTIVITY: IDENTIFYING BULLYING AND RELATIONAL AGGRESSION

Help girls identify girl-bullying behaviors and how their actions may be considered bullying and/or relational aggression. Individually or in small groups, have girls consider the following:

Do I

- gossip or spread rumors about other girls?
- post things on Instagram, Snapchat, or other social media that could be embarrassing to another girl?
- ignore certain girls on purpose or intentionally exclude girls from "my group"?
- make fun of the clothes, appearance, or financial status of another girl?
- tell my friends who they can or should be friends with?

Take the time to explore with girls how and why they engage in any of these behaviors, and help them strategize healthier ways to manage their anger and express their opinions. Also, discuss what girls can do when they observe other girls participating in girl bullying.

Why Are Girls So Mean to Each Other?

Researchers have attempted to understand why girls engage in relational forms of aggression more than physical forms of aggression and why girls seem to prefer engaging in more covert ways of harming their peers than boys do. Interesting research (Brown, 1998) has looked at gender role adherence and the way in which girls participate in and experience relational aggression. Specifically, the researchers found that girls who follow along with more of the traditional stereotypical female behaviors are also more likely to engage in more relationally aggressive behavior. This is not to say that girls who merely look or act feminine are more relationally aggressive but rather that girls (and women) who buy into the idea that girls are "supposed" to act in certain conventional or stereotypical ways tend to engage in these more covert forms of bullying, social isolation, and peer exclusion more than their peers who hold less stereotypical or traditional beliefs about how girls should act.

For many girls and women embodying the female role means, in part, engaging in competition with other girls and women; criticizing and demeaning others' looks, behaviors, and thoughts; and isolating oneself from other girls while seeking the attention of men and boys. Relational aggression is a covert way of expressing anger, being dominant, and resolving conflict and tends to be more consistent with the social expectations placed on girls.

This makes sense because, in general, girls have been socialized to be kind and nice and to not be physically aggressive (Simmons, 2009). While boys and girls both get angry at similar rates, they learn to manage their anger differently (Brown, 1998). Girls are taught from a very young age that aggression and fighting physically are not particularly acceptable or permissible for girls. Girls who get in physical fights often have a bad reputation and receive lower acceptance from peers than boys who physically fight with their peers. While there are certainly very physically aggressive girls and girls who pride themselves on their physical strength and ability to fight, *most* girls do not engage in a great deal of physical fighting or overt forms of aggression. So rather than physically expressing the anger that they are feeling, girls instead learn strategies to manage their anger via much more covert and manipulative ways.

I believe that when it comes to girls learning how to effectively form and navigate relationships with one another, they are lacking direction and support from the adults in their lives. Our advice to girls is often "Be nice" or "Be respectful" or even "Don't put up with disrespect," but very rarely are we working with girls on how to forge and grow effective relationships that are egalitarian, reciprocal, respectful, and communicative. How can we expect girls to demonstrate competencies in relationships if we haven't taken the time to break down the components of healthy and unhealthy friendships and relationships and actively teach them the skills that they need to navigate the give-and-take of effective relationships? We are not dealing with a generation of girls who have a character deficit that is keeping them from supporting one another; we are dealing with girls who have a skill deficit when it comes to effective relationship navigation. They haven't learned, practiced, and mastered the skills that will help them develop and maintain strong and supportive relationships with one another, and it is our responsibility to teach them.

☆☆ ACTIVITY: WHO IS MORE LIKELY TO . . . ?

Think about the ways in which boys and girls, or men and women, handle conflict. Who is more likely to

- get into a physical fight at a bar?
- rally a group of friends to ignore or exclude someone?
- punch a wall in frustration?
- spread a nasty rumor?
- be nice to someone's face and then talk about them behind their back?
- be on the same sports team and get into a physical fight during practice?

The unfortunate outcome is that girls may not learn effective communication skills to get their needs met in healthy ways. It is very difficult to tell someone something that they do not want to hear or to tell another person that something they said or did was hurtful. It can be much easier to simply spread a rumor or even cut a person out of our lives. Equally unfortunate is the way in which many girls move through their adolescent and young adult years and still fail to develop the communication skills that allow them the freedom to speak their mind and openly share their thoughts and ideas with others.

⚲ REFLECTION: HOW DO I MANAGE CONFLICT?

Consider the ways in which you generally manage conflict. What behaviors do girls see when they watch you handle a tough situation? Consider some of the following scenarios. What do you do when

- someone cuts in front of you in line at the coffee shop?
- someone forwards you a nasty email that a coworker wrote about you?
- you hear gossip about another person who works at your school?
- a coworker makes fun of another's appearance?
- the office is planning a happy hour but doesn't want to invite one person?
- your daughter tells you that her best friend's mother thinks you are superficial and controlling?

The way in which girls see adults manage conflict influences how they will approach similar situations. Providing girls with effective role modeling on how they can handle difficult and uncomfortable situations can help increase their ability to appropriately and confidently stand up for themselves and resolve conflicts in healthy and assertive ways.

Girls who have trouble speaking their mind often turn into adult women who continue to lack assertive and direct communication skills. Women then can fail to be effective role models for girls on how to communicate without being manipulative or relationally aggressive (Brown, 2003). An extreme example of this is seen currently on various reality television shows. Women are portrayed in relationships with one another as isolating, manipulative, backstabbing, and just plain mean. Women are often featured competing with one another for the affection of a guy (or perhaps for a single red rose), and the audience is inundated with depictions of women's relationships as competitive, dramatic, and divisive.

Even young girls are tuning into shows and following the activities of celebrities whose activities are so clearly designed for adults. Girls are constantly exposed to adult content in music, movies, social media, and television, and they are looking to adult women in their lives and in the media for the protocol of what it means to be a girl. The challenge is that there are few effective role models in any of these venues for girls, and there are even fewer examples of effective and supportive female relationships for girls to observe.

Do We Contribute to the Problem?

Unfortunately, the media is not exclusively to blame for how girls learn to relate to one another. Girls pay attention to the adult women in their lives in order to learn how to engage in relationships with other girls and women. As adults we continue to struggle to have authentic and communicative relationships. We still find women who are competing with other women, who demean and undermine one another in an attempt to make themselves look better, and who judge one another in very intense ways. While conducting a focus group of mothers with teenage daughters, one mom shared the following with me:

> I think that most women have a few close female friends that they can talk to and be honest with about things. But I also think that the majority of women can't stand other women. When I was growing up, I just couldn't stand to hang around other girls. I thought they were full of drama, and I would rather have hung out with guys instead. You just don't have to deal with all of that petty drama with guys. I admit I don't feel safe around other women. I feel like I always have to keep my guard up, because I am not sure when they might turn on me. I learned that strategy when I was in middle school, and I've kept my guard up ever since. I think it is easier to just keep everyone away than it is to let them in and wait to see if they are going to screw you.
>
> —Tanya, mother of a seventh-grade girl

Researchers have identified and isolated the role that mothers can play in the perpetration of their daughters' girl-bullying behavior. Specifically, they found that mothers who engage in relationally aggressive behaviors with their own friends, such as gossiping, excluding them from activities, and talking about them behind their back, have daughters who engage in these same kinds of behaviors. Additionally, it has been found that mothers who have a more permissive style of parenting and seek to be their child's friend as opposed to their child's parent also have daughters who are more relationally aggressive (Werner & Grant, 2009). This is not to say that mothers are solely responsible for the relationally aggressive behavior of their daughters; rather, it is to illuminate the fact that mothers have a significant influence on their daughters' development. When girls see adult female role models who are cooperative, supportive, and encouraging of one another, they realize that women can be their allies. When they are bombarded with divisive and competitive images of female relationships, they learn to divest from their same-sex friendships.

Relational aggression is one of those things that does not necessarily go away just because we grow up. The patterns of communication that we learned during our early years tend to persist throughout our adult lives. For many women this means the absence of strong and supportive female relationships. As girls go through school and their focus shifts to dating behavior, many abandon their relationships for dating and intimate relationships. They often proceed through their high school, college, and even adult years with few close relationships with women. They sacrifice their female friendships for intimate or dating relationships, and many never recover these relationships. For some girls college or adult life may bring them back to effective and supportive relationships with other women, but for others these relationships continue to be competitive and strained.

The challenge lies in the fact that we know that girls and women who lack effective and supportive relationships with other girls or women and who utilize their dating and intimate relationships for all their emotional and intimate support are at an increased risk of being involved in a violent dating relationship (Chesler, 2009). Girls and women need effective female relationships, and we need to teach girls how to have these relationships during their early years.

☆☆ ACTIVITY: HELP GIRLS IDENTIFY THEIR SUPPORT SYSTEMS

Girls say that they often feel alone and that no one understands what they are going through. They report difficulties in their relationships with other girls and can feel isolated and misunderstood throughout the lonely adolescent years. Helping girls identify the people in their lives who love and support them is a critical task that can have lasting implications. Girls need to be able to picture the people in their lives who they can go to for support. Work with girls to identify

- someone they can tell difficult things to.
- someone who can make them laugh.
- someone who always believes them.
- someone who they can trust.
- someone who really listens to them.
- someone who will protect them.

Impact of Relational Aggression

I guess I've always been a bit of a bigger girl. I mean, I'm not fat, I'm more athletic. I think I am really strong . . . stronger than my brothers. There has always been a part of me that wishes I were smaller and shorter. I don't really like being so tall. I always feel like a giant around my friends. They wear super cute little clothes, and my mom always makes me wear shorts that go almost the whole way to my knees, I look like such a dork sometimes. I know that other girls always make fun of me and my clothes—they say I look like a lesbian. They call me fat and make pig noises when I walk by. I hate going to lunch because I feel like they are always watching and criticizing what I am eating, so I hardly eat anything, and then I am starving all day. I guess the worst was about two weeks ago. We were in the locker room changing for gym class, and two of the girls started messing around with me and making fun of me. I tried to ignore it, but then they picked up my shirt off of the bench and screamed to the whole room, "Yup—size extra large! Just as we thought!" I was so embarrassed, and I didn't know what to do, so I just played it off like it didn't bother me.

—Malaysia, seventh grade

The impact of relational aggression on its victims is significant. Girls who experience social and relational bullying from their peers have negative academic, social, emotional, and mental health outcomes. They often do not know who to talk to about what is happening, and they feel embarrassed to report the incidents to an adult (Raskausas & Stoltz, 2004). Girls don't want to be perceived as tattle-tales, so instead of telling someone about what is happening, they act like it doesn't really bother them that much. Like Malaysia stated above, she "just played it off." Deep down inside she feels terrible, but the face that she must project to her peers is that it is "no big deal."

Figure 4.2 lists some of the common issues seen among girls who have experienced relational aggression; while this is not an exhaustive list, it provides a starting place for identifying girls who may be experiencing this type of aggression.

Figure 4.2 Common Problems Among Girls Who Experience Relational Aggression

Academic	Social	Emotional	Mental Health
Decreased school functioning	Social maladjustment	Stress	Depression
Desire to skip school or avoid peers	Difficulty making and keeping friends	Loneliness	Anxiety
Negative academic outcomes	Peer rejection	Decreased self-concept or confidence	Somatic complaints
		Withdrawal from peers and family	Suicidal ideation

Source: Merrell, Buchanan, & Tran (2006).

Perhaps most important, peer victimization and aggression influence the self-concept and self-worth of girls (Merrell et al., 2006). The experience of relational aggression can shake the core of a girl and make her question everything that she says or does. What is most difficult about this is that when a girl's confidence gets compromised during the adolescent years, she may not regain her confidence again until adulthood—if at all.

What Can We Do?

Is it possible to intervene and change the course of girls' relationship and communication styles? I think without a doubt the answer to this question is a resounding yes! We can't just resign ourselves to the idea that girls are mean and there's nothing we can do about it.

There are concrete ways to change relational aggression between and among girls. Part of this requires attention to the girls who are participating in the relationally aggressive behavior, as well as to the girls who are victims of girl bullying. At different times, all girls can be perpetrators, victims, or bystanders of relationally aggressive behavior.

Include relational forms of aggression in the definitions and discussions of bullying and cyberbullying. Ensure that students, parents, teachers, and administrators understand the severity and impact of relational aggression on its victims. Because of the ongoing emphasis on bullying in schools, coupled with the lack of inclusion of relationally aggressive behavior in many of the definitions of bullying, many parents, counselors, and educators lack a fundamental definition of relational aggression. Relational aggression is a form of bullying, and the consequences to perpetrators should be applied accordingly. Relational forms of aggression should not be viewed as "girls being girls" and deemed as less severe than other forms of aggression.

Teach girls about empathy and how to "walk in someone else's shoes." Provide girls the opportunity to develop a conceptual understanding of the fact that we don't always know what's going on in someone else's life—we don't always know their story or what they might be dealing with outside of school. Girls can sometimes judge one another on physical appearance, clothing, socioeconomic status, and a variety of other external factors without taking into consideration the reality of another's life. Having girls identify the times when others have been empathetic toward them and the times when they have demonstrated empathy to another allows them to begin to develop social competence around identifying and invoking empathy. Empathy must be practiced on an ongoing basis, so it is important to give girls the opportunity to identify situations where they can demonstrate understanding and concern for someone else.

Teach girls that they don't have to like everybody but they have to demonstrate respect for one another. We should not attempt to teach girls that they need to like everyone they meet and that they should be friends with everyone they interact with. (If we are being honest with ourselves as adults, we don't like everybody. We should not expect any different behavior from the girls in our lives.) Rather, it is much more important that we teach girls how to demonstrate respect for others, even people they don't really like. We don't need to like everybody, but we need to show them respect.

Teach girls that not everybody is going to like them, and that's okay. Sometimes we say or do things that other people don't like, and we may be criticized for doing so. It is only natural for us to want other people to like us, and for adolescent girls this pressure is even stronger. Prepare girls for the invariable fact that when they do stand up for themselves, other people in their lives may not appreciate it, particularly those people who are used to bullying or controlling them. In any relationship when we stand up for ourselves or speak to the other person in a new or different way, it changes the dynamics of the relationship. This is often a hard concept for girls and women because as girls we learn that it is important to be liked. I recently worked with a college student, Trisha, who had grown up in a family where she was the "pleaser." She was responsible for doing everything perfectly and was the one who kept the peace in the family at all costs. She never had a strong opinion about anything and could easily be directed by her family or friends to do whatever they wanted her to do. She told me that if everyone around her was happy, then she was happy, so she would go to great lengths to ensure the happiness of the people in her life. I asked her to share with me a time that she could remember when someone in her life had gotten mad at her. Trisha could not think of a single example of a time or situation where someone had been mad at her! This was an indication to me of a young woman who had an inability to speak her mind for fear that someone "won't like her," and unfortunately, this proved to be the case because Trisha had been repeatedly taken advantage of in a variety of different ways throughout her adolescent and young adult years.

Teach girls the difference between passive, aggressive, passive-aggressive, and assertive communication. We have found that one of the most powerful activities we have done with girls that resonates with them for years after our programming is teaching them the difference between passive, aggressive, passive-aggressive, and assertive communication. These tend to be definitions that many girls are unfamiliar with, and they generally don't realize that there are different and explicit ways of communicating. Girls need to learn that there are appropriate times for various types of communication. It is important that we teach them how to differentiate between the types of communication and when each is best utilized.

> *Passive:* Many girls, like Trisha, are extremely passive and have great difficulty speaking their mind or giving an opinion. The result tends to be that these individuals are easily taken advantage of and believe that everyone else's opinion or ideas are more important than theirs. They are girls who have difficulty getting their opinions heard or letting others know when their boundaries have been infringed upon. People learn to be passive for a variety of reasons. This may include being the peacemaker in a chaotic family structure, negotiating fighting between a mother and father, experiencing aggressive or authoritative parenting, lacking self-confidence, or experiencing abuse. Passivity is a learned response to external conditions and exists to try to maintain the peace or calm in often chaotic relationships. Extremely passive people rationalize that it's easier to go along with something that they don't agree with or easier to ensure that they don't "upset the apple cart" than it is to speak their mind. Some might say

that their opinions just aren't that valuable or that they don't really care enough to speak up. I always ask girls, "When there is something that you really want to say and you don't say it, who do you get most upset with?" Invariably, we get most upset with ourselves when we don't speak our mind and don't allow our voices to be heard. But for many girls this internal frustration or anger is easier to manage than another person's anger, frustration, or disappointment in them. Passivity can be a long-term and ingrained response to a variety of different external situations, and it can be very difficult for an individual to change their passive behavior or passive style of communication. Unfortunately, we know that girls who are passive and have difficulty standing up for themselves are at risk for a multitude of negative outcomes, including lack of equity in friendships, manipulative dating relationships, negative self-worth, low self-esteem, depression, and anxiety.

Aggressive: Conversely, we also struggle with the issue of dealing with very aggressive girls. Angry, physically intimidating, and verbally abusive girls are equally problematic as girls who are passive, if not more so. These girls attempt to rule the social hierarchy and dictate the behaviors of those around them. They respond to conflict or confrontation with an extremely aggressive response. They have difficulty engaging in effective conversations or participating in problem-solving activities because their aggression is unmanageable. What I found to be most interesting about aggressive girls is that they believe that they are standing up for themselves and "not getting taken advantage of" by other people. They perceive their behavior as a means to getting their own needs met. Unfortunately, this aggressive behavior rarely produces the desired outcome.

Passive-aggressive: Passive-aggressive behavior and communication is one of the more common types of communication style between girls. It is demonstrated when there is first a refusal or inability to take a stand or confront a situation, followed by indirect or hidden hostility toward the person. When girls are passive-aggressive, they may be nice to someone's face but then spread rumors and express anger about them behind their back. This damaging type of behavior is most often seen in girls who lack emotional regulation and are afraid or refuse to confront uncomfortable situations. There is a desire to express the negative feelings but an inability to do it directly. Passive-aggressiveness is perhaps the communication style that is the most damaging to relationships because it is manipulative and unpredictable.

Assertive: Teaching girls how to communicate effectively makes common sense; however, most girls and even most adult women find assertive communication a challenge. Standing up for yourself in a respectful and confident way sounds much easier than it actually is. Telling somebody something that they don't want to hear is actually quite a bit more difficult than it sounds. This could be as simple as telling your friend that you need the five dollars back that they borrowed or telling somebody that they cut in front of you in the line in the lunch room. It would be so much easier to complain to your friend, "Oh my gosh! I can't believe she just cut in line. She is such a jerk" than it would be to say, "Excuse me, you just stepped in front of me in the line. The line actually ends back there."

Teach girls how to appropriately use "I" statements. Using "I" statements is a significant part of communicating assertively. We cannot expect others to read our minds, so we need to utilize our expansive communication skills to be able to tell others what we want, what we need, and how we want things to happen. This does not mean that we are dictating the terms of every relationship that we have; rather, it means that we are communicating effectively and in a reciprocal way with the people in our lives. "I" statements are simple statements that are easy to use; however, even most adults have not adequately mastered the use of assertive communication and "I" statements.

The critical element of the "I" statement is that you teach girls to accurately name the behavior that is distressing, connect the behavior

to what they are feeling, and then tell the other person what they
need from them:

"When you_____,
I feel _____."
"I need you to _____."

**We must prepare girls for the responses that they may receive from
others when they stand up for themselves.** In our society assertive
women are not always viewed with the highest regard. When girls
and women stand up for themselves, it challenges the social norms
that exist around girls being quiet and passive. I have often heard
girls tell me that the first time they stood up for themselves to someone who was harassing them or trying to take advantage of them,
they were called a "bitch." For girls who've never been called a bitch
before, this initial reaction can feel startling or discomforting. Girls
who experience relational aggression on an ongoing basis or who
have difficulty standing up for themselves may need to learn that
when they stand up for themselves, they might get a negative reaction from others. Talk to girls about what possible reactions they
might get, and help prepare them for an uncomfortable response.

Provide girls with opportunities to be in girl-only spaces. It is not
often that girls have the opportunity to be in spaces that are female-
only. It is even less often that girls have female-only spaces where
they can explore the issues facing their lives and try out new skills
and behaviors. Because adolescents tend to believe that they are completely unique and their experiences are exclusively theirs, it is hard
for them to understand that other teens their age are experiencing
the same, or very similar, things. One of the most surprising things
to me is that after participating in girls' programming, a number of
girls say, "I love being in the girl-only group! It was neat to see that
other girls my age are going through the same things as I am. I didn't
really realize that." It's not just putting girls in a room together and
having them talk about their issues that is beneficial. While the mere
sense of shared experience is powerful, the desired outcome is that

girls develop new ways of interacting with one another and their environment as a result of bringing them together. This is where the purposeful engagement of an activity or an intervention can be most powerful. You create a safe space for girls to engage with one another, and then you provide them the opportunity to develop a new skill or competency that they can try out safely in that space.

Bring girls who are different from one another together in purposeful and intentional ways. It is of little importance whether or not girls are already friends with each other when they are in a group with other girls. In fact, it's probably more beneficial to have girls who are from different groups, different cliques, and different backgrounds to all come together to have the opportunity to share their individual experiences and learn with and from one another. Girls come to understand that while they are unique, their experiences may be more universal than they realize, and often girls find that they have a great deal in common with other girls.

Relationships, Dating, and Coercion

5

Developing Healthy Relationships in an Age of Sexting, Swiping, and Snapping

Guys want you to do things that you might not be ready for, but you know that if you don't do it, they will just go on to the next girl who will.

—Maya, seventh grade

I think girls are under a lot of pressure to send nudes. It's basically like if you don't send the picture, you know that another girl will.

—Taylor, eleventh grade

Dating. Fitting in. Flirting. Exploration. These are all typical aspects of the adolescent years, and in fact, they are normal developmental milestones that our girls should be learning how to navigate. Oftentimes, it can seem that these new behaviors come rapidly and without warning. I have talked to so many parents who say something like this:

I don't even know what happened to her. It is like she was one girl one day and then woke up the next day, and I didn't even know who she was anymore. She has become obsessed with her clothes, how she looks, meeting up with friends on the weekends, and sending texts that she doesn't want me to read. She spends hours by herself doing her hair and changing her clothes. I just don't get it. I remember being a little bit like that when I was a teenager, but that didn't happen until I was much older. She is 12 years old. . . . I am sure I was 15 when I started caring about that stuff.

It is hard to determine what the "right" age is for girls to start developing an interest in how they look, in dating and in developing independent friendships and relationships. Generally, this exploration happens a bit earlier than most adults are prepared for and earlier than the age most adults believe that *they* started trying out similar behaviors. When I asked fifth-grade girls to share with me some of the big things they are dealing with that adults don't necessarily understand, many talked about puberty and dating (and yes, they used the word *dating*). Posing the same question to high school girls revealed their belief that their parents don't take them seriously and, specifically, don't take the intensity, intimacy, and importance of their relationships seriously.

We know that in many ways girls are "getting older younger." Meaning that the attitudes and behaviors that they are developing are more advanced than may have been typical for their age, which can be associated with the increased exposure they have to adult-themed media and content. Youth today can easily access movies, YouTube content, pornography, political commentary, hate speech, and violence without warning, context, or parental oversight. Even with all of the technology controls and social media trackers that are available (see Chapter 2 for further discussion), the amount of information that is instantly accessible with a simple click is mind-blowing.

However, we also know that access to information is not the sole cause of early-adolescent curiosity. Their bodies are changing, their hormones are surging, and in turn their attitudes, behaviors, and desires are changing as well. Physically and developmentally these changes are a good sign—that growth is taking place in the way it should. However, socially and interpersonally, challenges may ensue as oftentimes the physical maturation that a girl experiences can outpace her psychological maturation, and her parents' readiness and willingness to take on this barrage of new changes may be the slowest of all to develop.

Developmental Issues

The Office on Women's Health website for teen girls, girlshealth.gov, reports that girls start puberty between the ages of 8 and 13 years and it usually ends by age 14. The age of puberty onset has declined by several months over the past 50 years, with girls starting physical puberty changes, such as breast and pubic hair development, around age 9½ or 10 years for Caucasian girls and as young as 8 years for African American girls. With menstruation generally following within 1 to 2 years, girls are gaining weight, developing breasts and hips, and physically looking more womanly at younger ages. These hormonal changes mean that girls are also dealing with sexual feelings, confusing urges, mood swings, and emotions that they have never experienced before.

As girls' bodies change, their hormones race, they feel awkward and self-conscious, and they can become overly concerned with their changing appearance. When they spend hours in front of the mirror obsessing about every pimple on their face, how their clothes fit, and whether or not they like the image they see in the mirror, we must recognize that they are simultaneously experiencing societal pressures to fit in and look a certain way as well as physical and hormonal changes that affect their physique, thinking, and emotions.

An additional impact of this early maturation is that girls start to receive sexual attention at younger ages and begin to develop sexual interest and curiosity. As adults, we can have a difficult time recognizing (or admitting to!) this reality, and in turn, we rarely prepare girls adequately for the physical, emotional, and social changes that are coming their way.

The nervousness to start the conversation is often the biggest impediment to having open and accurate dialogue with girls about their changing bodies. For some reason, we have taken basic biological information about what a healthy body should do and accomplish (i.e., a healthy biological female should have a period around age 11–14) and made ourselves feel uncomfortable, squeamish, and embarrassed to discuss it. We gear up to have "the talk" with girls in an attempt to provide them with their first insights into puberty and, in doing so, often make a seemingly straightforward conversation awkward and horrifying for both the adult and the girl.

In talking with a group of mothers of daughters in grades 4 through 7, I listened to them share their struggles over knowing *when* to start talking to their daughters about some of the topics that they viewed as more complicated or difficult. For example, if they talked to their girls about puberty or menstruation too early, would it scare their daughters? Similarly, if they talked to their daughters about signs of healthy/unhealthy dating relationships, would it "give them ideas" or "indicate approval" for behaviors for which they did not think their girls were ready?

Providing girls accurate information on the changes that the female body naturally experiences can help ease their anxiety and also help them realize that what is happening to them is normal. Starting these conversations well in advance of the actual changes helps girls begin to recognize the differences between children and adults and the processes that must take place to progress healthily through these transitions. Moms and dads alike can, and should, have these ongoing, open, factual conversations with their daughters and work to diminish the embarrassment that can often accompany the dreaded "talk." There is a small window of time that parents have to be the leading source of information in their child's life. When it comes to helping our girls develop an understanding of their bodies, their growth, and their emotions, wouldn't you rather be the one informing and influencing that conversation rather than the internet or her equally uninformed peers?

The bodily changes are normal and healthy, and the sexual interest that accompanies puberty is also normal and healthy. Think back to when you started puberty. Did your physical changes start earlier or later than your peers? Were you the first one in your class to hit that growth spurt, the last one, or somewhere in between? It is often most difficult to be among the first girls to develop physically, as it is to be among the last boys to hit puberty. Both are fraught with their own social challenges. From her receiving sexual attention that she might not be prepared to handle to him being teased and made fun of for his small stature, the adolescent years are an unpredictable mix of highs and lows. What, however, is predictable during this time, is that the physical puberty changes have a direct correlation to the romantic interests that begin to take shape, and dating takes on a whole new meaning.

Importance of Dating Relationships

With the hormonal changes of puberty come both internal and external pressures for girls to flirt, date, seek sexual attention, and engage in romantic relationships. Girls begin to see relationships as a type of social status and experience pressure from their peers to be viewed as attractive, to be desired by others, and to date. Many girls are exploring their sexuality and orientation during adolescence and are working to understand themselves and their complex emotions. My research found that issues surrounding boys and dating were near the top of the list of concerns for girls in all grades, starting from fifth grade. But what also exists for some girls is a concern that their sexual orientation does not match that of the majority of their peers and that their parents refuse to discuss or acknowledge their budding emotions or help them make sense of their complicated feelings. Being told that they will "grow out of it" or that they "don't really know yet what they like" is a surefire way to create, or increase, a divide in a relationship.

Girls who may have an alternate or nontraditional sexual orientation are going through all of the typical changes of puberty and adolescence, but they have even fewer places to learn, explore, and make sense of their emotions and have fewer people who are knowledgeable, accepting, and supportive of their developmental challenges. At a time where most teens feel awkward, different, and sometimes completely alone in their experience, we need to make a concerted effort to seek to understand their emotions and their insecurities through nonjudgmental and open communication. When girls experience acceptance, affirmation, and support, they have the opportunity to develop healthier relationship expectations and habits.

For many girls dating is a form of social capital, meaning that being in a relationship provides social value and becomes a desired social expectation. Even as early as fifth grade, girls begin talking about relationships as one of the "big issues" affecting their lives. Among this age-group we hear comments such as

> We start dating at this age, and our parents think that we're too young for that, but they just don't understand.

> We like attention from boys, and it is really important to have a boyfriend.

Eighth graders tell us,

> We have feelings and urges, and we can't really talk to our parents about that. Like about sex. Parents just tell you don't do it. . . . But they don't understand how hard it is. They don't know what we have to deal with every day.

> I think dating is one of the biggest things that our parents don't understand. I know it was really different when they were our age, but right now everyone is dating. And if your parents won't let you, then you just have to sneak around behind their backs.

By eleventh and twelfth grade, the tone of girls' comments around dating changes somewhat because girls tend to have more steady relationships during their later years in high school; however, they continue to have reservations about talking to adults about their concerns. They say,

> We are making decisions about whether we'll go to college near each other or if we'll just break up.

> By this point we start getting more serious, and our relationships are getting more serious. Parents just think that we are going to meet someone new in college, and I don't think that is always true. Some of us are in love with the person we are with right now.

> My parents refuse to believe that I am not into guys, but I am not. I am attracted to girls. They actually laugh at me and tell me that I will grow out of this. I don't have anyone in my family that I can really be honest with about this stuff.

> Parents are sometimes so hard to read. It's like they want you to tell them everything that's going on in your life, but when

you tell them a little bit, they freak out and go crazy. So you learn real quick that you can only tell them certain things . . . but make them feel like you're telling them everything.

It can be hard for adults to understand the importance that girls place on dating and relationships throughout their adolescent years. We often look at these early relationships as silly or juvenile, but for girls the emotions are intense. Girls have shared with us at length the pressures that they feel to date, to be in a relationship, and to engage in sexual activity—there is nothing juvenile about these issues.

I'm sure we've all seen it: the seventh-grade girl who's had her heart broken for the first time. She's crying, she's emotional, and she can't seem to eat or sleep. She's doodling in her notebook swirling letters with their names together with hearts and just seems devastated that this relationship has ended.

As adults we recognize that the girl may be hurting and upset in a situation like this, and we do want to soothe the emotions that she has. However, we often fail miserably in our attempts at doing this. We often tell the girl, "You're going to meet someone better; this person was a jerk anyway" or "There are other fish in the sea. When you get to college, you will meet someone really great. I didn't meet your father until I was in college."

Unfortunately, this is one of the worst mistakes we can make. By making statements that focus on the future and dismiss the current state, we fail to acknowledge the intensity of the girl's emotions in this moment. She doesn't want to hear that in two years she's going to meet someone who is better. She just wants the pain that she's feeling right now to stop.

I did use the word *pain*. It can be difficult for adults to look at adolescent emotions, particularly around dating relationships, and equate intense words such as *pain* to them. We look at their youthful relationships and see them as innocent and fun. We see their emotions as fleeting childhood emotions; however, for the teen who is experiencing them, they feel intense and, at times, overwhelming.

We've got to remember that the experience that the teen is having at this very moment may very well be the most intense emotion that she's ever felt up to this point. We cannot relate to her situation from our older and more experienced perspective, with our history of forging relationships as well as our age and wisdom. Girls do not have the luxury of looking abstractly at the situation and thinking, "This isn't so bad. I'm sure I will have to deal with more difficult things when I get older." Rather, her brain is saying to her, "I may not make it. I've never cared for somebody so deeply. My world has just been shattered."

When as adults we lose the perspective of what it feels like to be in that place of adolescence and how difficult relationships feel in that space, we can quickly become insignificant to the lives of teens. The first time we tell them that what they feel is silly, unimportant, or juvenile may be the last time they readily share their feelings or emotions with us. While it can be difficult for us to relate to what they're going through from our more experienced perspective, we can relate to them on how it feels to be hurt, betrayed, embarrassed, or sad.

Don't tell teens that you know how they feel. Tell them that you're sorry that they're hurting. Tell them that you want to understand how they feel and that what they are going through sounds really hard. Inside you might be thinking, "This is the silliest story I've ever heard. I can't believe she's crying this much over this stupid breakup," but outside you're saying, "Wow, this is really difficult, and I can tell this is hard for you. Tell me how you're doing."

Healthy Versus Unhealthy Teen Dating Relationships

Physical and hormonal changes take place during the adolescent years that contribute to increased body self-awareness, preoccupation with attractiveness and a newfound interest in dating. In fact, nearly 30% of girls report that they are happier when they are in a dating relationship (Hinkelman, 2017).

Sexual thoughts and desires often accompany the physical and physiological changes of puberty, with about 40% of 9- to 12-year-olds (both boys and girls) experiencing sexual thoughts, increasing to 66% by age 13 to 14 years (Larsson & Svedin, 2002). However, when these typical sexual thoughts accompany the common desire to be part of a relationship, there is a window of vulnerability that can begin to open up for some girls. At this juncture girls may begin to prioritize dating relationships over their existing friendships and sometimes ditch their friends in exchange for a budding romance. Worse, some girls begin to see other girls as their competition; nearly three out of four teen girls agree with the statement "Most girls are in competition with one another." When I ask girls what they are competing for, I get a wide range of responses, from popularity to grades, to beauty. However, more than any other response, girls say, "attention from boys."

One school counselor told me,

> I think the root of all girl drama is a boy. Usually, the boy is manipulating two girls, making them feel like the other one is the problem. Because girls are groomed to be pleasers, they are willing to take on the responsibility of being "the problem" in the relationship, and then they will work on changing themselves so that the boy will choose them over the other girl.

Let me share with you a conversation that I had with an eighth-grade girl, Sarita.

A CONVERSATION WITH SARITA, AN EIGHTH-GRADE GIRL

ME: It seems like girls have a hard time getting along with each other. Do you think that is true?

SARITA: I totally think that is true. Girls are drama and just look for reasons to fight, argue, and get in each other's faces. Girls are always competing with each other.

ME: What do you think girls are competing for?

SARITA: Boys. Everyone wants the boy to like them. If a guy is giving you some attention and then starts to pay attention to one of your friends, you get pissed off about it.

(Continued)

(Continued)

ME: Who do you get pissed off at?

SARITA: At your friend. She knows that he was talking to you, and she was just trying to get in there and mess it up. Guys always do that; they are going to talk to whatever girl will do what they want them to do.

ME: Tell me what the guys are looking for the girls to do.

SARITA: Everything. Guys want girls who have perfect bodies and sexy clothes. They want girls who will drop everything to pay attention to them. I think guys are also looking for girls who will do other stuff with them too . . . you know, like sexual stuff . . . send them dirty pictures and stuff. I heard some boys talking about "hitting it and quitting it," and I just don't think that is right.

ME: Ok, so let me make sure I've got this straight. Girls compete with each other for the attention of boys, but then sometimes the same boys can be pretty disrespectful to the girls. Does that sound about right?

SARITA: Yeah, I guess so. Sometimes I think that boys are one way with you and then they are a totally different person when their friends are around. They will be all sweet and nice, and then when they are in front of their friends, they act like they don't even know that you are around. I think boys our age are very immature. They don't know how to treat a girl. I think that's why lots of girls look for older guys to date.

For many girls, the adolescent years consist of a tremendous emphasis and focus on dating, and social status is based on who is in a relationship and who is not. This is where a connection between self-worth and romantic relationships can begin to develop. Girls begin to compete with one another for attention at a very early age, and as we often see, the competition does not stop when girls become adults. As one school counselor said,

Girls try to outcompete other girls. While adults may see this as being childish, we must admit that adults still deal with this and compete too! We need to listen to girls and help them define a positive body image and also define what they actually want in a relationship.

When a girl's identity and sense of self are connected in large part to her dating relationship, and that relationship is prioritized over all of her other relationships, we should begin to pay keen attention. While not universally alarming, there is some cause for caution. When girls become competitive with other girls, the result is often a lack of warm and supportive female relationships. Girls who have interest and attention for only the one person they are dating may actually be at an increased risk of being involved in a controlling or violent dating relationship. This can happen when

1. being in a relationship is of highest social value, and they will go to great lengths to secure and maintain a dating relationship.

2. they have few/no friends who give them honest feedback and support or help them to gauge the health of the relationship.

3. they get all of their needs—companionship, friendship, intimacy, and so on—met through their dating partners, and they rely only on them for all of their personal and social support.

When a dating relationship starts to get unstable, we may begin to see frantic attempts to maintain the relationship. Regardless of whether or not the relationship is fun, supportive, reciprocal, and healthy, there can be a tremendous overinvolvement in ensuring the status quo. Often this can evidence itself as placating or desperate behavior as girls work to keep something they perceive as critically important and of tremendous value.

Learning About Relationships

Many of the expectations and patterns of dating, as well as our coping strategies for managing conflict in relationships that we learn during our adolescent years, continue into our adult relationships. While the dating and romantic relationships of our youth generally dissolve over time, the understanding of how relationships work and what our role is in a relationship can affect our future dating and intimate relationships. Unfortunately teen relationships are often characterized by anxiety, jealousy, loneliness, desperation, and dependency. For LGBT youth these challenges may be amplified because dating may take place less openly due to social pressure or fear of negative repercussions from others. In many teen relationships there can also be high levels of exclusivity and a great deal of social dominance, with boys and girls alike reporting high levels of control and jealousy in their dating relationships. When these unhealthy patterns begin in the teen years, the same tumultuous patterns can more easily persist in college and adulthood.

Parents often have rules for when they believe their daughters should be allowed to date, and the general sentiment is the older the better. However, restricting her ability to date (or more specifically, to date with your knowledge/approval) also restricts her ability to develop important relationship navigation and negotiation skills that she will surely need as she gets older.

We have to teach girls the realities of navigating the dating world, and our best chance to do that is while they are living with us and likely developing their earliest crushes in the late elementary and early middle school years. With girls reporting that their dating relationships begin as early as fifth grade, it is important that these conversations start early so that the girl is best prepared to manage what she will invariably face in middle school, high school, and beyond. Helping her understand what a healthy and respectful relationship looks like goes beyond simply saying, "Don't ever let anyone disrespect you"; it must include specifics about what respect and disrespect actually look like and how she should respond in situations where she is ill at ease, uncomfortable, or embarrassed. She should also know what a fun and equitable relationship looks and feels like—one in which she is respected, appreciated, and valued.

We start this process by knowing the signs of healthy and unhealthy relationships and talking to girls about these signs while they are young. Regularly point out signs of respect or disrespect that you observe in friendships and relationships. Help ensure that girls learn from a young age that people who like them don't make fun of them, hit them, tease them, or embarrass them. Sometimes when girls are little and a boy is teasing them or hitting them, we say things like "He's only doing that because he likes you." At the earliest ages we need girls to understand the kinds of behaviors that are acceptable and unacceptable, what respect and disrespect look like, and how they can trust their gut and intuition in situations that make them uneasy.

A sign of a potentially unhealthy relationship is when one person pressures the other person to do things that they don't really want to do. The pressure can be related to lots of different things, but commonly it is connected to sexual behavior, sending nude photos or videos, drinking, doing drugs, going to parties, hanging out with an older crowd, and lying to parents about their activities. Sometimes girls are called "babies," "immature," or "frigid" when they resist some of these pressures.

A second common sign of an unhealthy relationship is when there is consistent monitoring and tracking of the other person's whereabouts and activities. With advances in technology and the fact that nearly 100% of teens have smartphones, it is now common to enable the "Find My Friends" or a similar tracking app so that there is a constant connection and the ability to know where the other person is at all times. The questions "Where are you?" and "Whom are you with?" are now replaced with the constant monitoring of one's whereabouts, often followed by questioning and/or jealousy if there is suspicion that the girl wasn't where or with who she was supposed to be. About 30% of teens report that they are or have been in a relationship where their partner checks in on them multiple times a day to know who they are with and what they are doing (Lenhart et al., 2015). Girls can sometimes mistake this type of oversight and control for concern and care. Helping them develop boundaries, privacy, and a sense of independence ensures that they are not easily swayed into the belief that monitoring, control, or manipulation should be equated with affection.

For many girls being in a relationship can be more important, in their minds, than staying true to their own principles or standing up for themselves in situations that cause discomfort. It is critical to teach girls that a person who cares about them should not want to pressure or coerce them into doing things that they don't really want to do. Similarly, monitoring their whereabouts and overseeing their behavior constantly is not a sign of deep love; rather, it is indicative of a controlling relationship. Providing girls the opportunity to identify these traits and characteristics well in advance of when their actual dating begins gives them the ability to define their boundaries and identify effective strategies for handling these types of situations. The challenge here is that this requires having the conversation before the situation arises.

⭐⭐ ACTIVITY: STARTING THE CONVERSATION

Adults say that they often have trouble starting conversations with girls about difficult topics. We've got to acknowledge that there may be embarrassment or discomfort, and then we have to forge ahead. When these types of conversations take place with regularity, they become less awkward. Here are some ways we might start a conversation:

- "I noticed that a lot of girls in the fourth grade are starting to wear bras and makeup. What do you think about that?"
- "I was watching a show last night that showed a bunch of women fighting and competing with each other over the same guy. Their goal was to get a rose from a guy who they've actually never met before. Why do you think women do that?"
- "I'm thinking that some time you're going to experience a situation where you may be pressured to go further sexually than you think you want to go. Let's talk about some things you might say or do if you are in that situation."
- "I've been hearing a lot about girls being asked to send nudes or revealing pictures and videos and then the pictures get spread all over the school. Have you seen anything like that happen?"

Starting the conversation in this way ensures that you don't put your own judgment or perspective into the conversation. This is key for opening up an honest conversation with a girl. The moment that she feels that you have an opinion or that there is a "right" answer, the ability to have an authentic conversation diminishes. How different would the conversation be if you instead said, "I've been hearing a lot about girls being asked to send nudes or revealing pictures and videos and then the pictures get spread all over the school. You would *never* think about doing something that reckless, would you?"

What's the Deal With Sexting?

Sexting is defined as sending sexually explicit photos, videos, and messages through electronic means, primarily cell phones. It has become increasingly common among adults and youth alike. By the time girls are in high school, about 75% report that most teens their age send sexually explicit texts and photos to one another, and two of three say that they have been asked to send a nude photo (Hinkelman, 2017). Data on the percentage of girls who have sent a photo are a bit harder to come by due to the legal reporting requirements that accompany knowledge of sexting (most school personnel are required to report incidents of sexting to administration, children's services, and/or law enforcement due to its being classified as production and dissemination of child pornography), but according to conversations with girls, the numbers are high. "I actually think that more than two-thirds of girls have been asked to send a nude. It is literally like every girl," Samantha, an eleventh-grade girl, explained to me as I shared our research findings with her and a group of her peers. The other girls nodded their heads in agreement, which prompted me to ask, "Is sexting a big deal?" The girls paused and looked at one another as they took a moment to think about their responses.

"I mean, it's a big deal because you can get in massive trouble for it. Or the photo can get posted or shared after you sent it," Nicole, a senior in the group, explained to me. As I listened to the girls talk through this question, I realized that for most, sexting felt like a big deal because of the potential for major negative consequences. They talked about their parents or their school administrators finding out and how awful that would be. I listened to them hypothesize about the various ways in which the photos could "never go away," which might affect their college admissions or a job prospect in the future.

Not once did the girls talk about not sending a photo because they actually didn't want to.

Next I asked, "Why do you think girls send nude photos?" Their reactions ranged from "Because they want attention" to "They think it will make the other person like them" to "They want to feel sexy." The girls talked about the fact that if they didn't send a photo, then "he'll just move on to the next girl who will." Their responses are consistent with what researchers report regarding girls' motivations for and participation in sexting. A relatively newer, yet well-researched perspective contends that consensual sexting is now a part of 21st century dating and courtship. Girls and young women report that sexting makes them feel sexy and is a way to flirt or show interest in another. Among teens, sexting appears to be a precursor to actual sexual activity. Teens who engage in sexting are more likely to engage in sexual activity sooner than their nonsexting peers. In this way, sexting is a part of the sexual exploration process, where teens try out new things as they work to increase their understanding of a new landscape. This is not to say that we should approve of such behavior and consider it simply "kids being kids," because there is an obvious "dark side" to sexting as well.

Most see the dark side of sexting as the potential consequence of the image being posted or shared, or in some way the sender being exploited. This is most certainly a cause for concern, as there are personal, social, academic, and legal implications. But this is not the only issue we should be addressing. Part of what we must consider in this discussion is the "why" behind the behavior. What is the motivation, and what is it rooted in? Understanding this can help us more readily connect with and support girls who are consistently facing requests and pressure. Research suggests that girls are more often repeatedly asked, pressured, or coerced to send sexually explicit pictures (Englander, 2015), and they feel compelled to comply for fear of losing their romantic partner or experiencing negative social consequences (Lippman & Campbell, 2014). It is estimated that among those who have sexted, 70% have felt pressure around sending a photo (Englander, 2015). Girls who are in relationships experience less pressure than those who are searching for a relationship, indicating that the need for approval and acceptance is a part of this complex equation.

So let's take it back to our discussion at the beginning of this chapter. Girls feel pressure to be in a relationship because it is a sign of social status and acceptance. They also feel pressure to send sexual photos of themselves to gain acceptance from dating partners or potential dating partners. It is important to think about how the pressure surrounding sexting directly correlates to the pressure they experience to be in a relationship:

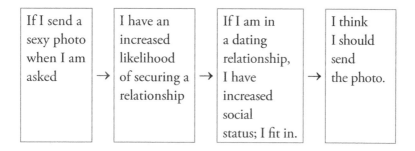

| If I send a sexy photo when I am asked | → | I have an increased likelihood of securing a relationship | → | If I am in a dating relationship, I have increased social status; I fit in. | → | I think I should send the photo. |

Helping Girls Identify the Signs of an Unhealthy Relationship

Sending sexual photos and videos is one area where girls experience a great deal of coercive behavior. Unfortunately, many girls don't recognize coercion, or pressure to do something that you don't want to do, as a sign of an unhealthy interaction or relationship. We need to help girls learn the difference between a healthy, equal relationship and an unhealthy, high-pressure or controlling relationship. This can be a much more difficult task than you might expect because so many of us think of unhealthy relationships as those that are physically violent. While physical violence is definitely unacceptable in relationships and certainly a sign of an unhealthy relationship, there are also more subtle forms of control that girls need to know are equally unacceptable and dangerous.

Unhealthy dating behaviors are much more prevalent than we might imagine. A 2011 research study by Kaukinen and colleagues found that nearly 30% of college women reported that their dating relationships in high school contained some violent or controlling behavior. Some girls have come to expect control, domination, and violence in relationships because that is what they are exposed to in their families, their communities, and the media. Other girls learn that when people are dating or married, they do have control over each other and are within their rights to exert this control at various points. A fifth-grade girl told me,

> My mother is so annoying; if I were my dad I would lose my mind. She is constantly texting him, asking him where he is, and when he is coming home. She calls him like 100 times a day, and then she gets all mad at him when he tells her he still has some work to finish up before he can come home. I've also seen her call him when she is paying the bills, and she'll be like "You spent $50 on gas last week, and you didn't tell me." Sometimes I feel like she is bored, so she needs him to come home and be bored too. If I were him, I wouldn't want to come home.

We want to instill in girls the fact that they can develop reciprocal, equal, and healthy relationships, and we want them to understand what this can look like. Let's take a look at some of the common signs of relationships that could potentially be unhealthy, or could become unhealthy.

#1: They always wants to know where I am and whom I am with. There is a natural interest and curiosity surrounding the person we're dating. We want to learn all about them, and we also have a tendency to want to know where they are and whom they're with. When the casual "What's up? What are you up to?" turns into a perpetual and constant "Where are you? Who are you with?" we need to pay attention to these signs. While this does not describe dating violence, it is a red flag for controlling dating behavior.

We want girls to know that if the other person has a constant need to know who they are with and what they are doing and gets upset with them on a regular basis, this could be a sign of a controlling person. There are very few people who have the "right" to know everything about you. This includes where you are, who you're talking to, and what you're doing at every moment of the day. In fact, depending on your age, there is arguably no one who should know all these things at every given time.

As we get older, our rights to privacy increase. While it's important that parents, teachers, and other caring adults have information to keep teens safe, it's also important that girls are able to define their own boundaries and the access that they provide to others in their lives. I've heard many girls say, "I just don't get it; they get mad when I am just hanging out with my friends. It's like they need to know where I am at every minute of the day, and if they don't like one person who's in the group, they get mad at me."

Teaching girls that they have a right to privacy and a right to a personal life is a critically important step. However, do we as adults actually believe that teens have a right to privacy? Often parents have so much information on where their teen is and what they are doing (and rightfully so!) that the teen can have a hard time differentiating among who actually should get access to this information. If we observe a teen meticulously describing which friends they are hanging out with, what they are doing, and who they are with, and going into excruciating detail as though to justify their behavior to their dating partner, we need to be mindful of the potentially controlling behavior that may be present.

#2: They want the password to my phone and my social media accounts. A current trend is for dating partners to have access to each other's cell phone, email, and social media passwords. It is seen as a sign of affection and trust that each partner can log onto the other's account and essentially track their communications and behaviors. Unfortunately, once again this does not allow a teen, or an adult, to develop a sense of individual privacy. Monitoring behavior and communication is once again a sign of control. So-called equal partners in a dating relationship should not maintain control of each other. Additionally, access to each other's technology among today's teen couples often produces catastrophic results once teens break up.

#3: They get mad when I hang out with my friends. Spending time with friends is an important part of the social development of teens, and when teens are dating, they are often eager to spend a lot of time with each other. However, when the expectation is that all of your free time will be spent with the dating partner and little, if any, time will be allocated to friends, there could be cause for concern. Girls who lack relationships with other girls and who look to have all of their emotional and intimate needs met through their dating relationships are at a higher risk of being involved in a violent dating relationship (Chesler, 2009).

Getting mad when the other person wants to spend time with their friends indicates an individual with high levels of insecurity and high levels of control. The difficulty here is that girls will often forgo their other friendships when they start dating relationships. As one tenth-grade girl stated,

> I just hated to see my best friend get into a serious relation-ship; we used to do everything together, and now I hardly ever see her. It's like she just dropped me once they started dating. And I've seen her do this before, and she thinks I'm just gonna be here for her when they break up. But I'm not having that happen to me again. If I'm not good enough for her now, I'm not gonna be good enough for her then.

#4: They keep track of where I am through my phone. With modern technology the ability to know another person's whereabouts at any given time is possible. GPS-enabled phones, tracker locating systems, and location and notification services provide information to another person about where an individual (or at least their phone) is located. Marketed initially as a system for monitoring children, GPS tracking has evolved into a way to keep tabs on teenagers, dating partners, and spouses. This, along with location services, social media check-in points, and geolocation photo tracking via smartphones, provides a great deal of detail on a person's activities throughout any given day. We need to teach teens about the safe and effective use of these technologies, while equipping them to set boundaries around what information they share and what information they allow others to access.

#5: They criticize my appearance. Criticizing the other person's body shape, weight, size, or appearance can be a sign of an unhealthy relationship. Putting the person down, making jokes, or demeaning them in this way can be emotionally destructive. To a girl's fledgling sense of self-esteem, negative comments about her body from her dating partner can leave real and substantial scars. As one girl stated,

> She always tells me that she thinks I'm pretty, but she thinks I need to lose a few pounds. She calls me thick or juicy. She makes comments about how pretty other girls are and how I would be so much prettier if I was more fit. It makes me really self-conscious and makes me not want to eat when I'm in front of her. She makes these comments about me when we are in front of her friends too, and it's really embarrassing.

#6: I feel like I have to "tiptoe" around them so that they won't get upset. For girls the tendency to be a "pleaser" can further compound negative interactions in already strained relationships. For many girls and women "keeping the peace" is their role within their families or relationships. They try hard to ensure that the other person is happy, even if that happiness comes at their own expense.

If you recognize that a girl is "tiptoeing" around in her dating relationship, it is a good sign that she has some fear that upsetting her partner will in some way negatively affect the relationship. This often means that she won't share her authentic self, or her authentic feelings, for fear of losing the relationship. She, in essence, will put the needs of her partner before her own needs and will maintain this dynamic throughout the relationship. This then becomes the expectation of her behavior.

When this happens, it makes it more difficult for her to speak her mind or share her opinions for increased fear of upsetting the other person. Many girls consider themselves so lucky to have a dating partner that they will go to great lengths to keep the person in their lives, regardless of the sacrifice of self that has to take place.

#7: They ask me to send nude or revealing pictures or videos. While the sexting rates of teens vary from less than 15% in some studies to more than 65% in others, girls report that they sext for a variety of reasons. Sixty-six percent of girls who have sexted say it is to be flirtatious, 52% say it is a sexual present to a guy, and 40% say it is as a joke (Lipkins et al., 2010). Girls report that they receive frequent requests from guys to "send a sexy pic" and that they often feel pressure to do it or else the guy will just move on to another girl who will. Often girls send the photos of themselves with little thought as to what might happen to the photos after the intended recipient views them. When teens break up, the photos and videos often get sent to everyone in the entire school. A recent example of this happened when an eleventh-grade girl made a sexually explicit video of herself and sent it to a classmate who was her boyfriend at the time. When the relationship ended, he sent the video to the entire football team at the school, and within days it went viral throughout the high school. School staff, parents, and even the police became involved in the situation. Possessing or distributing nude or sexually explicit materials involving minors can be considered possession or distribution of child pornography—a felony. The administrators were not sure how to handle the situation or how to discipline the students. The parents were mortified, and the girl who was in the video was beside herself with embarrassment and depression. She ultimately withdrew from school.

Additionally, teens are using video chat apps or other live stream technologies that are used for video chatting and sending video messages to engage in sexual exploration with their peers. While there may be a record that a call was made or the message disappears after a specific amount of time, teens may perceive that there is no record of the activity or the content of the call. As technology advances, it is important to know what pressures girls may be under to engage in this type of sexualized activity. While some argue that sexting and video chatting are merely technologically savvy ways of exploring adolescent sexuality, girls need to be aware of the very real potential for exploitation that is often a result of engaging in such behavior.

#8: I try to make him or her look good in front of my friends so they don't think he or she is a jerk. Sometimes when girls are in difficult relationships and their friends recognize the deficits, they go out of their way to express how wonderful and fantastic their partner is. "Oh, they are so sweet; I got a note in my locker this afternoon." "He loves me so much and bought me flowers, candy, and a card for Valentine's Day." "She is just so thoughtful; she remembered that I had a big test today and sent me a special good luck text." Granted, all these things are really sweet, but when placed in a context of patterns of behavior that are compensatory, or trying to make up or cover for the bad or controlling behavior, we see girls attempting to normalize their relationships to their friends. Their logic is that if they show everyone how wonderful and caring their partner is, their friends will overlook the other behaviors that aren't so attractive.

Part of this is a need to save face with one's friends, and part of this may the girl trying to convince herself that her relationship is healthier than it actually is. My gauge of this behavior is to consider whether or not a good deed by a dating partner is as important, or as special, if it happens and we aren't able to share it with others. For example, if we get a dozen roses delivered to us at work, does it feel different from getting a dozen roses delivered to us at home? If no one is there to witness the sign of affection, does it still feel the same? Sometimes it seems that our need to promote our relationship to others is an attempt to convince ourselves or our friends what a fantastic person we're with.

#9: They won't talk to me when they get upset; they just ignore me. Often, when girls think of unhealthy dating relationships, they think exclusively of physical intimidation or threats. However, there are nonphysical ways to control someone's behavior, and one of them is through utilizing the "silent treatment" or "giving someone the cold shoulder." Instead of talking about what it is that is bothering them, the other person will ignore their partner for a period of time. Generally, this results in the person who is being ignored trying to figure out what they did to upset the other person. This, more subtle form of manipulation ensures that the person being ignored knows that they did something wrong and also learns not to do it again.

#10: They say that if I ever break up with them, they will kill themselves. Finally, when one partner threatens to leave the relationship and the other person is so distraught that they threaten to harm themselves, we must recognize this as a very scary form of manipulation. This puts pressure on one person to try to fix the situation so that the other will not harm themselves. Fearing that the other person is unstable or may kill themselves is not a good reason for staying in an unhealthy relationship. However, it is a strong force of control because no one wants to believe that they did something to make another person hurt or kill themselves.

It is important to take all suicidal threats and behaviors seriously; however, relationships cannot be maintained on the basis of this type of behavior. Generally, it's not until middle school, high school, and beyond that adolescents and even adults will make these kinds of threats. The messages can be confusing as well. Should I be flattered because they care so much about me? Will anyone ever love me this much? It is important that girls recognize that this kind of behavior is extremely controlling and that the person who is making such threats likely has more substantial behavioral or mental health issues.

What Can We Do?

Provide opportunities for girls to learn about their changing bodies and to ask questions in a safe, low-risk setting. If you work with elementary or middle school girls, they likely are interested in talking about their bodies and the changes that are happening but too terrified to bring the subject up with you. When we give girls the opportunities to ask questions and explore, we are amazed at how much they don't know about puberty! One school counselor who runs groups with girls told me that she passes out index cards to the girls before the lesson to write down any questions that they have about puberty and what is happening to their bodies. She then collects the cards (without any names or identifying information), brings in the school nurse to the session, and then addresses the girls' questions within the group. More often than not, many girls have the same questions.

Teach girls how to set boundaries, practice refusal skills, and stand up for themselves in dating relationships. Girls and women have a difficult time standing up for themselves in a variety of settings but perhaps most often in romantic relationships. Help girls understand that the feelings of both people in the relationship are of equal importance and that neither person gets to dictate the terms of the relationship. One of the hardest things for a girl to do is to say "no" or "I don't want to do that" or "I'm not cool with that" to a person she likes or cares about. The result is that girls often end up going along with things that they don't want to do for fear of upsetting the other person. Girls need to think about their boundaries and limits and practice saying "no" when they are not in a precarious situation so as to increase their ability to say "no" when there is more pressure to say "yes."

Help girls identify trusted adults they can talk to about these issues. It can be difficult for girls to know who they should talk to when they feel confused, pressured, threatened, or unsure of themselves. Many do not want to tell their parents about the bad things that have happened to them or the concerns that they have for fear of upsetting or disappointing them. This can leave girls feeling very alone. If they don't think they can talk to their parents, who else is in their support system? Some of these people could be grandparents, aunts, pastors, teachers, counselors, principals, or coaches. Help girls create a list of the people they trust and could talk to about difficult issues.

Acknowledge that it can be very hard to leave a controlling or abusive relationship. You may be working with girls who are involved in unhealthy relationships or who live in a home where there is an unhealthy relationship. It is important that we don't make statements such as "Why haven't you broken up yet? I don't know what you are waiting for." It is extremely difficult to get out of an abusive relationship, and many girls are fearful for their physical and emotional safety, so they continue to stay in unhealthy situations. This is why it is so critical that we give girls the tools to identify the signs of a potentially unhealthy relationship while they are young, so that they have awareness and can make decisions about their relationships as they mature.

"Lighten Up," "I Was Just Joking," "Boys Will Be Boys," and Other Stuff Girls Hear

6

Addressing Disrespect and Sexual Harassment

When we change classes we basically expect that we are going to get our butts hit or grabbed in the hallways. It literally happens to me everyday. But then if I say something, the guy says, "Geez . . . relax; I was just playing." So you can't really win.

—Estelle, seventh grade

There are a lot of sexual comments. Stuff about our bodies, stuff about what they want us to do to them or that they want to do to us.

—Reagan, ninth grade

We get a lot of pictures that we don't ask for. Like AirDrop will pop up on your phone, and you'll see a picture of something normal, like a puppy, and then you accept the photo, and the next 10 pictures behind it are porn.

—Jayden, tenth grade

By the time girls get to high school 80% report that boys their age are disrespectful to girls, up from 50% in fifth grade (Hinkelman, 2017). When I dug deeper into the research, I found that this statistic held steady across all demographic factors. It did not matter whether girls attended a high- or low-poverty school; whether they were from an urban, suburban, or rural environment; or if they were Black, white, Asian, Hispanic/Latinx, or multiracial—nearly all girls reported similar perceptions of disrespect, with consistent increases as they got older. I wanted to dive deeper into the statistics to understand more specifically what girls were experiencing. I was interested in knowing how to provide more context for the survey responses so that the stories and examples could help explain the girls' responses; so I conducted dozens of focus groups with hundreds of girls across the country. This opportunity to listen to their concerns, hear their stories, and understand their realities gave me a much deeper appreciation of the complexities of their relationships and the intricacies of their interactions.

The saddest and perhaps most frustrating part of this is that many girls acknowledge that they experience lack of respect from boys. They see it as the norm. In my conversations with them I would say something like "So in this big survey I did with almost 11,000 girls, I learned that about 80% of the girls in high school believe that boys their age are disrespectful of girls. Does that seem accurate to you?" Then I would just sit back and listen to the girls talk, share their stories, debate with one another, and work to articulate their own definition of respect. They would give examples and talk about specific situations and at times specific people (although we made an agreement to keep the names of others out of our conversations) who routinely demonstrated respect or didn't act respectfully toward them. It was interesting to listen to how they categorized their male peers and, more specifically, how they segmented the guys' behaviors. Overwhelmingly, girls agreed with the 80% statistic, although many would give examples of one or two guys in their lives who "were cool." Some had specific friend groups of both boys and girls where they reported feeling safe and respected. Others shared that their "best friend but not boyfriend" (this must be clarified as a notable difference) was a guy and that they did everything together. In listening to example after example, it became increasingly clear to me that their positive experiences were based on specific relationships but their negative experiences were with "guys in general." When taken as a group, their perceptions and experiences of their male peers were of disrespect and even harassment; however, their individual relationships could offset their generalized perceptions.

I wanted to further understand where the disrespect starts and how, if unchecked, it can escalate into bigger challenges (Gartner & Sterzing, 2016). We'll begin by examining the negative, and sometimes hostile, climate that girls experience, which can lend itself to increased acceptance of disrespect and harassment toward them.

General Disrespect Toward Girls

Disrespect that girls experience simply because they are girls can include the various ways they can be excluded, made fun of, or put down based on their gender. The comments or behaviors can be so insignificant, even trivial, that some may truly perceive that there is no real or long-standing impact. They might be policies (e.g., school dress codes that are unfairly biased against girls), comments that can put girls at a disadvantage or leave them out of an opportunity (e.g., telling girls that a particular activity is likely to get them messy so they might not want to participate), or long-standing practices that disproportionately affect girls (e.g., girls' high school sports are relegated to the middle school facilities or the less desirable fields/courts when compared with boys' sports).

Oftentimes, these instances of disrespect seem innocuous, as they are not often called into question because they aren't seen as being a big deal. The small aggressions are rarely attention grabbing and are not typically viewed as singularly damaging or traumatic. However, the repeated experience can contribute to bias, insensitivity, or degradation. When behaviors or comments reinforce the stereotype that there are certain things that are accessible and appropriate for girls and other things that are for boys, often there is a differential negative impact on girls. Such comments can often happen unintentionally, without acknowledgment, and may even be a poor attempt at humor. Here are some examples that girls (and women) hear regularly:

Examples of Gender-Based Disrespect

- "That's just boys being boys . . . you know, locker room talk. You can't really take that seriously."
- "He really needs to man up and take responsibility."
- "I need three strong boys to help me carry these boxes."
- "These girls need to have some self-respect and act like ladies."
- "To be honest, if you register for that class, you'll be the only girl there, and it might be uncomfortable for you."
- "She's such a good athlete . . . and she's actually pretty too!"

We might read these or similar examples (or perhaps have even said a few of them ourselves) and not realize that the comments are in fact damaging and also quite a bit sexist. In many cases the person who has made the statement may have little idea that their comments are negative and demeaning, because the behavior is not in their conscious awareness—they are simply saying what they are thinking.

Despite the discomfort that we might feel when we hear such comments, we are often at a loss for words because we don't want to overreact. After all, it was just a passing comment, right? "I shouldn't make a big deal about it," "They didn't mean anything by it," "They didn't even realize they were being offensive," "I don't want them to think I'm a crazy feminist," we may think to ourselves. However, we rarely think about the cumulative impact that these types of comments can have on our girls. We may not fully grasp the fact that passing comments can turn into pervasive belief systems, and before long girls have internalized the message that there are indeed separate and unequal rules and expectations for boys and girls. The expectations become so ingrained because "that's the way it has always been" that they don't even question why their team has to practice at the old facility with the hand-me-down equipment while the boys' team has a sparkling new court and fresh new uniforms each season. They silently wonder to themselves why they aren't allowed to wear tank tops for gym class when the boys routinely take class shirtless. Girls recognize quickly that behaviors are judged differently based on whether one is male or female, and unfortunately, they can learn to accept this gender-based disrespect and differential treatment.

As the adults who are influencing, supporting, and encouraging girls, we have a responsibility to develop an awareness of these subtle forms of disrespect, and we may want to determine how to address the behavior without intentionally escalating the situation. Responding without making the other person feel defensive ensures that we aren't mistaken for agreeing with the comment and also gives us the chance to gently point out the concern that we have. Here are some suggestions (Nadal, 2014) for how you might think about responding:

Nonescalating Responses to Gender-Based Disrespect

- "You might not have realized this, but when you told Jamie that she might be uncomfortable as the only girl in the robotics class, you may have inadvertently made her feel like she shouldn't take the course. Maybe we can follow up with her and ensure that she recognizes the situation but also realizes that we believe in her and know that she is up for the challenge!"

- "You just said that 'boys will be boys.' . . . What does that mean? I don't get it."

- "Why is that funny?"

- "Actually, in my experience the girls in my class are really strong and would love to be asked to carry those boxes alongside their male peers."

- "I think that is a stereotype. What I have learned is _____."

- "Another way to look at it is _____."

Once we start doing this as regular practice, girls notice the way we stand up for them, and their awareness of these subtleties also changes. They begin to develop more keen insights into this type of behavior and come to realize that they too can confidently and respectfully respond in situations where they feel uneasy or disrespected. When girls have the skills to respond to lower levels of threat or disrespect, such as those mentioned earlier, they are then better equipped to effectively handle more severe situations that they might encounter, such as sexual harassment or even violence. But if they don't develop these very basic skills, their ability to employ more assertive strategies to stand up for themselves is increasingly unlikely. I liken this to the learning concept of *scaffolding*. We help them develop the basic skills of recognizing the situation as one of concern and practicing the skills to address or confront the issue. In doing this girls learn how to use their voice and stand up for themselves in lower-risk situations, such as the examples above. Then as they build confidence and efficacy in their ability to successfully master that skill, they are able to take on situations that may be complex or higher risk, such as sexual harassment.

Sexual Harassment

Sexual harassment has gotten much more attention with the proliferation of the #MeToo movement, founded by Tarana Burke and elevated to mainstream awareness through the film and entertainment industries. Long-hidden and pervasive sexual harassment was shared by dozens and dozens of victims, which broke open long-hidden and pervasive sexual harassment in the film and entertainment industry. Here we saw dozens and dozens of victims of harassment coming forward to share their stories with the public in a systematic way that was never seen before. Most of the women who shared their experiences talked about men who used their positions of power and influence to degrade and abuse them and then ensured their silence with blackmail, threats, and exclusion. Business dinners that turned overtly and uncomfortably sexual, role auditions or job interviews that started pleasantly and then turned to something more nefarious. The consistent patterns of taking advantage of younger, less powerful women who were trying to launch their careers in an industry that they loved and were working diligently to succeed in.

Now when we think of sexual harassment, the #MeToo movement is part of the narrative; however, it is not without its critics and detractors. Some feel that the movement has gone too far, has put boys and men on the defensive, or has created an unsafe climate for both men and women in the workplace. However, I believe that it has started an important dialogue and has uncovered generations of disrespectful, manipulative, and abusive behavior toward women. It has been effective because it has shifted the narrative to encourage and emphasize women's autonomy and agency in determining how and when they disclose their experiences of sexual violence. When we think of sexual harassment and #MeToo, we think about adults who are part of Hollywood, movies, and entertainment and high-powered executives. While this has been critical to the elevation of the issue, I have wondered if girls see themselves in the #MeToo movement. Do they equate their experiences in school to the movement they observed in the media?

How Do Girls View and Experience Sexual Harassment?

While the vast majority of high school girls report that boys their age are not respectful to them, they don't necessarily define the behavior as *sexual harassment*. I believe this is often due to the fact they may not fully understand the definition of the term. However, through conversations with girls I see clearly that this is what many girls experience on a very regular basis. From subtle comments about their bodies to pervasive and ongoing sexualized behavior, girls are not immune from the confusing, demeaning, and extremely hard to navigate hormone-infused reality of the social landscape. While harassing behavior is not indicative of the way *all* boys treat *all* girls, it is an indicator of the way many girls experience their social climate and the boy-girl interactions that are a part of their day-to-day lives. They truly see some of the disrespectful behavior as how boys *generally* talk about and treat girls.

However, the sexualized culture is not exclusively perpetrated by boys; girls can contribute to the behaviors as well. One school counselor shared with me that her seventh-grade girls will smack each other's butts in the hall—specifically directed toward the girls with the "bigger butts." The girls who have "smaller butts" are at risk of having their pants pulled down by other girls. Girls also make fun of one another for their physical development—for developing curves, breasts, and hips either before the majority of their peers or later than their peer group.

While *most* sexual harassment and coercion continue to be situations where boys are the aggressors and girls are the victims, girls are not immune from making sexually charged comments to boys, spreading sexual rumors, and contributing to a sexualized climate that can be extremely uncomfortable for boys.

What Actually Is Sexual Harassment?

Sexual harassment is generally defined as any unwelcome sex- or gender-based verbal or physical contact. According to the Office for Civil Rights, U.S. Department of Education (2010), sexual harassment is defined as

> unwelcome conduct of a sexual nature, which can include unwelcome sexual advances, requests for sexual favors, or other verbal, nonverbal, or physical conduct of a sexual nature. Thus, sexual harassment prohibited by Title IX can include conduct such as touching of a sexual nature; making sexual comments, jokes, or gestures; writing graffiti or displaying or distributing sexually explicit drawings, pictures, or written materials; calling students sexually charged names; spreading sexual rumors; rating students on sexual activity or performance; or circulating, showing, or creating e-mails or Web sites of a sexual nature.

One can see how some of the more subtle gender-based disrespect can lead to attitudes that are more accepting of language and behavior that are both sexual and unwanted (see Figure 6.1). Sexual harassment is more egregious and more harmful than the disrespectful comments that were previously discussed, and if unchecked, it can have lasting impacts on the victim. Girls who experience frequent sexual harassment at school are less likely to want to attend school, less likely to feel safe at school, and more likely to develop social, emotional, and mental health issues (American Association of University Women Educational Foundation [AAUW], 2011).

Figure 6.1 Continuum of Disrespect, Aggression, and Violence Toward Girls

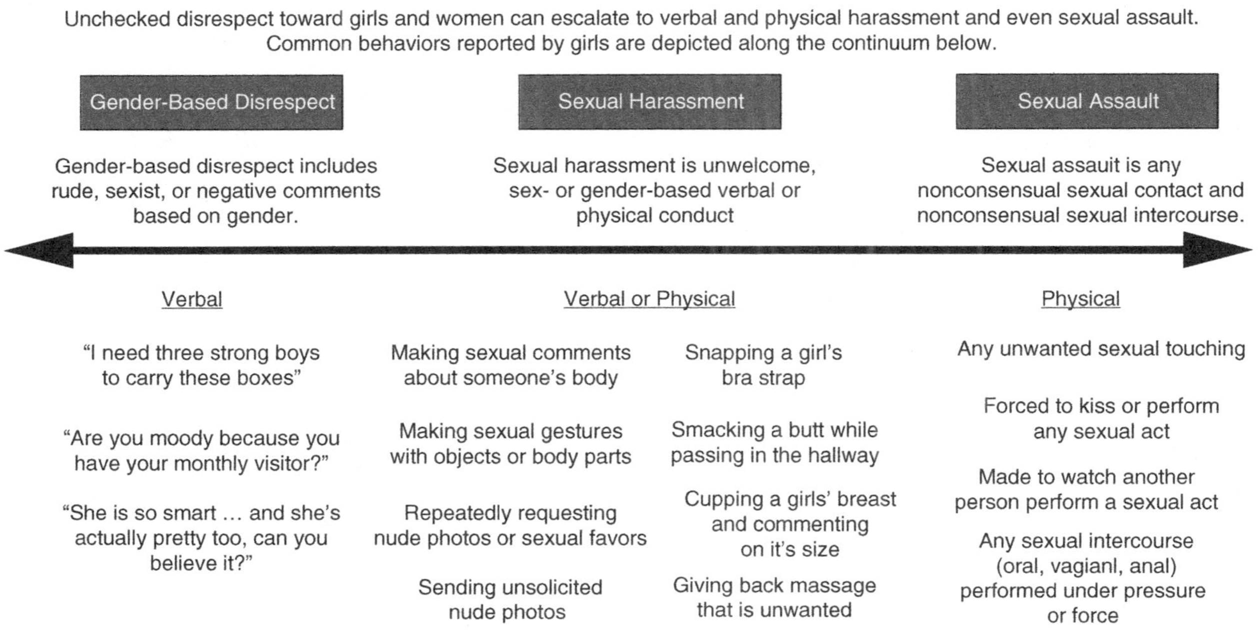

Unchecked disrespect toward girls and women can escalate to verbal and physical harassment and even sexual assault. Common behaviors reported by girls are depicted along the continuum below.

Gender-Based Disrespect	Sexual Harassment	Sexual Assault
Gender-based disrespect includes rude, sexist, or negative comments based on gender.	Sexual harassment is unwelcome, sex- or gender-based verbal or physical conduct	Sexual assault is any nonconsensual sexual contact and nonconsensual sexual intercourse.
Verbal	_Verbal or Physical_	_Physical_
"I need three strong boys to carry these boxes"	Making sexual comments about someone's body	Any unwanted sexual touching
"Are you moody because you have your monthly visitor?"	Making sexual gestures with objects or body parts	Forced to kiss or perform any sexual act
"She is so smart … and she's actually pretty too, can you believe it?"	Repeatedly requesting nude photos or sexual favors	Made to watch another person perform a sexual act
	Sending unsolicited nude photos	Any sexual intercourse (oral, vagianl, anal) performed under pressure or force
	Snapping a girl's bra strap	
	Smacking a butt while passing in the hallway	
	Cupping a girls' breast and commenting on it's size	
	Giving back massage that is unwanted	

Statistically, by the time girls graduate from high school, upward of 90% have experienced sexual harassment at least once, with 62% being called a nasty or demeaning name and 51% receiving unwanted physical contact at school (Leaper & Brown, 2008). Girls might not label the behavior as "sexual harassment," but they will talk at length about what they experience daily at school. Fifth-grade girls report getting their bras snapped on a regular basis, seventh-grade girls speak of pervasive butt gabbing when they are walking down the hall in between classes, and high school girls have gotten used to unsolicited comments on their bodies, lewd requests for sexual activities, and a sexualized culture where girls are the fodder for the joking that takes place both in and out of the locker room. A group of middle school girls in a suburban school shared with me their experiences of boys "asking for oral sex and making sex gestures to us in class," "talking about who has the best boobs and the nicest butt and comparing your body to everyone else's—basically rating you and saying why you aren't good enough," "asking for nude pictures *literally* every day," and "pressing their bodies up on yours while you are trying to get stuff out of your locker."

Girls often find themselves in a precarious position because they don't see an easy and clear response when they are faced with some of these situations. On the one hand, we tell girls not to put up with disrespectful behavior, but at the same time we also say things like "Guys are just immature. He is only teasing you because he likes you" or "You should just ignore them; that is just boys being boys." This dual messaging can be confusing, and it does not give girls a clear boundary or direction regarding what they should do and how they should react.

In many of these uncomfortable situations girls don't have a good understanding of how to respond, and so they laugh awkwardly, brush away the hand with an uncomfortable smile, and may even jokingly say, "Quit it!"—as they laugh and attempt to address the situation in the only way they know how. They want the behavior to stop but don't want to be seen as rude, as overreacting, or as a prude (my word, not theirs). So instead of confronting the situation directly, they respond in much more passive ways. As Mariah, a seventh grader who attends a diverse middle school suburban, explained to me,

> We leave class and walk to our lockers or to our next class, and it's like a free for all. You know that guys are going to come up behind you and smack your butt and make lots of sexual comments. They will like lick their lips and say stuff about what they want you to do to them—you know, sexually.

When I pressed further to understand how she and other girls responded to the boys' behavior, Mariah said,

> I guess I don't really feel like there is much we can do. If you yell at them to stop, they make you feel like you are totally overreacting and will say that they were just joking and that you need to lighten up. If you tell a teacher about what is happening, it honestly can just make things worse for you because everyone will find out that you were the one who told. So basically, you just deal with it.

What About the Girls Who Are "Asking for It"?

Unsurprisingly, this is a question that I get often from parents, teachers, and administrators, both young and old, male and female. There continues to be a pervasive sense that much of the sexual harassment that girls experience is something that girls enjoy and even something that they seek out and "bring on themselves." Girls routinely hear comments such as "If these girls wouldn't dress like that, we wouldn't have so many issues" and "Girls need to respect themselves and their bodies more and cover up. What do they think is going to happen to them when they are clearly flaunting their bodies?" and (my all-time favorite) "We implemented a stricter dress code because the boys can't concentrate when the girls are wearing revealing clothes."

The belief behind these sentiments is that (a) a boy's behavior is directly correlated to a girl's appearance and (b) a boy does not have the ability to limit his verbal or physical responses or reactions to a girl. A third belief embedded in this perspective is that girls enjoy being harassed. When broken down in this way, it is relatively easy to find the fault in this logic. Boys, without a doubt, have the ability, dignity, and wherewithal to learn and know when their behavior is inappropriate or demeaning. To assert that boys have a biological basis for lacking behavioral restraint around girls is terribly degrading to boys. Inferring that basic self-control is not a learned and practiced behavior trait but rather an innate and uncontrolled force is inconsistent with every theory of learning, discipline, and executive function that we tout and teach as counselors, parents, and educators.

Perhaps this view is less about boys' innate abilities and predetermined behaviors and more about the long-standing roles and expectations that society places on both boys and girls. Both grow up in a world that directly or indirectly teaches them the unwritten rules about what it means to be a boy or a girl. This includes how they should look, act, dress, and behave in relationships, so it is no surprise that these roles and expectations extend to the interactions that they have with each other. In many ways we expect that boys will be the ones who are more aggressive and persistent and that girls will be the passive recipients of attention, interest, or overtures. If boys aren't always interested or if girls are the initiators, there can be a sense of discomfort that the scene is somehow wrong because it is outside the social norm.

We have to be diligent in countering the message that girls are ever "asking for" harassment or violence. In schools this sentiment is most often connected to clothing choice and dress code. Inferring that if girls wear certain types of clothing, they should expect a level of degrading treatment from others is placing the responsibility for the behavior on the wrong person. The clothes that we choose to wear can say something about our personality, our style, or even our socioeconomic status. Sometimes girls wear clothing that is ill fitting or too tight because they don't have the means to purchase new clothes as their bodies are rapidly changing during adolescence.

Girls feel tremendous pressure surrounding their appearance as they approach middle and high school, and nearly 40% report that they think about their appearance "at least once a period" or "nearly all day" (Hinkelman, 2017). Styles and fashions change over time, and throughout history there has never been a time when popular sentiment told girls and women that they were dressing *too* modestly. There has always been an undertone of disapproval in the fashion choices that women and girls make—that they are "showing too much skin," "not leaving anything to the imagination," or "flaunting their bodies."

We must be clear with ourselves and with girls that a clothing choice never says, "I would like to be *assaulted* today." Wardrobe choices could say, "I'd like to be noticed," "I want others to find me attractive," or even "I want to look sexy." As a girl approaches puberty and finds that her physique is changing to look more womanly, she may be receiving more attention from peers and even from strangers regardless of the clothes that she is wearing. There are aspects of this attention that can feel affirming, flattering, and wanted. However, it can also feel confusing and unsettling. If she is met with disrespect or threats, the attention can feel uncomfortable, unwelcome, or even frightening.

To be clear, girls receive both appropriate and inappropriate attention from others regardless of their clothing choices and their physique. Girls who are not yet physically developed or who dress modestly are not immune from harassment or violence. In fact, there is actually no correlation between the type of clothing a girl wears and her experience of harassment or violence. (See Chapter 7 for a more in-depth discussion of this topic.)

It is really important to help girls discern between behaviors that make them feel good, attractive, happy, and desired and behaviors that make them feel objectified, degraded, or demeaned. This differentiation is a critical one as it sets the baseline for how girls allow themselves to be treated and what comments and behaviors they think are both expected and acceptable. This can start with an awareness of the simple negative comments that are made about or to girls (gender-based disrespect) and can progress to more extreme behavior (sexual harassment). We'll discuss the issues of violence and sexual assault in Chapter 7, but we can see how these behaviors can build on one another, setting the stage for a climate that is disempowering for girls. We have an opportunity to address the inequities that we observe while we also help girls develop the skills and courage to stand up for themselves when faced with such challenges.

How Can I Help?

Teach Girls How to Identify Disrespect and Harassment and How to Appropriately Address Situations That Cause Them Discomfort

Recent Harvard research confirmed that while most girls and women have experienced sexual harassment, fewer than 25% have had a conversation with their parents about addressing sexually harassing situations; yet most report wanting guidance from the adults in their lives (Weissbourd et al., 2017).

While ignoring disparaging comments or harassment is a strategy that girls often employ (AAUW, 2011), it is not always effective in stopping the behavior from happening again in the future. While there is no "proven" strategy that will work 100% of the time, we do know that passive strategies such as ignoring the behavior or laughing it off are much less effective than more direct or assertive strategies. We need to equip girls with tools and skills so they have options and choices for how to respond in an uncomfortable or threatening situation.

- *Give a firm and clear verbal response:* Teach girls that being clear and direct in their request leaves no question to the perpetrator that the behavior that they are experiencing is unwanted. Saying, "Stop doing that!" or "Don't touch me" is a much stronger response than saying, "Why do you keep touching me?" Responding in the form of a question can provide an opportunity for justification of the behavior and can simply extend the interaction. Telling the other person exactly what you need them to do (i.e., stop touching you) ensures that they do not mistake your perspective.

- *Project strong and confident body language:* Helping girls learn how to project strong and confident body language means that we help them learn how to take up more space. Girls are often taught to make themselves small and to ensure that they aren't too big or too loud. When we teach them to stand up to bullying, harassment, and disrespect, we have to encourage them to take up room with both their bodies and their voices. Standing with their head up and their shoulders held back, making eye contact with the person they are speaking to, sends the message that they are serious in their request.

- *Deliver the message with a serious facial expression:* Oftentimes when we are uncomfortable or embarrassed, we smile or even laugh. While our words might indicate that we want the other person to stop their behavior, if we are smiling or laughing while we say, "Stop it," our message can be confusing to the other person. If we truly want the behavior to stop, our words and our affect need to match. Give girls the chance to practice their delivery of a clear message with a serious face (no laughing!), so that they experience the difference for themselves.

Ensure That School Personnel Know Their Legal and Ethical Responsibilities Related to Identifying and Addressing Sexual Harassment in School

Every individual school employee has a responsibility to ensure the safety of all students within the school and can be held personally liable if they have knowledge of sexual harassment and do nothing with their information. According to the May 2020 Title IX regulations released by the U.S. Office of Civil Rights, schools are required to respond when they have "actual knowledge" of a complaint of sexual harassment, which can include a report to any employee of an elementary or secondary school. Additionally, schools are required to provide "supportive measures" to students, with or without a formal complaint. In short, if you know about sexual harassment taking place, you are ethically and legally required to do something about it.

Each school district that receives federal funding from the U.S. Department of Education is also required by law to have a Title IX coordinator—a person responsible for training the staff on issues of gender equity, identifying sex discrimination and sexual harassment, and resolving grievances. Title IX is a civil rights law that prohibits educational institutions from discriminating against students on the basis of sex. Often when we think about Title IX, we may think about girls' and women's access to, participation in, and funding for athletics, as this was one of the areas of vast inequity in schools when

Title IX was originally introduced in 1972. Title IX continues to address all areas of gender discrimination in schools, including sexual harassment.

Educators, parents, and students can access a plethora of free resources provided by the nonprofit organization Stop Sexual Assault in Schools (stopsexualassaultinschools.org), which is committed to providing information and tools on sexual harassment, Title IX, and sexual assault. This is one of the few organizations that are focused on tracking and addressing these issues in the K–12 environment.

Enforce Strict but Fair Rules, and Engage Students in Creating and Enforcing Policies, Procedures, and Protocols That Promote a Safe and Harassment-Free School Climate

While sexual harassment policies are mandated by law, the way the policies are enforced can vary dramatically from school to school. A school's climate is a direct reflection of the leadership's priorities and practices. When the school leadership takes a strong and visible stance for respect and equity and against sexual harassment, the educators, staff, and students follow suit. Specifically, authoritative school climates are associated with positive outcomes for schools, particularly as they relate to student violence and aggression. Authoritative schools are characterized by a strong disciplinary structure and the sense that rules are strict but fair, alongside a commitment toward intense student support so kids get care and respect from school personnel. These environmental shifts alone are associated with significantly less student experience of sexual harassment (Crowley et al., 2019). In schools where girls feel safe and protected, teachers and school administrators take them seriously, listen to their concerns, and address issues that they bring to light.

Schools that engage students in creating norms around school climate, that promote student participation in conversations centered on respect and social justice, and that welcome student voice in the drafting and enforcement of student behavior expectations enjoy improved student behavior and engagement. Give students the chance to contribute to the drafting of school policies, assemblies focused on student conduct, and schoolwide campaigns that address healthy dating and relationships.

Looking Out for the Girls 7

Identifying and Preventing Sexual Violence

About 30% of girls will experience some type of sexual violence at some point in their lives. We must instill in our girls the idea that they are worth defending and that they have the capacity and the right to successfully defend themselves.

Sexual violence may be one of the most difficult topics for parents, educators, and counselors to think about when it comes to the girls they care deeply about. As a result, this chapter might be the easiest one to skip because most of us have difficulty believing that our lives could be affected by sexual violence. We often think that sexual harassment is something that happens to someone else . . . to *those* girls . . . to the ones who dress sexy and "ask for it." The actresses who had the misfortune of being on the wrong side of a powerful movie producer. The overtly sexually dressed college girl who is headed out for a night of partying. We believe that sexual assault is one of those violent issues that we see on crime shows on TV and that it only happens to people we don't know.

Unfortunately, the reality is that most of us know people whose lives have been affected by sexual violence, whether or not they have ever shared their experience with us. If you are an educator, there is a strong possibility that you have observed sexual harassment in the halls of your school and a statistical probability that you have encountered many individuals who have been victims of a more egregious sexual crime. Among college women nearly 30% reported that they had experienced sexual violence from a dating partner while they were still in high school (Smith et al., 2003), and according to the Association of American Universities and the Bureau of Justice Statistics, about one in four women experienced an attempted or completed sexual assault during their college years.

When we look at data from 15- to 19-year-old girls, between 12% and 28% report being forced to have sexual intercourse at some time in their lives (Centers for Disease Control and Prevention [CDC], 2012; Morrison-Breedy & Grove, 2018), and nearly half have been coerced into performing other sex acts, excluding intercourse. It is hard to think that for every classroom of 30 girls there are likely 10 girls who have experienced or are experiencing some type of sexual pressure or violence.

A sexual violation—either harassment or abuse—is one of the most intimate violations that can happen to a person, and it can have lasting consequences. Unfortunately, many of us lack a sound understanding of what sexual violence is and often do not have accurate information on how to identify a situation that meets the definition of sexual harassment or sexual assault.

The CDC (2015) defines sexual violence as

> a sexual act that is committed or attempted by another person without freely given consent of the victim or against someone who is unable to consent or refuse. It includes: forced or alcohol/drug facilitated penetration of a victim; forced or alcohol/drug facilitated incidents in which the victim was made to penetrate a perpetrator or someone else; nonphysically pressured unwanted penetration;

intentional sexual touching; or non-contact acts of a sexual nature. Sexual violence can also occur when a perpetrator forces or coerces a victim to engage in sexual acts with a third party.

A key aspect surrounding sexual violence is the presence, or lack thereof, of freely given consent. Meaning that if the sexual activity is completed under pressure, duress, force, threat of force, impairment, or incapacitation, there is no presence of consent (Basile et al., 2014). The CDC (2015) expressly discusses consent as follows:

> Sexual violence involves a lack of freely given consent as well as situations in which the victim is unable to consent or refuse:
>
> *Consent*
>
> Words or overt actions by a person who is legally or functionally competent to give informed approval, indicating a freely given agreement to have sexual intercourse or sexual contact.
>
> *Inability to Consent*
>
> A freely given agreement to have sexual intercourse or sexual contact could not occur because of the victim's age, illness, mental or physical disability, being asleep or unconscious, or being too intoxicated (e.g., incapacitation, lack of consciousness, or lack of awareness) through their voluntary or involuntary use of alcohol or drugs.
>
> *Inability to Refuse*
>
> Disagreement to engage in a sexual act was precluded because of the use or possession of guns or other non-bodily weapons, or due to physical violence, threats of physical violence, intimidation or pressure, or misuse of authority.

Many of us incorrectly believe sexual violence to be a violent, forced sexual activity or rape, when in fact sexual violence includes *any* unwanted or coerced sexual activity (Dichter et al., 2010).

Examples of Sexual Violence

- Unwanted sexual touching (touching a person's genitals, buttocks, or breasts; forcing someone to kiss or touch another person)

- Forcing another person to perform a sexual act (undressing, posing for photographs, genital or oral contact, oral sex, intercourse)

- Pressuring, coercing, convincing, or tricking someone to engage in sexual activity

- Unwanted noncontact sexual experiences (exposure to pornography, unwanted filming or dissemination of sexual photographs, creating a hostile environment through the use of technology)

- Engaging in sexual activity with a minor (the age of consent to sexual activity varies from state to state, so it is important to know what the laws in your state say regarding sexual consent)

Often when we think of sexual violence, we think of a college-age or adult woman who is wearing a short skirt and is accosted in a dark alley by a stranger. While some sexual violence does take place in this manner, the unfortunate reality is that sexual violence affects people of all ages and most likely happens between people who know each other, not between strangers. Forty-four percent of victims of sexual violence are under the age of 18, and girls between the ages of 12 and 14 are at the highest risk. A peak occurs again at age 18 (CDC, 2012), with the first year of college being a particularly vulnerable year. The new-found freedom, the party and hookup culture, experimenting with drugs and alcohol, and exposure to higher-risk situations create an environment where girls can be taken advantage of by others who may exploit their vulnerabilities.

Conversations about sexual abuse and sexual violence do not occur with any regularity, and many perceive the subject as taboo. It is easy to believe that sexual violence happens to "those other people" but not in my school or community. Unlike other forms of child maltreatment, sexual abuse occurs with similar frequency in urban, suburban, and rural areas to children of various races, genders and socioeconomic statuses. Educators, counselors, and parents find it extremely difficult to talk to children about sexual violence and report not knowing what to say or how to approach the topic (Hinkelman & Bruno, 2008). When I surveyed teachers and counselors about their training to identify and address issues of sexual violence, most reported that their college training programs spent little, if any, time discussing the topic.

We learned that few adults have accurate information on how sexual violence happens and most believe that their daughters are well insulated from risk. Parents generally believe that their supervision of their children is so intense that there are no opportunities for an unwanted sexual incident to take place. As one parent of a 12-year-old said,

> She is almost never by herself, so there is really no opportunity for her to get into trouble. I make it my job to ensure that she is safe.

A father of a 13-year-old girl told me,

> My daughter is not allowed to date, and if she spends any time with a boy, it is when I or another adult is around. We would not ever allow her to be in a situation where she could get hurt or make a bad decision.

Similarly, girls report that they don't drink, aren't promiscuous, and dress modestly, so they do not perceive themselves as potential victims:

> I think about what I wear and how I act so that I don't send the wrong message. I see girls who are wearing clothes that are very sexy and girls who are always flirting with or doing stuff with guys. I don't do any of that stuff, and that is how I keep myself safe.

Isn't It Enough to Say, "Don't Talk to Strangers"?

When my colleagues and I teach sexual violence prevention workshops, we begin by asking the girls to discuss some of the things that we know about people who take advantage of others in sexual ways.

So I ask you to think about this as well. Describe below the person who sexually assaults another person:

- What do they look like?
- What are they wearing?
- What is their state of mind?
- Where are they when the assault takes place?
- What kind of job do they have?
- Where did they meet the victim of the assault?

If your reactions are like those of most girls, you may have thought of things like "He's crazy," "He has low self-esteem," "He's scary and creepy," or "He's mentally ill." There is a clear stereotype that persists surrounding who is capable of sexual assault. It is very rare to hear reactions such as "They are attractive and sexy," "A mentor and a coach," "A family member," or "A close friend."

Girls are generally surprised to learn that the notion of a scary guy jumping out of the bushes and abducting and raping a woman is usually way off base. While stranger assaults do occur, they happen rather infrequently. For children and teens who experience sexual abuse or violence, only 7% of the time is the perpetrator a stranger. This means that in 93% of the cases, the girl knows the person. Girls are most likely to be sexually assaulted by a family member, friend, or date, or someone they know and even trust. In fact, about 34% of the time the perpetrator is a family member, and 59% of the time the aggressor is an acquaintance (U.S. Department of Justice, 2000).

We've got to expand our thinking from the traditional "stranger danger" mentality, where we simply tell girls not to talk to strangers or walk alone at night. This approach fails to account for how sexual assault actually happens to girls. From childhood through their teen years, girls are most likely to be sexually assaulted by a family member or friend of the family. Because few elementary-age girls are "dating," their exposure to potential abusers tends to occur within the family system or within close proximity to the family (e.g., a coach, neighbor, family friend, etc.). In instances where the abuser knows the victim, there is often the presence of grooming behavior. *Grooming* refers to the actions of the abuser working to gain the trust of the child, and often her parents, in order to have increased access to her and, in some cases, authority over her (McAlinden, 2006). This is generally a gradual process of gaining trust through giving attention, having fun, flattering, and buying gifts. Sounds a bit like how a dating process between adults might take place. However, an additional component of the grooming process in abuse situations is the affirmation of loyalty through the confirmation of secrets. Kids begin to develop loyalty to the adult such that when the abuse begins, the child may feel admired and cared for while simultaneously confused and fearful. Grooming can be a lengthy process that can place over the course of weeks, months, or years, often ensuring that the child develops a dedicated attachment to the abuser. This is one of the ways in which child sexual abuse can persist for many years without the child reporting it to another adult or the authorities (Hinkelman & Bruno, 2008). Another of the main reasons that prevent children from reporting is that the victim often feels some responsibility for the abuse.

She Was Asking for It: Addressing Victim Blame

One of the most difficult aspects of talking about sexual assault and violence in girls' lives is the pervasive thinking that girls and young women have some responsibility for an assault that happens to them. I often hear adults make comments such as "She needs to watch what she is wearing. She is sending the wrong message to the boys" or "What did she think was going to happen when she went to that party by herself?" Even girls can be extremely critical of one another when it comes to sexual assault. One tenth-grade girl shared the following:

> I know this one girl whose uncle has been having sex with her for like two years. She hasn't told anyone else but me, and I secretly think she likes it. I mean—that's nasty—if she didn't like it, she should just tell him that she's not going to do that anymore . . . or tell her mom or a teacher or something.

This type of thinking, called victim blame, places some of the responsibility on the victim for the sexual assault, rather than on the perpetrator. As a society we tend to have very rigid ideas surrounding who is a sexual abuser and who is a victim. Several studies have shown that up to 59% of mental health, law enforcement, and school professionals often attribute some of the responsibility for sexual abuse to the child victims. Researchers have also found that teachers tend to attribute more blame to the victims than do social workers, school counselors, and school psychologists (Ford et al., 2001).

The following are a few scenarios to help you gauge your own reaction to situations where some type of sexual violence occurred:

CASE #1: AMANDA AND KANDICE

Amanda and Kandice are friends and classmates in the eighth grade. Both girls are quite athletic and play softball and basketball on the school teams and also on local traveling teams. Kandice has a huge crush on Amanda's older brother, Chad, who is in eleventh grade. Amanda thinks Chad is a jerk and sees that he treats his girlfriend horribly, and she can't understand why Kandice has absolutely any attraction for her brother. Amanda gets really annoyed when Kandice constantly flirts with Chad and, as Amanda says, "acts like a ditz" when Chad is around.

After a weekend softball tournament, Amanda and Kandice are at Amanda's house getting ready to go to a dance at the school that evening. Amanda's parents are not at home, and Chad is "in charge" of the girls until the parents arrive. Amanda is completely annoyed at Kandice because she thinks that she is "throwing herself" at Chad. Kandice is laughing way too hard at his jokes, play wrestling with him, and generally being friendly and flirtatious with Chad.

After Kandice gets out of the shower, Amanda takes her turn. Kandice is in Amanda's room in a robe and is brushing her hair and picking out her outfit for the dance. Without warning, Chad bursts into Amanda's room looking for his sister and finds Kandice there—completely startled and somewhat embarrassed. Chad realizes that no one is around and says, "Wow, Kandice! I've never seen you quite like this." He smiles at Kandice and looks her up and down. She doesn't know if she should feel flattered or embarrassed, so she smiles nervously clutching the front of her robe. "You don't need to close that—let me just have a look; I've always thought that you are such a cute girl," Chad says. Kandice is overwhelmed by Chad's sudden attention toward her and really can't believe that he is interested in her! She says playfully to Chad, "I can't do that; you better get out of here!"

Chad takes a step toward Kandice, and she doesn't know what to do. He leans in to kiss her and simultaneously opens her robe and fondles her breast. She is exhilarated and panicked at the same time! Kandice has only kissed one other person, and that was at a party during a silly game with her classmates. This was very different, and she wasn't sure how she felt about it. Kandice shakes her head and pushes Chad away, but he pulls her in close to him. He fondles her buttocks and then traces his hand down in between her legs. She jumps away from him and rushes out of the room. Chad follows and catches her in the hallway and says, "Kandice, you are more grown up than I realized. I'd like to see more of you, but we need to keep this between the two of us, ok?" Kandice doesn't know what to do, so she smiles and nods obediently.

CASE #2: MACY AND ZOE

Macy is an eleventh-grade girl who looks a bit older than her age. She is popular and outgoing and generally does well in school. Her older sister, Zoe, is a sophomore in college and invited Macy to spend the weekend in the dorm with her. Macy was so excited to be spending the weekend on a college campus and hoped that Zoe would take her around the town and to a couple of parties. On Saturday night Zoe and

(Continued)

(Continued)

Macy were in the dorm getting ready to head out to the party. Both girls were in party mode and were having a few drinks while they were getting dressed. Zoe gave Macy a mini dress to wear and helped her with her hair and makeup. She commented that Macy looked like she was in college and that the guys were going to be all over her! These girls were ready for a party!!

When they arrived at the party, Macy noticed that there were way more guys there than girls. The girls got in free and got plastic bracelets that meant they could drink for free all night. While Macy had been to many high school parties where alcohol was present, this was her first experience at a college party, so she drank slowly at first and took in the scene. Lots of people were dancing, and some were in another part of the house playing drinking games. Macy and Zoe began dancing with the rest of the crowd, and shortly thereafter, a few guys came up to dance with them. Both girls were dancing in openly sexual ways and grinding with the guys. As the night went on, Macy could tell that the one guy, Trevor, was really into her. She couldn't believe it—a college guy was paying attention to her!

Trevor was touching Macy all over as they danced, and she was enjoying the attention. He made sure that her drink was always full, and at one point Zoe looked over and saw Macy and Trevor making out in the corner. Macy was clearly enjoying herself and seemed to be totally into this guy. Trevor takes Macy by the hand and leads her upstairs, away from the other partygoers. He says, "Let's go somewhere a little more private and quiet." Macy is feeling the effects of the alcohol and wants to continue kissing Trevor. She follows him up to his bedroom, where they sit on the bed and continue making out. He starts to unbutton her dress and she pushes his hand away as she continues to kiss him. His hands continue to wander over her body and begin to make their way up her inner thigh under her dress. Macy laughs nervously and pushes his hand away again. "Stop it, Trevor!"

Trevor responds to Macy by saying, "Baby, you've been teasing me all night. You are looking so good in that little dress. I just couldn't wait to get you up here and get that dress off of you." Macy is feeling a little nervous at this point and is wondering what she has gotten herself into. She doesn't resist when Trevor further unbuttons her dress, but when she realizes that he plans to have sex with her she freezes. "Stop Trevor, I can't do this. I need to find my sister." He tells her to relax, that he's not going to hurt her, and once they are finished he will take her back to her sister. Macy doesn't know what else to do, so she doesn't do anything.

Self-Reflection

1. My initial reaction to each of these cases is

   _____

   _____

   _____

2. When I think about who is responsible for the assault, my mind first goes to

   _____

   _____

   _____

3. If I were working with Kandice, the first thing I would tell or ask her is

   _____

   _____

   _____

4. If I were working with Macy, the first thing I would tell or ask her is

   _____

   _____

   _____

When you read each case, did you initially identify each place along the way where Kandice and Macy could or should have done something differently? How easy it would be to say to Kandice, "Why didn't you yell at him and tell him to stop as soon as he came in the room?" or "You should have hit him when he tried to kiss you!"

We could tell Macy that she was irresponsible for going to a college party while she was in high school and that it is illegal for people under the age of 21 to drink alcohol. We could point out that she was wearing a revealing dress, making out with Trevor, and essentially leading him on or "sending him the wrong message."

The unfortunate reality here is that both Kandice and Macy were sexually assaulted—they were part of a sexual activity that was not consensual. While it seems easy for us to examine these cases after the fact and identify all the seemingly wrong things that each girl may have done, the fact remains that another person overstepped their bounds and took advantage of the girls' vulnerabilities. While there may have been actions that both Kandice and Macy could have taken, neither is responsible for the behavior of the other person, and neither should carry the burden of responsibility for the assault.

What if Chad had apologized and hurriedly walked out of the bedroom when he realized that Kandice was not fully clothed? What if, after Macy told Trevor to stop, he said, "Oh, I thought we were on the same page here. I didn't realize you weren't into this" and then stopped pressuring her? It is likely that these situations would have ended very differently. Sexual violence happens because there is a person who is willing to commit the assault, not because there is flirting, leading on, alcohol, or any other host of variables that are often wrongfully attributed as causal factors.

Our tendency is to analyze every behavior of the girl to determine at what point she brought the assault onto herself. Victim blame can be a particularly hard concept for us to come to terms with, particularly because it is easier for many of us to think that *we* would have responded differently in each case—that *we* could have easily prevented the situation from happening. We think to ourselves that if we were in that situation, we would have yelled at Chad or maybe even punched him if he came close. Then we would have told his sister and parents what happened. Perhaps we would rationalize that we would have never gone to a college party in the first place, let alone get tipsy and then be escorted upstairs to a bedroom. We may easily find fault with every minor decision that the girl made and only secondarily, if at all, find culpability for the abuser. Unfortunately, in this situation Kandice and Macy, like most victims of sexual violence, also blame themselves for the assault. They continually question what they should have done differently, why they didn't say or do something sooner, and what they did to provoke the other person.

Take, for example, the following statement from a young woman, Carrie, who was sexually abused by a soccer coach when she was a teenager. Even as an adult, she struggles to not blame herself for the abuse:

> I was 14 when he started paying attention to me. He was probably in his 30s at that point, and he was married, with a baby. I looked older for my age and really hadn't been in any relationships before. I had kissed maybe two boys up until that point but never anything else. I would see him every week at soccer practice, and it started with flattering comments about my body and how sexy and curvaceous I was. At 14 I didn't know what to do with that! It was exhilarating and confusing at the same time, and I found that I liked the attention and wanted it to continue. It was like when we were at practice or at a game, we had this little secret between us, and that felt sort of special. I was really attracted to him and wanted him to like me, but I didn't know what to do when he started to touch me. I mean, there was a part of me that really liked it, but then there was another part of me that knew it was wrong and that it had to stay as a secret. No one could ever find out because I should have stopped it from the very beginning. I should have told him that he needed to stop and that I was going to tell an adult what was going on. I should have reported him to the school. But I couldn't—I knew people would ask me why I didn't do something right away. I let it go on for years. I knew they would say that I could have stopped this earlier if I really wanted to. I couldn't deal with that, or what my teachers' or parents' reactions would be, so it was just easier to stay quiet.

In this situation Carrie was 14 years old and was slowly and purposefully pursued by an adult man. He clearly knew that his behavior was inappropriate and illegal, yet he was able to effectively manipulate the situation so that Carrie kept his secrets and subsequently blamed herself for the abuse. Unfortunately, this scenario is far too common for thousands of girls and boys, and it keeps sexual abuse hidden and stigmatized.

Let's return to the self-reflection based on the cases of Kandice and Macy. Was your initial reaction to question the behavior of Kandice and Macy or to question the actions of Chad and Trevor? For many of us our initial reaction is to pinpoint all the opportunities that the girls had to make a different decision, get out, or report the event. Our secondary response is to identify the fact that Chad and Trevor could have made different choices as well. If we are to be effective in changing the culture around sexual violence, we must be willing to shift our thinking as it relates to who is responsible for the acts.

If we are fortunate enough to be the adult in a girl's life who she will actually talk to about such a sensitive issue, we must handle her concern with the utmost respect and care. If we fail to do this, she will likely think twice before she ever confides in us again. Responses such as "Now Macy, what did you think was going to happen when you went up to his bedroom?" or "Kandice, do you think that was a good idea to kiss Chad back when he first kissed you—don't you think that could have sent him the wrong message?" sound paternalistic and judgmental. Girls want adults to validate their reality, acknowledge their confusion, and help them make sense of the situation. She probably already blames herself, and we do not want to add to her insecurities.

WHAT DO I SAY?

Suggestions for Talking With Girls Who Have Experienced Sexual Violence

"Whatever you did to survive was the exact right thing to do at the time." "You did what you needed to do to get out of the situation, and I am proud of you." "What happened to you is not your fault." This is the language that girls need to hear when they finally have the courage to share their experiences of assault or abuse with us. They are taking a risk and making themselves extremely vulnerable by sharing the details with us, and our responsibility is to honor their vulnerability and provide support and care. Because survivors of sexual violence are extremely likely to blame themselves (and other people are likely to blame them as well), they will often reconstruct the situation and identify everything that they could, or should, have done differently to prevent the violence from taking place. Here are some suggestions for how we might talk with Kandice or Macy after the events.

Kandice

- I am sorry that this has happened to you. I can imagine that you felt pretty confused and you might even still feel confused about what happened.
- Sometimes it is easy for us to blame ourselves when situations such as this happen. I want you to know that even though you are attracted to Chad and may have been flirting with him, it does not give him the right to touch you in the way that he did.
- You have the right to decide who can touch you, where they can touch you, and when they can touch you. Chad did not have your permission or your consent to touch you in the way that he did. What he did was wrong.

Macy

- Macy, I am sorry this has happened to you. I bet it was a pretty scary experience and a difficult place to find yourself.
- I get the sense that you think that you should have prevented this from happening. I want you to know that you are not responsible for what Trevor did.
- I want you to know that even though you made the choice to go to the party and dance with Trevor, you did not make the choice to have sex with him. Dancing and kissing are not an invitation for sex.

Consequences of Sexual Violence

The impact of sexual violence in the lives of girls varies tremendously. Previously, I read in the paper a story about a young girl who had been sexually abused by a teacher. At the sentence hearing her parents told the judge, "She will never be whole again. He robbed her of her innocence, and she will never get that back. My daughter will never have a normal life again." While I certainly recognize the horror that parents feel when they learn of a crime against their child, especially a sexual crime, I also believe that people can recover from these situations and grow up to lead healthy and productive lives. Sexual violence affects girls in substantial ways, but I refuse to believe that the impact of this crime ruins a girl for the rest of her life. I refuse to believe that she will never have healthy relationships and will forever lack self-esteem and confidence. Our reactions and responses to girls who have experienced sexual violence are critically important, and to communicate a lifelong sentence of pathology and doom is unfair and unrealistic. We do not want girls to believe that their lives are "ruined" and that they have no chance at a productive future.

Are the impacts of sexual violence far-reaching and intense? Yes, most definitely. Girls who experience sexual violence are more likely than girls who are not victimized to experience low self-esteem, depression, suicidal thoughts, and drug and alcohol use. Additional impacts include eating disorders, mood and anxiety disorders, delinquent behavior, risky sexual behavior or sexual acting out, and even *learned helplessness*—the belief that they do not have any control over the outcomes of different situations or relationships. If girls who have experienced sexual violence are in a relationship that is controlling or where they are fearful, they may have difficulty setting boundaries, making decisions, and being an equal partner. Girls who are involved in violent dating relationships may lack the ability to distinguish between a healthy and an unhealthy relationship and may not have the skills or confidence to change the dynamics and expectations of the relationship, thus exposing themselves to the risk of being victimized in the future.

We additionally know that the greater the degree to which a person blames themselves for the assault, the worse their mental health outcomes may be and the less likely they are to tell anyone about what happened. Girls who believe that they are responsible for an assault or that there was something they could have done, but didn't do, to prevent the assault have higher levels of depression, anxiety, and self-blame, and they rarely tell anyone that they were assaulted. If they already blame themselves, they are afraid that others will blame them as well.

When girls receive support, encouragement, belief, and care from their friends, families, and support systems, they are more likely to recover more quickly and to have fewer mental health issues and long-term effects. Our response can determine the health of the girl's future—we need to make sure we do it right.

What Works in Preventing Sexual Violence?

Many schools and organizations are concerned with the safety of their students and implement programs that attempt to decrease the vulnerability of students. There are programs available that provide information and skills to students related to preventing sexual violence. As we consider such programming, we must be cognizant of what actually works, and is research based, when it comes to effective prevention programming for girls.

As soon as I began working in the field of sexual violence prevention in 1997, I began to receive "tips" and "strategies" from friends and family members regarding how to keep women safe. I can't tell you how many email messages I have gotten over the years with directives to girls and women about ways to stay safe, avoid rape, or avoid the "wrong kind" of men. Some of the most unrealistic suggestions were for girls to never wear their hair in a ponytail, to never park next to a white van, to always ask the security guard at the mall to escort her to her car, and to never get on the elevator if a man is on it. Unfortunately, there is no evidence that doing, or not doing, *any* of these things is related to avoiding sexual violence. Often the messages that girls receive on how to keep themselves safe encourage them to engage in elaborate self-protective behaviors and can provide a false sense of security (i.e., "I am headed to the mall to meet someone I have been chatting with online. When I get to the mall, I will not park next to a white van; thus, I am keeping myself safe"). Girls and women often develop misplaced fears in that they may be afraid to walk alone at night yet have no reservations about being alone with a date. Let's consider the actual realities of some of the most commonly heard self-protective strategies:

Myth #1: Never Walk Alone at Night.

While this might be easier for very young girls to follow, from middle school on through adulthood, most girls find that they need to walk alone at night at some point. While there is certainly strength in numbers and having girls look out for one another is great, there has been no research that correlates walking alone at night to an increased likelihood of rape. The available research is to the contrary, indicating that the majority of sexual assaults occur in the home of either the victim or the perpetrator, rather than outdoors or in unfamiliar places.

Myth #2: Never Talk to Strangers.

Girls are only sexually assaulted by strangers in about 7% of cases. This means that 93% of the time juvenile sexual assault victims know their attacker. About one-third of the time girls are assaulted by a family member (parent, grandparent, sibling, cousin, etc.), and about 60% of the time girls are assaulted by friends or acquaintances (dates, family friends, coaches, neighbors, friends of friends, etc.). So the idea that we only need to teach girls to stay away from strangers fails to account for how sexual assault happens most often to girls.

Myth #3: Just Go Along With It so You Don't Get Hurt.

A large body of research over the past 20 years has indicated that girls and women are much more likely to prevent a sexual assault from occurring if they utilize assertive or aggressive verbal and physical resistance and protective strategies. In fact, nonforceful verbal responses, such as begging, pleading, or crying, have actually been associated with an increase in completed sexual assault and an increased likelihood of being injured. Teaching girls to respond assertively or aggressively to potentially threatening situations gives them a much improved chance of getting away and the ability to use their voice and their bodies to keep themselves safe.

What Can We Do?

Provide girls with accurate information on how sexual violence happens and how they can respond to potentially threatening situations. Girls need to learn the above myths and facts about sexual violence and recognize when they might be vulnerable. Teach girls who the most likely offenders are, as well as strategies they might use to keep themselves safe. We would use different strategies when we feel uncomfortable or pressured on a date from those we would use if we were confronted by a stranger. Oftentimes, it is actually much more difficult to be assertive or aggressive with someone we know. We don't want to overreact, hurt someone's feelings, or have them think that we are crazy, so sometimes we just let things go instead of speaking up. Help girls think of ways they could respond to the other person in various uncomfortable or threatening situations, such as the following:

- A classmate is giving them an unwanted backrub while they stand at their locker

- A stranger on the bus is sitting too close

- A coach walks in on them in the shower after a game

- A person at the mall keeps showing up at every store they visit

- A date is pushing them up against a wall and forcefully kissing them

Having the chance to think about different situations (girls may have their own, more relevant examples to consider) and practice various responses gives girls confidence in their abilities to actually use the skills when they find themselves in similar situations.

Teach very young girls that they have a right to set boundaries and stand up for themselves. Very young girls through elementary school need to learn that they have a right to stand up for themselves. Young children are often expected to follow along with any adult directive and are not given the chance to ever say "no" or not do something that is asked of them. Young girls should be taught that they do not have to hug or kiss people they don't want to hug or kiss—even if the person is a family member or a friend of the family or Santa Claus or the Easter Bunny. Some parents have difficulty with this and expect that children will obey them at all times. Letting young girls know that people should not touch them on the parts of their body that would be covered by a bathing suit can help them understand what the "private parts" of their body are. Giving a girl the power to set that boundary and make that decision will enhance her confidence and her sense of having ownership over and respect for her own body. By instilling this idea in younger girls, we will experience less difficulty when we expand on the information with older adolescent girls.

Know the signs of sexual abuse and violence, and consider the possibility that the distress in a girl's life could be related to experiencing violence. There are many different signs that we would look for if we believe that a girl may have experienced some type of sexual violence. Figure 7.1 gives a list of these signs, which while not exhaustive, provides some general information on behavioral and physical indications of abuse. It is important to note that these indicators are

Figure 7.1 Signs That May Indicate Sexual Abuse and Violence

Younger Children	
• Bed-wetting, thumb sucking, fear of the dark	• Sexual acting out with peers
• Nightmares	• Tension stomachaches
• Separation anxiety	• Age-inappropriate ways of expressing affection
Prepuberty and Teenage	
• Truancy	• Alcohol or drug abuse
• Excessive bathing	• Anxiety or depression
• Withdrawn and passive	• Delinquent behavior/acting out
• Sexual inference in artwork	• Sexual promiscuity
• Decline in school performance	
Physical Indicators	
• Bruises or bleeding	• Sexually transmitted diseases
• Pain or itching in the genitals	• Pregnancy
• Difficulty sitting or walking	• Frequent sore throats, urinary tract infections, yeast infections

Source: Child Welfare Information Gateway (2012).

not a confirmation that a child or a teen has experienced violence; rather, they are characteristics that would tell us that there is some level of distress in the girl's life. The distress could be due to many different things, such as parental divorce, being bullied at school, or a behavioral health issue, but the distress could also mean that there has been some sexual violence. So our role, as difficult as it may be, is to consider the possibility that abuse could be present.

Teach Girls Assertive and Physical Responses to Violence

Girls can learn simple verbal and physical responses to situations of potential threat. However, before any assertive response can be taught effectively to a girl, we must first instill in girls the idea that they are worth defending and that they are capable of defending themselves. Girls have not generally been reinforced for being strong, physical, or loud. When we teach sexual violence prevention to girls, we are asking them to push back against some of the traditional ideas about girls' strength, so that they begin to experience themselves as powerful and as possessing the capacity to influence the outcome of a potentially violent situation. Even the smallest girl can learn skills that can be used on the strongest offender. Effective sexual violence prevention for girls teaches them how to exploit the vulnerabilities of a stronger attacker. As girls get older, they can learn more sophisticated protective skills and can utilize different strategies in various situations. Enrolling girls in girls-only self-defense classes can help them learn and practice these skills.

Provide girls the opportunity to identify their support systems and the trusting, caring adults in their lives who they could talk to about sensitive topics such as sexual violence. Girls rarely tell others when they experience sexual violence because they are often embarrassed or believe that they did something to bring it on themselves. I have worked with many women in counseling who were sexually abused as children or sexually assaulted in college but who have never told a soul because of fear and embarrassment. Helping girls to identify who they could talk to if they were assaulted and who will believe them and support them is critically important. Girls do not want to be questioned or met with suspicion if they tell another person what happened to them; they just want someone to believe them and comfort them. Sometimes the reaction of the adult can make the girl close up, stop talking, or recant their story. If we, as adults, react with horror, disbelief, or anger, then girls will be hesitant to share their experiences with us. While it can be difficult, we need to meet their disclosures with care, concern, and support.

Help girls understand that adults and children should not have "secrets" with each other. One of the common ways in which child sexual abuse persists for many years is that the adult tells the child that they have a special "secret" that they are not allowed to tell anyone. Often, breaking the secret is associated with threats: "If you tell anyone, I will hurt your mother/kill your dog/send your father to jail," and so forth. Young children have difficulty knowing that this is a bad secret and one that they can and should tell another person. Talk to girls about the difference between "good" and "bad" secrets. An example of a "good" secret is a surprise birthday party. Overall, it is a good idea to tell girls that adults and kids shouldn't keep secrets between each other.

Know your ethical and legal obligations. Many of us feel ill prepared to handle situations involving alleged child abuse and feel even less equipped to work in an academic setting with students who have been sexually victimized. We often do not know what our reporting responsibilities might be and don't understand when we need to call Child Protective Services. Some research has suggested that many school professionals lack the ability to recognize and understand the pervasive effects of child sexual abuse and they report sexual abuse cases less often than they would if they had more and better training. School and counseling personnel need to know their legal responsibilities regarding reporting sexual violence and protecting children, and professional development opportunities can address this requirement.

It is mandatory for educators, counselors, social workers, and other helping professionals to report child abuse. This means that if we have a suspicion that a child is being abused and we do not report it to Child Protective Services or the police, we can face legal consequences. While educators and counselors are legally required to report child abuse to a child protection agency, any person can freely make a report if they have a suspicion of abuse taking place. Parents, family members, coaches, and friends can notify the police or a child welfare agency if they believe that a child is being abused. Most agencies allow an individual to make an anonymous report if there is a hesitance to identify oneself. When addressing these difficult situations, the first step is to know what to look for, and the second step is to know how to intervene. The goal is to create an environment and a relationship where a child feels safe to disclose the abuse, and then the adult can take action to stop the abuse and protect the child. Schools and organizations should have clear policies and procedures that all staff should follow regarding reporting requirements, chain of command, and documentation of all activities. Allowing child sexual abuse to go undetected or unaddressed is both an ethical and a legal issue for adults who work with kids.

The Pressure to Be Perfect

8

Stress and Coping in an Age of Perfectionism and Helicopter Parents

There is just so much pressure. Pressure to look perfect, to get perfect grades, to be perfect in your sport. I am a swimmer, and I have to swim really well, and I also have to get really good grades because I have to get into a great college.

—Emily, age nine

How does a nine-year-old already have extreme pressure around having to do everything perfectly? Shouldn't she be living a carefree life where swimming is for fun and college is so far away that her fourth-grade self can hardly imagine it? Unfortunately, this reality is all too common as girls report that they are under increasing pressure to be, look, and do everything perfectly. The stakes keep getting higher, and their coping skills can't keep up. Where is the pressure coming from? Does she really think that she has to be perfect at everything? Is the pressure any different from what it was 10 or 20 years ago?

What Is Perfectionism?

Perfectionism is not simply an attitude, belief, or work ethic that an individual holds or demonstrates. It goes beyond simply striving to do something well or being detail oriented. Rather, perfectionism is a combination of personality traits that includes excessively high personal standards alongside extremely critical self-evaluations. We often use the term *perfectionist* to describe someone who is very detail oriented, who is concerned with doing everything right, and who spends excessive amounts of time to ensure a perfect outcome on a particular task. Perfectionism actually goes a bit deeper than this as it is a measurable set of attitudes and behaviors with a lot of intricacies and different dimensions (Curran & Hill, 2019). Perfectionism is less about a person's personality and more about how they view and cope with the world around them.

One type of perfectionism is when the excessively high expectations, behaviors, attitudes, and tendencies are directed toward the self (self-oriented). We see this happen when girls attach an extremely high level of importance to doing things just perfectly. This doesn't mean that they are simply doing their best or that they have great attention to detail. Rather, they hold consistently and unrealistically high expectations for themselves, and they rarely believe that their own performance is adequate (Curran & Hill, 2019; Hewitt et al., 2017). These are the girls who are continually hard on themselves. They never truly feel that they are "good enough" or have accomplished enough, despite the actual outcome. They earn 100% on their exam but beat themselves up because they didn't get the five points of extra credit that was available.

Another type of perfectionism is when girls strive to be perfect so they can gain the approval of others. This is when girls consistently perceive that they are being observed and judged by the people around them, and so they feel that they have to do everything perfectly in order to be accepted (socially prescribed perfectionism). These girls pay attention to the messages that they believe they are getting from others, and they view their environment as judgmental, harsh, and unfair, as a place where they will never earn enough approval. When girls experience this type of perfectionism, they live in a constant state of feeling inadequate in the eyes of others. They feel that no matter how hard they try, they will never live up to the expectations that others have of them.

There are subtle differences between these two types of perfectionism, but without a doubt both are detrimental to the happiness and mental health of girls. Girls who truly struggle with perfectionism are also more likely to experience depression, suicidal ideation, social phobias, anxiety, body dissatisfaction, and eating disorders (Curran & Hill, 2019). Perfectionism creates unhappiness, low self-worth, and a sense of inadequacy. Even if perfectionism is connected to actual high achievement, the end result is not a guarantee that girls feel better about themselves or their accomplishments; rather, they continually feel that they aren't living up to their full potential.

Is Alexis a Perfectionist?

Alexis is a girl who seems like she has it all. She is in eleventh grade, captain of the basketball team, a high honor roll student, and this year's homecoming queen. She's got a great group of friends, and she works really hard in school and also at her sport. It has been rumored since she was in middle school that a college scholarship is a possibility for her, so she is diligent about her physical training, diet, and basketball practice schedule. When she missed a key foul shot in a big game, she stayed back after practice every day for two weeks and shot 100 free throws by herself. In addition to high school basketball, she also plays on an Amateur Athletic Union team and a regional travel team. Academically, Alexis shines. She is taking three Advanced Placement classes and works really hard to keep her grade point average (GPA) well above 4.6. She often stays up late in the evenings to complete her assignments and rarely turns in work that she has not double- and triple-checked.

Is Alexis a perfectionist? She is diligent in major areas of performance, namely sports and academics. She spends a great deal of time getting things right, and when she doesn't succeed, she works harder to get things right. Most people on the outside looking in would say that Alexis is the total package—smart, athletic, popular, and a good friend. But is she a pressure cooker inside with the stress continually building up until she's ready to explode? Does she internalize the message that she has to do everything perfectly? Is she constantly driven to ensure that she is gaining the approval of her parents, teachers, coaches, and peers?

Research indicates that the girls who seem to "have it all" may actually be at risk for negative outcomes, because they are often overlooked as in need of any additional support. Parents, teachers, coaches, and counselors rarely think about these "total package" girls as the ones who might need some extra help or encouragement. This girl is one who no one worries about much because her grades are good, she has friends, she is not getting in trouble, she's playing sports, she's not skipping school or doing drugs. But inside she dislikes herself, she battles daily with feelings of inadequacy, she feels like a constant failure, and despite her achievements she truly doesn't think she is good enough. Girls who struggle with self-confidence are particularly vulnerable to the stress of perfectionism. When confidence is low, girls often develop perfectionistic tendencies because they are trying to compensate for their lack of self-worth.

In my research we actually found that the highest-achieving girls, the ones with GPAs above 4.0, were actually the most likely to say that their parents pressure them to be perfect. Compared with girls with lower GPAs, these high-achieving girls are also less likely to think that they are smart enough for their dream job and less likely to speak their mind or disagree with others because they want to be liked (Hinkelman, 2017). High-achieving girls, whether actual perfectionists or not, struggle profoundly and often do so under the radar, because excellence does not set off a warning light. They are rarely identified as needing support, because for the perfectionist communicating to others that they need help only contributes to their sense of inadequacy.

So is Alexis a perfectionist? From the description provided, it is still a bit unclear. We would actually need to know more about her to make a more accurate assessment. We would need to understand how she is internalizing her perceived failures and how she is making sense of the expectations that others hold for her behavior or performance. We want to be sure that we aren't confusing hard work, persistence, and grit, which are all healthy and productive assets, with perfectionism, which is a troubling and paralyzing state of being.

How Do I Know if She Is a Perfectionist?

Helping girls develop a strong and healthy work ethic and a drive to succeed without developing the debilitating trait of perfectionism requires careful attention. You may have already noticed perfectionistic traits in the girls in your life and want to better understand if this is a potential area of concern. Adopted from Smith's (2016) and Hewitt and Flett's (2004) perfectionism scales, the following give you a sense of some of the attitudes and behaviors that may indicate perfectionistic tendencies:

1. She has a strong need to be perfect.
2. If she's working on a project, she can't relax until she finishes it perfectly.
3. She thinks others are disappointed when she doesn't do things perfectly.
4. When she messes up, she feels like a failure.
5. She often feels that she can't meet others' expectations of her.
6. She's never sure if she's doing things right. She often doubts herself.
7. She's worried or afraid that she will make mistakes.
8. She believes that the people around her expect her to do everything perfectly.
9. She thinks that her parents expect her to be perfect.
10. She feels more successful when she pleases others.

You might be reading this list and thinking that many of these statements represent the girl(s) you parent, teach, mentor, or coach. You might be thinking to yourself that you don't put undue pressure on her, so you wonder where it is coming from. We know that girls are more susceptible to perfectionism because they, more than boys, tend to place greater importance on what others think of them and they more readily internalize the messages they receive from their environments.

Do Adults Contribute to Girls' Perfectionistic Tendencies?

> I want my daughter to be perfect. I want her to know that if she doesn't do everything just right, I will be disappointed in her and I will likely love her less. I put excessive pressure on her to get perfect grades, to look perfect, to act perfectly, and to basically be an all-around rock star.
>
> —Said no parent ever (I hope!)

While most parents don't overtly tie their child's performance to their love for and acceptance of the child, kids can often perceive this to be the case and will work diligently to avoid disappointing their parents. About one in three girls feel that their parents pressure them to be perfect, with high school girls nearly twice as likely to believe this than elementary-age girls (Hinkelman, 2017). When girls are young, they learn how to read the emotions of their parents and how to modify their behavior accordingly so that they are pleasing them and gaining approval as frequently as possible. Girls hate to see their parents upset, sad, frustrated, or disappointed and will work hard to avoid being the cause of such emotions. Think back to when you were a teenager. It was always so much worse to hear an adult say that they were "disappointed" in you than they were "upset" with you. Even as adults we'd likely rather have someone mad at us than disappointed in us. Disappointment carries with it an increased level of personal responsibility and the lingering sense that we should have done something differently to control the outcome.

When girls develop a hypersensitivity to an adult's worry, concern, or disappointment, they also develop an aversion to making mistakes. They relate their behavior or performance to the expressed emotional state of the adult. This adult could be their parent, their teacher, their coach, or anyone else whose opinion they hold in high regard. Basically, they develop a sense of responsibility for the feelings they observe in the adult. They believe that their behavior has caused the adult's emotions. What a heavy thing for a teenage girl to take on!

And let's be honest, parents are also living in a hyperstressful environment, with a lot of pressures both on themselves and on their children. In my conversations with mothers, I constantly hear of the intense pressure mothers feel to be the "perfect mom." Exhausting themselves in an attempt to achieve the elusive goal of "work-life balance" by being the CEO of their family and the CEO of their career. Moms consistently report feeling like they are "bad moms" because they aren't able to attain perfectionism in all aspects of their lives. They report feeling like they are failing at work when their family responsibilities increase and then experiencing a sense of failure at home when they aren't able to be as present or as responsive as they desire, which they describe as *mom guilt.* Interestingly enough, in all of my parent symposiums and workshops with thousands of parents, I have never heard of fathers using the term *bad dad* or *dad guilt* when describing their own parenting style or perceived faults. For some reason the self-deprecation in the term *bad mom* seems to have comfortably settled into the subconscious self-descriptions of women. In the same way that perfectionism is more likely to affect teen girls than teen boys, the debilitating traits of perfectionism often persist into adulthood, continuing to affect more women than men.

Nonetheless, we also know that both men and women can feel a tremendous sense of responsibility for the successes and failures of their children. Many parents are trying desperately to succeed themselves and often describe their lives as stressful, overwhelming, and exhausting. They may be working diligently to experience personal or career success, but they simultaneously feel an intense sense of responsibility for the performance of their children. They may see their child's failure as their own failure and actually find that their own self-esteem is contingent on their child's performance or success (Verhaeghe, 2014). This is not merely a parent feeling a sense of pride when their child gets an amazing report card, plays wonderfully in the softball game, or gets into their first-choice college. This child-centric self-esteem is most readily observed when the performance of the child has a significant positive or negative impact on the parents' sense of self.

When parents experience success through the successes of their children, they can become increasingly more involved in and controlling of their children's lives. With this increased parental expectations also comes an increase in the way children internalize the need to please their parents. In time, this results in everyone—both parents and kids—intensely attuned to the performance and success of the child. The child understands that their behavior and performance have an impact on the parent, and the parent is continuously seeking opportunities for their child to demonstrate success.

This laser focus, from both parents and kids, often results in both developing an intense aversion to disappointment and failure. In turn, parents work diligently to protect their kids from failure, and kids work equally hard to not let their parents down by messing up.

Helicopter Parenting and Fear of Failure

The term *helicopter parent* is often used to describe a parent who is constantly hovering over their child to keep them from experiencing negative outcomes. Physically, emotionally, academically, and interpersonally, a helicopter parent is intensely involved in their child's life and steps in to intervene, support, or rescue, even when the child doesn't ask for or need help. Swooping in to take care of a situation when it becomes tense or difficult, a helicopter parent essentially communicates to the child a very clear message about the child's own safety and/or ability. Basically, they are saying, "You can't do this right without me, so I will just take care of it." Helicopter parents seek to maintain high levels of control over their kids' behavior, while simultaneously insulating them from disappointment, hurt, or failure.

A helicopter parent may hover over her toddler so she doesn't make a misstep and fall at the playground. A helicopter parent may immediately call the parent of another child who refused to play with his child at recess. As kids get older, helicopter parents may compulsively check their child's book bag and complete their kid's homework that is overdue. They send emails to sports coaches to complain about their kid's playing time. When I was a college professor overseeing graduate school admissions for my academic area, I actually had a parent call to inquire about their student's standing in the admission process. I was incredulous because this student had already graduated from undergraduate school and was pursuing a graduate degree! (Dear parent, please know that this type of behavior will *never* help your adult child's graduate school admission.)

Helicopter parenting is characterized by an intense aversion to allowing a child to fail, or even struggle. When insulating the child from hurt feelings or disappointment is of primary importance, the child doesn't have the opportunity to learn the coping skills or strategies that would allow them to successfully handle the situation in the future. The double whammy here? Helicopter parenting tendencies often co-occur with the perfectionist tendencies that were previously discussed and can result in compounded negative mental health outcomes for kids: anxiety, depression, self-confidence issues, and intense fear of failure. If adults who engage in helicopter parenting behaviors realized that their parenting practices actually resulted in creating kids with higher levels of depression and anxiety, lower levels of emotional and academic functioning, decreased decision-making ability, and impaired social outcomes, they would *never* engage willingly in these destructive behaviors.

To be sure, failure feels awful. It is never the experience or emotion that you wish on yourself or someone you love. It can be painful and embarrassing and can really rattle your confidence. But failure is an essential component of learning, and when embraced versus avoided, it is one of the most effective growth-producing experiences that we can have.

Failure and Mindsets

To *fail fast* and *fail forward* are terms that have gained popularity in recent years. "Fail fast" comes from the business world and is often employed as a strategy for new product development. The principle behind the fail fast philosophy is that you develop a prototype and you test it straightaway. You learn quickly what doesn't work (i.e., what failed), and then you make modifications for improvement and test again. Each round of revision and testing happens rapidly so that the best possible product is able to go to market in the fastest amount of time. Each iteration of failure provides new insights into how to make the product better. When failing fast is the tactical approach to development, the built-in expectation is that failure is embedded in the learning process. It is critical to effective growth and development.

The term *failing forward* holds a similar sentiment. It is a philosophical approach to learning that can help kids see and incorporate failure as a tool for progress rather than something that should be avoided. The failing forward approach starts with the mindset that making mistakes is an important and necessary part of growth and learning. When learning something new or trying to master a new skill, mistakes and failure are a consistent and required part of the journey. Think of this tactic as it relates to playing a piano. If a girl decided that she wanted to learn to play the piano, she would not simply sit at the piano and bust out a difficult Beethoven symphony on her first try. She would start by learning which keys correspond to which notes and where her fingers should be placed on the keyboard. She would learn how to read sheet music and how to connect the notes on the page to the keys on the keyboard. She will mess up way more often than she gets it right, but with practice she will start to develop mastery over various aspects of playing the instrument. Each time she sits at the piano, she knows that there will be errors and mistakes, but she uses each as an opportunity to correct her playing and improve her performance. Using the mistakes and failure to propel herself forward, she is learning how to incorporate them into her own growth and development.

This approach is what the esteemed Stanford psychologist Carol Dweck (2006) calls a *growth mindset*—the idea that intelligence, skills, and abilities are malleable and that at any point in time, we have the ability and the capacity to learn and to improve. Individuals who possess a growth mindset see mistakes and failure as opportunities to get better. They are eager to continually put themselves out there in ways that give them the chance to grow. They aren't discouraged by setbacks; rather, they are excited by the challenge.

What if she sat at the piano for the first time, without training or practice, and tried to play that symphony? Likely, she would be wildly unsuccessful. If her response was "Well, I guess I'm just not good at playing the piano," she would quickly become bored and frustrated with the piano and would convince herself that this instrument is clearly not for her. Even more damaging, what if her parents observed her first attempt at playing the piano and said, "Honey, you're just not good at the piano. Don't worry, I wasn't good at playing the piano either. We can find something else."

I think we would all agree that playing the piano is not a one-shot deal. It is a developed skill that requires thousands of hours of practice and refinement. As far-fetched as this example might sound, it has tremendous relevance for how we as adults approach growth and learning and how the girls in our lives approach their own development. I have heard parents say, "I wasn't good at math, and she's just not good at math either," completely discounting their third-grade daughter's ability to become better at math. Dweck (2006) calls this a fixed mindset—the belief that abilities are finite and that you are either good at something or not. Individuals with a fixed mindset view failure as a limitation of their own abilities—the belief that "I can't do it because I don't have the capacity." Also, when parents have this fixed mindset, they see their children's failure as debilitating. They can feel anxious and worried about their child's performance and, in turn, try to help their children avoid the activities that could cause disappointment or failure (Haimovitz & Dweck, 2016).

When adults view failure as an opportunity to learn and enhance one's skills, they approach performance with a focus on growth and improvement. This sends the message to kids that intelligence can be built through the process of learning and teaches kids to not fear failure but to see it as part of the process of getting better.

Stress, Anxiety, and Anxiety Disorders: There Is a Big Difference

We live in a culture that has normalized, and even glorified, stress. There is a tremendous pressure to maintain a feverish pace of life alongside the necessity to perform, achieve, and exhaust ourselves in the pursuit of the perfect outcome—perfect grades, job, house, family, and so on. Girls are not immune from this stressed-out culture, and many begin to see stress as a badge of honor. Scheduling so many extracurricular and enrichment activities that they have no free time, pulling all-nighters to prepare for an important exam, achieving the perfect physique through dieting and working out—girls' lives are full of real and, at times, manufactured stress.

Stress is an important and necessary part of life. As Lisa Damour (2019) explains in her book *Under Pressure*, experiencing stress warns us of danger, keeps us safe, and also motivates us. Stress is not always a bad thing! Stress generally comes from an outside source—a big term paper with a looming deadline, the final penalty shot in the championship soccer match, an intense argument with friends. In the simplest of terms stress is a response to a threat. As adults we face stressful situations daily, from running late for work to delivering an important, high-stakes presentation to our boss, to rushing to the hospital before visiting hours are over to visit a sick family member. Daily activities and hassles can cause us stress, but typically, when the event or hassle has passed, the stress level subsides.

Anxiety, on the other hand, is the way in which an individual specifically responds to stress. Anxiety is internally based and persists even when the stressful situation has passed. Stress causes anxiety; the two concepts should not be considered interchangeable, and one (anxiety) is definitely more debilitating than the other. I think many of us, girls included, struggle with the differentiation between stress and anxiety and then simply default to describing their emotional state as "anxiety."

To be fair, girls are being diagnosed with anxiety at the highest rates in history. However, many of the girls who describe themselves as anxious may just need support to more effectively manage their stress so that it does not actually spiral into anxiety or, even worse, an anxiety disorder.

Our goal is not to try to create a life that is free from stress or to encourage our girls to have stress-free lives. That is just not practical or realistic. However, we must be clear with girls that facing and handling stressful situations effectively is a critical skill that they will use often and consistently throughout their lives. Individuals who effectively manage stress are more productive, have an increased sense of accomplishment, and are happier and more satisfied in their lives. It is not the mere presence of stress that results in negative outcomes; it is the individual's ability to manage the stress that dictates how they will fare.

Stress	Anxiety	Anxiety Disorders
Stress is a normal part of life that everyone experiences at various points. It is the brain's and body's reaction to a demanding or challenging situation.	Anxiety is a normal stress response that persists even after the stressful event passes. Anxiety can include tension, worry, fear, and nervousness.	Anxiety disorders are a disproportionate response to stressful or typical life events, and they interfere with daily activities and relationships. They include both anxious feelings and physical symptoms that are persistent, irrational, and overwhelming.
In most cases stress subsides when the event or task is complete and the body re-regulates itself. Managing stressful situations can include exercise, deep breathing, setting goals and deadlines, and envisioning positive outcomes.	Anxiety can be effectively managed with the implementation of coping skills and strategies such as identifying triggers, managing thinking patterns, and journaling.	Anxiety disorders can be effectively treated with mental health counseling, specifically cognitive behavioral therapy, which may be used alongside anti-anxiety medication.

How Does This All Tie Together?

Perfectionism, helicopter parenting, failure, mindsets, stress, anxiety. We have covered a lot of concepts in this chapter, and I am hopeful that the connections between these concepts has become clear. Girls are living in a time when stress is normalized and performance is always high stakes. However, when the need to perform or to "get it right" outpaces the need to learn and grow, girls will take on fewer difficult challenges, because doing so increases the risk of missing the mark or failing. Additionally, when girls' parents, teachers, or coaches have an aversion to accepting failure as a critical component of learning, they will, intentionally or unintentionally, lead girls away from opportunities that have the potential to expand their skills and competencies.

When girls fail to develop adequate resilience and coping skills because they have been insulated from disappointment and failure, they experience increased levels of stress and anxiety. Their lack of coping skills results in an inability to manage typical life hassles in healthy ways, and their confidence in their own abilities can become compromised as well.

What Do I Do?

Identify your own mindset, growth or fixed, and pay attention to how that affects how you teach, compliment, reinforce, or coach the girls in your life. Do you have a fixed or a growth mindset? Gauge the degree to which you would agree or disagree with the following statements: "Your intelligence is something very basic about you that you can't change very much" and "Truly, smart people do not need to try hard." These are a few of the questions that are part of Dweck's (2006) mindset quiz. You can find lots of mindset quizzes online, and when you answer them honestly, you'll find whether you lean more toward a fixed or a growth mindset. This can help you recognize your own beliefs and motivations, but perhaps even more important, it will give you insights into the ways you interact with and influence others. Having a growth mindset means that you see intelligence and skill development as expandable and see effort as the path to mastery. Growth comes from embracing challenges, experiencing setbacks, and learning from criticism. Promoting a growth mindset in girls can help ensure that they don't limit their options or opportunities because of a fear of failing. They see themselves as capable of trying new things and developing new competencies with less perfectionistic tendencies because failing is a part of the growth process.

Motivate and support her without further stressing her out. Parents are intellectually mindful of the overt stress that they place on their children, but they often feel that they don't quite know what to say or do to minimize the intense expectations while simultaneously ensuring that their daughter has access to every opportunity to be successful. A parent of a 14-year old girl shared with me, "You don't want to add to her stress, but you also don't want her to lose her competitive edge." When your girl understands the tremendous investment that you have in her happiness, her achievement, and her success, she is keenly aware that reaching her goals is as much about her as it is about everyone else's investment in her. Recognize that you may be a source of stress for her, even if you believe that the majority of her stress is self-imposed. High-achieving girls are already striving to meet their fullest potential. Often their motivation is not just to reach their own personal best but to ensure achievement that stands out from the crowd. Compounding her perfectionistic tendencies with pressure to please you or meet your expectations can only exacerbate her feelings of inadequacy.

Teach and practice stress management skills. Girls report that they are swimming in a "sea of pervasive stress" (Spencer et al., 2018) and that there are high expectations for them in all aspects of their lives. While we cannot remove all stress from girls' lives, we can teach them how to anticipate and manage the stressors they are likely to face. Healthy coping mechanisms are not innate; they are taught and practiced. Help girls recognize the mental and physical signs of stress that they might experience, including a racing heart, sweaty palms or underarms, an upset stomach, tense muscles, difficulty sleeping, and ruminating thoughts. We all experience stress a little differently, so the cues for one person may differ somewhat from the cues of another. When I get stressed, my heart races, my stomach is upset and tied in knots, and I get uberfocused on the task or activity at hand. Once I complete the task, there is a huge release of energy and endorphins!

Stress can paralyze us or motivate us. When we possess and practice adequate coping skills, we can thrive in tremendously challenging situations. Deep-breathing techniques, physical exercise, healthy eating, maintaining relationships and social connections, keeping a schedule and effectively managing time, ensuring adequate sleep, laughing, praying, or meditating are all effective techniques to manage stress. Encourage your girl to try a variety of different strategies in order to determine which ones will work best for her.

Academic or Instagram Influencer? 9

Why Girls Feel They Have to Choose

I think sometimes girls think that they should not be too smart around boys.

—Audrey, sixth grade

As I stood in the auditorium before a group of giggling and excitable sixth-grade girls, I posed a few questions. "Who thinks that girls can be anything they want to be?" Without exception, every hand in the room was raised. "Who thinks that one of you young ladies, here in this room, could be the president of the United States someday?" Once again hands rose throughout the room. The girls laughed, made jokes, poked their neighbors, and were generally excited. The next question I asked was "Who thinks boys can be *too* smart?" The girls responded with a resounding "No! Absolutely not." Then, "Do you think that girls can sometimes be *too* smart?" It was so interesting to watch the dynamics that happened next. Several girls raised their hands; many shouted out, "No!" Others put their hands up halfway as they looked around the room to see what their peers were doing. The girls were not sure what to make of this question, and it clearly wasn't an easy question to answer.

Girls today live in a society that holds a lot of confusing expectations and gender stereotypes. The confusion that the girls felt around being smart or even *too* smart is, unfortunately, a real thing. Girls are very aware that there are negative characteristics associated with being smart, and they learn how to strategically balance the multiple aspects of their identity. While they don't readily admit that they would rather be pretty than smart, they do recognize that there is embarrassment associated with being smart (see Figure 9.1).

Research with adolescent girls demonstrates that, on the one hand, girls place a great deal of value on their academic success and see their achievement as a form of validation. On the other hand, they recognize that there is some danger in being too focused on school and getting good grades, or being seen as a know-it-all. So girls will often play up or down their smarts based on the situation and environment, depending on the perceived risks of being viewed as too studious (Raby & Pomerantz, 2013). How do they play down their intelligence? They do this mostly by conforming to conventional views of femininity—by being more "girly" or more "sexy." Girls often hold a belief that if they express this more socially desired side of themselves, they can more easily balance their intellectual side as well.

The pressures that girls are experiencing today aren't new, but they are more pervasive. With pressure to have the perfect social media feed,

Figure 9.1 Girls and Intelligence

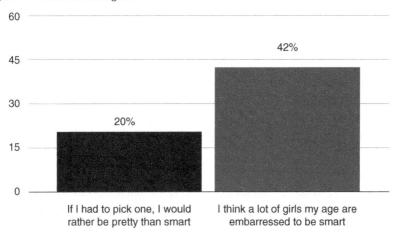

Source: The Girls' Index, 2017.

the perfect body, perfect grades, and essentially the perfect life, girls are working hard to present themselves in the most appealing light to all who may be paying attention, particularly online. Girls also figure out relatively quickly the kind of social media content that gets the most attention, and it's no surprise that it's not the academic type.

In general, girls get more likes on the social media content they post than guys. More specifically, researchers have found that female users who post images of beaches and bikinis, lingerie, and workouts will get the highest levels of male engagement. Girls will engage most with other girls' appearance-related posts, like the outfits of the day, hairstyles, or makeup (Davies, 2017).

In general, we increase or decrease specific behaviors based on the feedback that we receive from others. If we wear a particular outfit and we get degraded and made fun of all day, we will likely consider whether or not to wear that outfit again. Similarly, if we post an image of ourselves winning the championship chess tournament and our impressive trophy and we get very few positive responses, we are unlikely to post similar content in the future. However, if we post an image of ourselves in a bikini at the beach and it gets a massive amount of likes and comments in a short period of time, we are getting major positive reinforcement and will be much more likely to post something similar again in the future. We feel a real rush of dopamine, which fuels our decisions.

This new social media landscape reinforces girls more than ever before for their appearance-related traits rather than their competence-related traits. It makes sense then that when faced with decisions surrounding which aspects of themselves to emphasize, girls often prioritize sexiness and attractiveness over other traits that they see as incompatible with appearance—like intellect. By the time girls are ready to head to middle school, many girls already believe that attractiveness and intelligence can't coexist (Stone et al., 2015).

Smart = Intimidating

Girls feel the pressure to be feminine, desirable, and well liked. They recognize that "fitting in" is extremely important, and they often internalize the expectations that they should be accessible and not intimidate the people around them. And for some reason the idea of girls and women being smart has often been equated with them being intimidating. Girls, who are socialized to be nice and kind and to ensure that the people around them are comfortable, can have difficulty when they hear that they are intimidating. The idea that their brains, smarts, knowledge, and hard work can intimidate someone else can make girls feel that they need to tone themselves down and not appear *too* smart.

Many adults believe that this trend has passed and now it is "cool" for girls to be smart; however, many girls would disagree:

> I think that people look at girls and think that, first and foremost, they are supposed to be pretty. There is a pressure to look a certain way and act a certain way, and I think that girls want people to like them. That is really one of the most important things. Girls who are really into their school work get made fun of and are called "nerds" or "geeks." I think that some of us, myself included, try to see that as a point of pride. Yes, I am smart, and I like to learn, but that doesn't mean that I don't like to have fun with my friends. I don't get how people think that you are either fun, silly, and stupid or that you are smart and serious and boring.
>
> —Meghan, twelfth grade

Apparently, the pressure for girls to not be "too smart" can become a bigger concern when there are others to impress. Girls have fewer concerns about being smart in front of other girls than when they are around boys. There is a pressure to not be perceived as too intelligent around boys because that could be seen as intimidating in some ways. Instead of being proud of their intellect, girls often play down this aspect of themselves when they are around others:

> One of my friends is supersmart, and she always gets 100% on our assignments and tests. Our teacher does this thing where people who get 100% have to come to the front of the room and the rest of the class is supposed to clap for them. I know she always gets embarrassed, and I know that the rest of the class isn't really clapping because they are proud of her. They basically roll their eyes every time she

gets called to the front. Last week she told me that she was going to intentionally miss a couple of questions on the next test so that she didn't get called to the front again.

—Isabel, seventh grade

Hundreds of online blogs, discussion forums, and advice columns are focused on "smart girls who intimidate guys," "girls playing dumb to get a date," "how to pick up a smart girl or a dumb girl," and "hot versus smart: which would you pick?" The conflict remains for girls—you can't be both smart and desirable, and being desired is really important:

There is a girl I know who acts dumb to get attention, but she is really, really smart. I don't understand why she does it, because it is so annoying. She is like trying to be that dumb blonde.

—Klaudia, seventh grade

I was speaking with a group of teachers recently, and several commented on the way in which very intelligent girls would play down their intelligence, and even more so when there were boys around. They shared stories of girls in their classrooms who are highly capable and high achieving yet are self-deprecating about their own achievements. They watch girls downplay their intelligence and accomplishments so that others don't think they are being too proud or cocky. The teachers believe that it is "safe" for girls to get attention for being popular, pretty, sexy, athletic, or even a party girl and that, in general, this type of attention was desired. However, if girls are perceived as being too invested in school, then they won't be viewed as fun, interesting, or social. Basically, smart girls are boring.

Research actually supports these observations, particularly the part about getting attention for being attractive or sexy. When girls hold sexualized gender stereotypes—meaning they believe that they can enhance their social status by prioritizing their sexual attractiveness—they demonstrate lower levels of academic performance. Essentially, girls deprioritize their academic outcomes to ensure that they are seen as sexy rather than smart (Nelson & Brown, 2019).

I wanted to hear what the girls themselves thought about being proud of their intelligence, but I knew I had to ask the question in a specific way. If I asked the girls, "Do you ever act stupid in front of boys to get their attention?" I probably wouldn't get very useful responses. So instead I asked them why they think girls are sometimes embarrassed about being smart. I didn't connect the question to boys in any way; however, the girls' responses were overwhelmingly connected to boys' opinions of them. Among sixth-grade girls, I heard the following responses to the question "Why do you think some girls are embarrassed about being smart?":

> 'Cause if you seem like you are smart, the boys will say, "Oh you are too smart for me; you can't be my girlfriend." They think you are a geek.

> You don't want people to think that you aren't fun—that all you do is stay home and study all the time.

> Guys don't want a girl who is smarter than them. They want to be in control.

⭐ ACTIVITY: ASK GIRLS WHAT THEY THINK

Ask the girls in your life about their perceptions of "smart" girls or women. Depending on the messages that have been reinforced for the particular girls, they may have a wide variety of responses to these questions. What is most important in your conversation is that you provide them with a safe place to talk about these questions. If girls feel that there is a "right" answer that you want to hear, they may limit their responses:

- I've heard that sometimes girls feel pressure to be either smart or pretty. What do you think about that?
- Who are some of your female role models you believe are intelligent women?
- Some people think that girls can "dumb themselves down," or pretend that they aren't as smart as they really are. Is this something you have ever seen?
- How do you think intelligent women are portrayed in the media? Who are some of these women?
- Do you think girls, in general, would rather be smart or pretty?

Hardwired: Boys Are Good at Math, Girls Are Good at Reading

What do you tell your daughter or the girls in your classroom when the president of Harvard University says that girls just aren't capable of doing high levels of math and science in quite the same way as boys? Larry Summers, a former president of Harvard University, stated that girls and women have a "different availability of aptitude" that prevents them from being as successful as boys and men in the sciences and science-related careers, he essentially told girls and women everywhere that there is really nothing they can do about their deficits—they were just born that way.

In much the same way that careers have become stereotyped into male and female categories, specific subjects in school also maintain specific gender expectations. Historically, it has been thought that boys are good at spatial tasks, including subjects in school such as math and science, and girls are good at reading and writing, and so they flourish in subjects such as English and literature.

When children are three and four years old, boys and girls perform the same on assessments of spatial skills, counting, and math computation (Eliot, 2009). Girls in early elementary school perform as well as boys in math and science. However, as they get older, their scores begin to slip, and the discrepancy between the genders becomes a bit larger throughout high school. By high school graduation there is a noticeable gap on achievement tests such as the SAT and the ACT, with boys outperforming girls in the math sections of the SAT and girls outperforming boys on the verbal test. But while boys have outperformed girls for more than 20 years on the math section of the SAT, the gap has diminished considerably over the past several years.

As we saw an improvement in girls' achievement tests, high school graduation rates, and college attendance rates, some social scientists, sociologists, researchers, and educators have questioned whether the gains for girls have come at the expense of boys. They suggest that if girls are doing better, it must mean that boys are doing worse and we are experiencing a "boys' crisis." The reality is that *both* boys and girls are doing better. While girls are graduating from high school and attending college at slightly higher rates than boys, the proportion of boys who are graduating high school and going on to college is at an all-time high (AAUW, 2016). Similarly, when it comes to achievement test scores, there has not been a decrease in boys' scores and an increase in girls' scores; rather, both boys' and girls' scores have improved.

There has been a great deal of sociological, neurological, and psychological research that has attempted to understand the variance between the learning and achievement of boys and girls. Some scientists argue that there are innate differences between boys and girls from the time they are born that are responsible for the discrepancies in achievement in different subjects. This is the "nature" approach—that we are genetically predisposed to excel at certain things based on our gender.

Others argue that children are born as a blank slate, with boys and girls being relatively equal. Every experience and opportunity that children are presented with throughout their formative years help shape who they are, what they are good at, and what they will ultimately become. This is the "nurture" approach, which contends that we are shaped by societal influences and by our experiences.

Research Focus: The Plasticity of the Brain

As we try to answer the question of nature versus nurture, we must consider both the biological brain differences that exist between girls and boys as well as the differences that we develop based on how we are socialized and educated by our parents, our friends, the media, and the rest of our environment.

Biologist and scientist Lise Eliot has conducted extensive research on the brain and, specifically, on the brain differences between boys and girls as well as the way the brain grows and develops in relation to what it is exposed to and the experiences it has. In her book *Pink Brain, Blue Brain*, Eliot (2009) discusses the very small ways in which children's brains are different based on their gender. In her review of hundreds of research studies that looked at brain size, brain activity, differences in sensory processing, and frontal lobe development, she found that there is actually "surprisingly little solid evidence of sex differences in children's brains." The brains of young boys and girls are much more similar than they are different!

So how is it that men and women become so different that by the time they are adults there are more marked differences between their brains? Enter the term *plasticity*—a term that describes the way the brain reacts, changes, and responds to different experiences. The brain is likened to a muscle that changes in response to the way it is used. As we go through changes, experience new things, have new relationships, and develop new skills, the brain changes its structure to respond to our life experiences. Every time we do something new or experience something different, our brain reacts accordingly, so that over time the structure of our brain is shaped by all the influences and experiences of our life.

Dr. Eliot (2009) asserts that

> learning and practice rewire the human brain, and considering the very different ways boys and girls spend their time while growing up, as well as the special potency of early experience in molding new neuronal connections, it would be shocking if the two sexes' brains didn't work differently by the time they were adults. (p. 6)

This research tells us that the exposures we provide to girls as they grow up and the things that we reinforce in their lives will help shape the way their brains develop. Through providing girls with diverse learning opportunities, we can have the option of expanding their cognitive as well as their interpersonal skills.

We know that our abilities are expandable and that learning has a significant role in our intelligence, our interests, and our personality. When we consider cognitive differences such as speaking, math, mechanical ability, or interpersonal skills such as empathy and competitiveness, we must consider both the degree to which these differences have been shaped by our social learning as well as how these differences have been innately programmed. In other words, we must consider how our experiences impact the genetic predispositions that we have.

Most contemporary scientists look not exclusively at nature versus nurture, but how nurture influences nature—that the experiences we have, the things we are exposed to, and the interactions that are part of our lives impact the genetic predispositions that we have. This would suggest that our approach to helping girls must take into consideration the fact that their brains are moldable and pliable throughout childhood and adolescence and that despite any hardwiring that girls or boys experience, they have the ability to develop social, emotional, behavioral, and academic skills. And this ability to learn outweighs the genetic or biological predisposition that we may or may not be born with.

💡 REFLECTION: NATURE VERSUS NURTURE— WHAT DO YOU THINK?

As you think about your own life experiences and your own academic skills and achievement, what were the big things that influenced you? How much of your academic and career decision-making was connected to your genetics, and how much can you attribute to what and who you were exposed to? Some of the questions you might consider are the following:

- Do you have same- or opposite-gender siblings?
- When you played as a child, do you remember building, or constructing, things or taking care of, or nurturing, things?
- Do you remember reading books, completing puzzles, doing flashcards, or writing stories as a child?
- What was your parents' level of educational attainment?
- What peer group did you hang around with in school? (Were you an athlete, in the band, in the chess club, a loner? Did you skip school all the time, or were you a serious student?)
- Were you encouraged to take certain courses or participate in specific activities (sports, dance, choir, debate, student government, etc.)?

Can Girls Be "Both-and" Rather Than "Either-or"?

Clearly, there is a stigma for girls around being smart. It is one that many won't readily admit to parents or teachers but is certainly one that girls recognize and internalize. For many girls it means that you can be smart at the expense of being pretty or desired by boys. High-achieving girls report having a difficult time negotiating their studies, their femininity, and their social lives (Skelton et al., 2010). More simply stated, girls struggle to try to "have it all." Achieving good grades, being popular, being pretty, and being liked by boys are areas where girls say they feel pressure. Girls say that as long as you are pretty and popular, you can also be smart—that these traits (attractiveness and social skills) can "balance out" the intelligence.

This either-or thinking seems especially prevalent during the younger years, when girls are really trying to figure out who they are and what they value. When fitting in is of the utmost concern, any area of real or perceived difference can be mortifying for girls. They want to fit in, and they want to be liked by their peers, and during adolescence this can be more important than being smart or high achieving. We have an opportunity to help girls see that they don't have to choose—they can have it all.

CASE STUDY: "THAT IS FOR BOYS"

I was interviewing a group of female engineers and discussing with them their own process of coming to identify engineering as a career. I was interested in knowing what influenced and motivated them to enter such a male-dominated profession (only about 11% of engineers are women). Each woman spoke of their aptitude in science and math; however, they also reported that they were often encouraged by teachers or counselors to become math or science teachers, not engineers. The women spoke of being one of the few girls in their advanced classes in high school and feeling tremendous pressure to try to "fit in" and not always be the "smart girl."

One participant said, "My mother and father are both engineers, and I think that had a lot to do with me becoming an engineer as well. I had constant reinforcement from the time I was little that I was good at designing and building things and that I could become a scientist or an engineer. I remember when I was about 9 or 10 years old and I was invited to a birthday party for one of the girls in my class. My mom and I went shopping for a birthday gift, and I bought my friend this very cool build-your-own-robot kit. I was super excited about the gift and couldn't wait for my friend to open it. Everything she had gotten so far were clothes, stuffed animals, and sparkly nail polish kits. When she finally opened my gift, she looked confused and disappointed and just sort of shoved it to the side.

(Continued)

(Continued)

One of the boys at the party said, "That is a boy present. Why would you give that to a girl?" I was so upset because I thought it was so cool. Then I got embarrassed and became really self-conscious about it and said, "Sorry, my dad picked it out."

From that day on, I found myself thinking about everything that I said or did and wondering what other people would think. I questioned the things that I was good at and the things that I liked and became embarrassed about my academic strengths and interests. I questioned whether I was doing things that people would say boys are supposed to do. In retrospect, I found that I would play down my intelligence and my curiosity so that I wouldn't stand out from the other girls. It really wasn't until I went to college and met a few other women who were really into the same things that I was that I started to feel comfortable again in my own skin. I realized that I could like what I like and that it was okay.

Promoting Girls' Academic Achievement

There are many factors that contribute to the academic achievement, persistence, and motivation of girls. Support from parents, peers, teachers, and counselors is critical as a girl seeks to identify her strengths and interests. When girls believe that they have support from these important people, they are more motivated to achieve in specific areas. Leaper et al. (2012) looked at girls' participation in the subjects of math, science, and English. They found that when girls felt that they were supported to excel in particular areas by the people they care about, they were more likely to do well in those areas. They found that this support was most needed when girls were participating in subjects or activities that have been more stereotypically typed for boys, such as math and science.

What is so interesting about this literature is that the researchers found that when girls are supported and encouraged in a specific area or subject (e.g., math, science, or English), their motivation in that area increases. When girls feel that their achievement in a particular subject is not supported by peers, family members, or teachers, their motivation for that subject decreases. Thus, general academic support and encouragement are important, but content- and subject-specific reinforcement may have a stronger impact.

Subject-Specific Support and Encouragement	
Providing girls specific and instructive feedback and encouragement can help improve their academic motivation and performance. Here are some examples of general and specific feedback:	

General	Specific
You are so smart.	You are doing a great job with long division. I can see how hard you are working.
You did well on your science test.	You clearly have a solid understanding of the process of osmosis; nice work!
That math test was hard, but you did a good job.	Algebraic equations can be really difficult, but you figured it out and nailed that test. Awesome!

While parents and teachers are tremendous influencers, the importance of peers in the lives of girls cannot be overstated. Girls' friendships and social circles can have a big influence on their academic interests, persistence, motivation, and achievement. The characteristics of the friends that girls have, coupled with the girls' own characteristics, can affect how girls perform academically. Most often, girls hang around with other girls who are somewhat similar to them. They may have shared interests and attitudes and, subsequently, similar behaviors. Friends can have a mutual influence on each other, and this can be positive or negative (Veronneau & Dishion, 2011). Friends can affect school success in the following ways:

- *Problem behaviors:* Teens who have friends who participate in delinquent behaviors such as substance use, aggression, or destruction, or who have attitudes or behaviors that are inconsistent with school success, have lower levels of academic achievement.

- *Academic achievement:* Higher-achieving friends can help contribute to a girl's school success and academic achievement. If it is "cool" to be smart and girls can learn effective study and learning strategies from their peers, they may be challenged to achieve at a higher level than they would be if they had average- or low-achieving friends.

- *School engagement:* Friends who are more engaged with school, follow the school rules, and put effort into learning and participating can have a positive influence on their peers.

While other people are critically important influencers in girls' lives, we also know that the way a girl feels about herself can also affect her achievement. Confidence and self-concept are connected to academic achievement. In fact, self-concept and achievement are reciprocal in that each influences the other. When girls have a low self-concept and low confidence in their abilities, it is likely that lower levels of achievement will follow. Conversely, girls who have higher levels of self-concept, specifically academic self-concept, and approach school tasks with increased confidence tend to have higher achievement. Success reinforces one's self-concept, and people with a high self-concept achieve even more. Our work with girls must focus on what we can do differently to encourage them and help them develop, while also focusing on what girls can be doing differently to build themselves up and to experience success in a variety of academic areas.

What Can We Do?

Teach girls that their skills are expandable. Parents will often say, "I wasn't good at math, and so it is no surprise that she's not good at math." When I learn that the child they are referring to is only in second grade, I worry that they have already written off their child's math abilities. As children grow and become more cognitively complex, they also can develop new ways of thinking and reasoning. Our skills are expandable, and while certain subjects may be more challenging, we all have the ability to learn new skills. Especially for a child so young, her competencies should not be predetermined based on the parent's perceived strengths or deficits. This connects back to the discussion of growth mindsets in the previous chapter. We want girls to know that they can improve their performance in all subjects and can learn to be better students of math, science, reading, or writing.

Teach girls that their value comes from who they are and how hard they work, not how pretty, popular, or sexy they are. Girls perceive that boys prefer girls who are not necessarily their intellectual equals. While this may not be the prevailing sentiment of all the girls you come in contact with, there are many who do believe this—at least in part. I do meet lots of girls who are extremely proud of their intelligence and excited to put their intellectual merits on display. But I also see girls who are embarrassed about the grades that they earn and do not want to share their high grades with their peers, both boys and girls. Because the need to fit in, get attention, and be liked by peers is so important for teen girls, we have to try to understand why they would "dumb themselves down" in certain social settings. Girls can struggle with demonstrating their intelligence for a variety of reasons. They are afraid to be smart because they fear the potential negative social implications. What will everyone think? Will everyone roll their eyes at me? Will they think that I am no fun? Regardless of the "why," we must recognize that this is a legitimate, albeit sad, reality for some girls. It can be frustrating to watch girls compromise themselves in this way. We need to help them redefine beauty, intelligence, work ethic, grit, and confidence so they can understand that all these traits can coexist harmoniously. From very young ages we want girls to believe that being smart is fantastic and that who they are intellectually and cognitively says more about them as an individual than who they are externally.

Encourage girls to build relationships with positive and high-achieving friends. Girls can have a positive or a negative influence on one another and can be highly influenced by their peers, especially during the middle school years. Helping them connect with friends who are also focused on academic achievement and success can foster their continued growth and development. It can be hard to set limits on girls' friendships, particularly when their peer groups can seem to change so rapidly, but it is important to know who their friends are, who their friends' parents are, and how their values, actions, and behaviors are consistent or inconsistent with your own. Admittedly, girls bristle when parents tell them, "It's not you that I don't trust. It's them" or "I don't know their parents; I don't think you need to spend the night." However, ensuring that girls are surrounded by positive social and academic influences can help set them up for a successful future.

Refute the stereotype that certain subjects in school are better for boys or girls. Adults and teens alike continue to hold stereotypes that boys and girls are better at, or designed to do, certain subjects or tasks. When adults hold stereotypes about particular school subjects and their appropriateness for boys or girls, there can be a significant effect on students' later achievement and career choice. Interestingly, researchers have found that as fathers' belief in gender stereotypes increases, girls' interest in math decreases (Davis-Keane, 2005). This means that when a girl sees that her dad has traditional ideas about what girls should do or be, the girl's academic performance in typically male-dominated subjects gets worse. From very early ages girls pay attention to the messages that they get from others regarding what they are supposed to enjoy and be good at.

Provide girls the exposure/opportunity to engage in math- and science-supportive environments. Parents provide their sons with more opportunities to develop math and science skills than they provide their daughters. From buying math and science toys to engaging in math and science building activities, parents place greater importance on these subjects for boys compared with girls (Davis-Keane, 2005). It is then no surprise that girls become less interested, and subsequently less skilled, in some of these areas. Encourage girls to be on the robotics team, the STEM (science, technology, engineering, and mathematics) interest group, the environmental club, and the math team. Help them find online communities, interest groups, apps, and camps where they can connect with other girls who have similar interests and aptitudes.

Create a classroom environment that is safe for girls to take risks. Girls want to learn in a classroom environment that feels safe and predictable. They want to know that if they raise their hand to answer a question and get it wrong, they will not be made fun of or maligned by their teacher or their peers. Girls prefer teachers who are in control of the class and who create the space for inquiry, learning, respect, and academic risk taking. They want encouragement and challenge, with equalized interactions between the boys and girls in the class.

What Do You Want to Be When You Grow Up?

10

How Stereotypes Are Holding Girls Back

While girls now have more occupational options available to them than ever before, there are still some very clear issues that exist regarding their ability to acquire many positions traditionally held by men. Women's representation in many areas has been steadily growing, such as in law, science, and medicine; however, there are still vast disparities in the access that women have to many higher-paying and higher-influence positions.

Some argue that women just aren't interested in these professions, that they don't like these fields as much as men do. Others argue that women aren't cut out for these roles and cite long hours, stress, and the inability to balance family and work as reasons why female representation is so low. Even among the STEM professions, which have been pushing to increase women's representation for nearly two decades, men still outpace women in nearly every discipline. Clearly there are major societal factors that contribute to (the lack of) access and acceptance for women in many arenas, but there are also historical, family, educational, and interpersonal factors that we must consider when we enter into discussions of occupational choice and career development.

It is important to explore the historical context of women in the workforce to recognize where there have been great strides and where there continue to be barriers to access. Women began to enter the workforce with regularity during World War II to assist the nation in a time of warfare. In doing so many women realized that they enjoyed, and were good at, various jobs outside the home, and at the end of the war they wanted to maintain their employment. Girls and women began to explore their occupational interests and found a whole new arena from which to gain satisfaction and a sense of accomplishment.

Our occupations are a part of our identity, and our careers help define who we are. When we initially meet new people, invariably the question is asked, "So what kind of work do you do?" We categorize and rank one another based on these social and economic categories, and we place great importance on our work identity. There is often a hierarchy that surrounds different jobs—white collar jobs, blue collar jobs, and so on. A hierarchy exists based on the education required for the position, the pay that the position provides, and the power that the position wields. Unfortunately, few girls and women spend very much time engaged in rigorous career-related research and planning. In fact, many of us experience the process of career development as a sort of planned happenstance, where chance events and environmental factors determine our ultimate career path.

When you think about your own career development, what comes to mind? Consider the following questions:

Career Survey

1. When I was a child, I thought I would be a _____ when I grew up.

2. When I was in middle school, I wanted to be a _____.

3. When I started college, I majored in _____ and thought I would be a _____.

4. The career that I currently have is
   a. the worst ever. I can't wait to leave.
   b. fine for now, but I'm always looking for the next opportunity.

   c. good and stable. I know what to expect from day to day, and I'm comfortable.

   d. the perfect fit for me. I can't imagine myself doing anything else!

   e. I don't really have a career right now.

5. The biggest influences on my career choices have been

_____

_____.

6. The biggest regret I have about my career decision is _____

_____.

7. If I had known in high school what I know now, I would have _____.

How much of your own career decision-making happened by chance? Perhaps you stumbled onto an internship that helped develop your passion for a particular field, or you chose a college major because your parents pushed you toward a particular discipline. What were the interests, curiosities, life circumstances, and realities that helped influence your career decisions?

When I was in kindergarten, we had a career day where each student had to choose a career and then memorize a poem that described the profession. I can't remember if I was assigned this particular career or if I chose it, but I was to be a nurse. I wore a nurse's uniform (which at the time was a little white dress with a hat with a red cross on it) and said, "When I grow up, I'll be a nurse to help you when you're sick. I'll do the best things I can to make you better quick." By the time I got to middle school I was heavily involved in sports, so I thought I might want to be an athletic trainer or a physical therapist. Then, once I got to college I was convinced that wearing a white coat was in my future as a pediatrician, so I started college as a pre-med major. After breaking one too many glass beakers and test tubes in chemistry class and gagging while dissecting a tiny pig in biology, I thought I might need to reconsider this career path. It wasn't until I took a Psychology of Women course with one of the most inspiring professors I have ever had that I realized that I had found an interest and a passion that I had never experienced before, and thus, I began my studies in psychology and education in earnest. This connection and alignment between the subject matter and myself was a completely new feeling! Who knew that there was an ability to pull together your interests, passions, curiosities, skills, and competencies and create a synergistic career and life path!

I've talked to many adults about their own career development. Some could easily say that they knew since they were in elementary school the career that they would have. One teacher told me, "I knew that I would be a teacher from the time I was in second grade. I never wanted to do anything else, and I never even considered another career path. It was what I was meant to do." Others have less intentionality and a less clear and direct path. One very successful business owner told me,

> I started out as a high school history teacher, but I was so close in age to the students that I didn't think I would last long at that job. I quickly moved on to sales and found that it was something that I was pretty good at. I kept seeking out opportunities for promotion and increased responsibility and was successful at that for a time. But there was a point that I realized that I wasn't going to make it any further in that particular company, so I took a risk and started my own business. It has turned out to be the best decision I ever made but at the time was one of the scariest things I had ever done.

It is interesting to compare these two career paths. Both people are content and fulfilled in their work, but they had two very different paths. The teacher was female, and the business owner was male. Can we draw any conclusions about gender differences in these career paths?

What Kind of Jobs Are for Girls?

Many of us would answer this question by saying that *any* job is accessible and available for girls and that there is no gender divide regarding who can or should do what type of job. At its core this statement is true. Girls *should* have access to the complete and unrestricted world of work; however, the reality is that there is a very strong gender gap in many professions, and the road for girls and women to access certain types of careers can be fraught with barriers and challenges. These barriers actually begin with the stereotypes that are held regarding the types of jobs that are viewed as more appropriate for men or women. Take a moment to see if you hold any conscious or unconscious biases by reading through the list of the following professions. Think of the very first image of the person that comes to mind when you read each word:

- Construction worker
- Hair stylist
- Kindergarten teacher
- Police officer
- Labor and delivery nurse
- Truck driver
- Software engineer
- Heart surgeon
- Florist
- Administrative assistant
- Auto mechanic
- Stockbroker

If you are like many people, the images that popped into your mind were overwhelmingly traditional in regard to gender. While you may have had a few of the occupations listed conjure up a specific person who was not of the stereotypical gender, in general, we tend to have very rigid ideas about who we see in different professional environments and settings.

Often, this happens without conscious awareness, and we find that our ideas about who does what type of job is ingrained in us as long as we can remember. This is probably because much of our career understanding and conceptualization happen during our childhood and elementary school years.

Learning About Jobs: The Early-Childhood Years

Some of the early career influences for girls are related to the types of exposures they have when they are very young. Let's consider the types of toys that are marketed to boys versus girls. Boys' toys tend to be much more action oriented and skill based, such as robots, Legos, Erector Sets, science kits, cars, and trains. These are toys that promote movement, skill acquisition, and spatial reasoning. Girls' toys overwhelmingly include baby dolls, ironing boards, kitchen sets, makeup, and clothes and fashion. These toys promote nurturing, caretaking, and domestic work—girls can even have a baby doll that wets itself so girls can learn how to change a dirty diaper. (See Peggy Orienstein's [2012] book, *Cinderella Ate My Daughter*, for a more in-depth and humorous discussion of kids toys.)

While it is hard to know the precise impact of these activities and exposures on children, it can be reasoned that some of the earliest ideas that children develop about skills, activities, and the world of work happen during play. Children learn and create understanding of the world around them through play. If a girl is repeatedly presented with and surrounded by toys that teach and promote the more domestic skills mentioned above, it is likely that her comfort with and skill development around those particular toys will be enhanced. The same can be said for the building and construction toys that are often given to boys.

The concept of plasticity of the brain discussed in the previous chapter applies to exposure to toys and activities. Boys are allowed to play in the mud, while girls are told not to get themselves dirty. Dolls are for girls and cars are for boys. Girls learn how to cook, while boys learn how to build. Children understand very quickly the toys and activities that are for boys and the ones that are for girls.

These early exposures not only help shape the brain development and pathway construction of young children, they also help shape their early ideas of who does what—what kinds of toys, activities, and even jobs are right for girls, and which are right for boys. Because kids begin to develop these ideas when they are quite young, we want to ensure that their exposure and ideas are vast and varied from the earliest ages.

⭐ ACTIVITY: TAKE A FIELD TRIP TO THE TOY AISLE

Take a walk through the toy aisles of your local store, or do a quick search online for "toys for girls" and "toys for boys." Look at the various toys that are marketed to boys and to girls. What do you notice? First of all, you are likely to notice a big difference in color schemes. The girls' toys are overwhelmingly pink, but the boys' toys are all different colors! See if you can find the exact same toy in a boy version and in a girl version. What colors do you think define the boy and the girl version? For example, you might find PlayDoh available in primary colors as well as in pastel colors.

Over the past few years some retailers have addressed this gender binary when it comes to how they display and itemize toys, but overwhelmingly, there continue to be very clearly defined categories delineated by blue or pink. Now think about the skills that you think each toy would help develop in a child. Do you see different opportunities for boys and girls? Are there chances for boys to learn the much-needed nurturing and domestic skills they'll need later in life? Do the toys provide girls the opportunity to create, design, measure, build, and operate—skills they will need in the future?

Next time you are choosing a toy for a child, think about what your choice says to that child (and their parents) about your perception of their roles, skills, interests, and competencies!

Understanding Careers: Elementary Years

During their early-childhood years there is a great deal of career education that happens for children. Between the ages of three and five children begin to understand the concept of work and develop an early understanding of the professions (Gottfredson, 2002). They understand that adults go to work and have jobs. Kids this age might start to talk about what they want to be when they grow up and will begin to identify real-life occupations rather than say they want to be a superhero, a cartoon character, or an animal.

Between six and eight years children form an understanding of who does what type of work. At this stage the initial gender assignment begins (Gottfredson, 2002). Kids tend to believe that nurses are women and construction workers are men. They see scientists as men in white lab coats and kindergarten teachers as women who teach the youngest learners.

Even at these young ages introducing students to the idea that men and women can perform any job can be a daunting task. Individuals tend to hold very rigid expectations about occupations and gender, and to consider men and women in careers that seem to be gender incongruent can be difficult. One middle school counselor said,

> When I talk about nontraditional careers for boys or for girls, I experience the "giggle" effect. It is really difficult for kids to think about men who work in salons or as nurses, or women who are construction workers. What makes this so funny, and what are we teaching them that results in this?

This is an extremely valid question. Where do children construct their ideas about the various occupations and who does what type of job? Historically, professions have been dominated by one gender or the other, and overwhelmingly, careers are stereotyped as male or female. I remember when I was growing up—and even today—I would hear people saying, "He's a male nurse." While this is unnecessary, providing the gender clearly points out that the person occupying the position is in some way unusual. This type of stereotyping is damaging to both girls and boys because it limits their career options from very young ages. It makes both boys and girls feel that they should not consider specific careers because they are not meant for people of their gender.

☆☆ ACTIVITY: DRAW A SCIENTIST

Ask your student or child to draw a picture of a scientist. Do not provide them with any additional instruction, and see what they draw. Next, ask the student to draw a picture of a nurse. Take note of the gender of each drawing. Use this as an opportunity to discuss gender stereotypes and careers and to dispel the myth that boys and girls can do only certain types of jobs.

I asked a group of fifth-grade girls about their career aspirations. Each took a turn sharing what they wanted to be when they were older. The range of responses included stylist, lawyer, fashion designer, teacher, singer, YouTube star, and pediatrician, to name a few. With a few exceptions the girls had identified careers that were much more female dominated than gender neutral or male dominated. Next, I asked the girls if they believed there were some careers that were better suited for men than for women. There was an emphatic "No!" followed by one girl saying, "Well . . . maybe there are some jobs men should do instead of women. Like construction and stuff. I am not saying that women can't do it; I just think that women wouldn't really like to do it." Another girl said, "I think there are jobs that people think men can do better than women, but I think we can do anything that we want to do."

Their assessment is consistent with what girls across the country believe about jobs and careers for men and women. In The Girls' Index™ survey we asked girls about their perceptions of leadership, their thoughts about working for a male or female supervisor, and their beliefs about whether certain types of jobs were better for men than for women. While only 8% of girls reported that they think men are better leaders than women, 13% said they would rather work for a male supervisor than for a female supervisor, and 44% believe that there are certain jobs that are better for men than for women (Figure 10.1).

Figure 10.1 Leadership and Career Perceptions of Girls

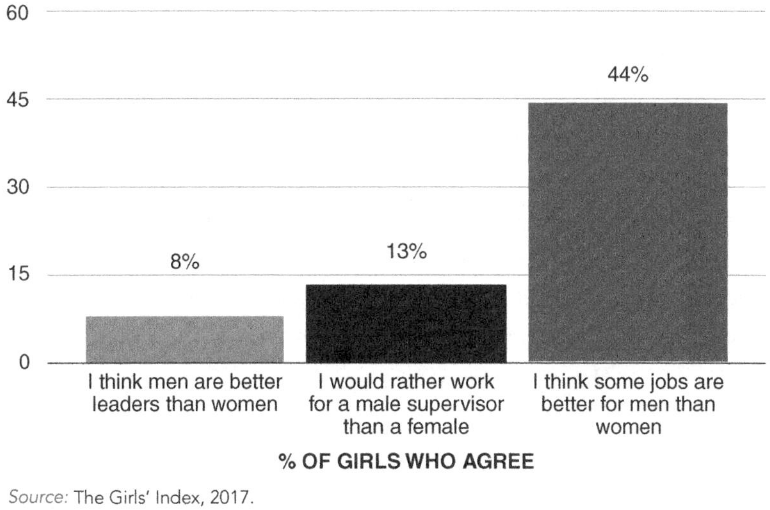

% OF GIRLS WHO AGREE

Source: The Girls' Index, 2017.

It was interesting to note that even in elementary school, girls believe that they can be or do anything they want. However, they still hold traditional ideas about the kinds of careers they are considering as well as the type of careers that are better for women. This perceived gender incongruity causes both boys and girls to avoid specific careers based on gender even before they assess whether that job is accessible to them or is a good fit for them (Gottfredson, 2002).

I conducted similar focus groups with mothers and asked them questions about their daughters' career aspirations. The mothers' responses were interesting as it became clear that many had never seriously talked to their daughters about their career ideas. A few mothers had a vague idea of the interests of their daughters. One of them said, "I have never really heard her talk about anything specific." Another mom shared, "I told my daughter that she doesn't have a choice when it comes to her career; I'll tell her what she will be."

When I asked the moms about jobs that were more appropriate for men or women, their initial response was similar to that of the girls: "No!" This was followed by "but . . . ." The "but" was connected, in large part, to the mothers' concern about their daughters' ability to effectively manage a career and motherhood. One mom stated, "I told my daughter, 'You can be anything that you want. You can be a doctor or a lawyer or a CEO. But just know that it will be hard to have a baby too.'" Girls learn from a very early age that motherhood and career success may conflict, and this message is reinforced to them throughout their lives. One high school girl who excels in science shared with me that her teacher suggested that she consider becoming a science teacher. When she told her teacher that she was thinking about engineering, her teacher said that if she became a teacher she would "get to spend her summers at home with her kids." I wondered if the teacher would make the same recommendation to an equally gifted male student?

⭐⭐ ACTIVITY: WHO DO YOU KNOW?

This activity is designed to help girls identify real people in their own lives who have nontraditional roles or careers. Help girls identify people they know who fit into the following categories:

1. A working mother with a child under the age of 2
2. A stay-at-home father
3. A dual-career couple who have decided to remain child-free
4. A woman who is a scientist, engineer, or IT professional
5. A man who is a nurse, elementary school teacher, counselor, or social worker
6. A woman who is a high school athletic director

If girls have difficulty identifying people they know who are any of the above, this is an ideal opportunity to have a conversation about some of the long-held stereotypes about men's and women's roles. Talk with the girls about why each of the above individuals would make the choice that they have made. Ask the girls what they see as some of the challenges that each might face in their daily lives.

You might be in a more traditional role yourself. You can use your own valuable experience to share with girls how you came to your decision around your career or family role. What were the pressures you experienced or continue to experience? Is there anything you would have done differently?

Seeing Myself in a Career: Middle and High School Years

Once kids have a firm understanding of gender and gender roles, they begin to notice other characteristics of individuals and careers. Between the ages of 9 and 13, kids begin to pay attention to the prestige of different jobs. They start to recognize that there are socioeconomic differences between people, and they begin to make correlations between socioeconomic status, prestige, and various occupations. At this point also, teens start to make decisions about how they see themselves fitting into certain occupations based on their perception of themselves (Gottfredson, 2002). Similar to what happens with gender incongruence, when youth perceive a disconnect between how they view their own level of prestige and the prestige levels of various careers, they again eliminate some desirable but perceived unrealistic choices. Because men, overall, have more prestigious careers than women, girls may have a more difficult time identifying with higher-powered, higher-paying jobs. Boys and girls are again narrowing their options in very different ways, yet probably don't even realize that this is happening.

To further illustrate the variance between men and women in the world of work, one need not look any further than the average compensation of men and women. According to the AAUW's 2019 report, women are paid 82 cents for every dollar paid to men. The statistics are even more disparate for women of color. Compared with white, non-Hispanic men,

- Black women make 62 cents on the dollar.
- Hispanic women make 54 cents on the dollar.
- Asian women make 89 cents on the dollar.
- Native Hawaiian or Other Pacific Islander women make 61 cents on the dollar.
- American Indian or Alaska Native women make 57 cents on the dollar.

An additional challenge is that while women currently make up about 49% of the nation's workforce, they comprise 59% of the low-wage workforce (people who are in the lowest 20% of earnings).

At ages 14 through 18, teens begin to consider internal characteristics such as motivation, values, and ability. Many begin to explore their perceptions of their own mental ability, academic skills, and determination. How hard am I willing to work for a particular outcome? What is my dream job, and do I think I am smart enough to have it? If there is an inconsistency between how teens see themselves and how they view a particular occupation, the career options are further reduced.

As adolescents go through this process, they begin to develop a sense of the level of career attainment and accomplishment they want to have in life. Throughout the years they have eliminated careers that don't fit the perception they hold of themselves. If I think that I am interested in chemistry or chemical engineering but I don't see any one of my own race or gender in that field, I may have difficulty seeing myself there. This, often subconscious, process results in the development of a *social space*—a zone of potential and acceptable occupational options that fit with one's self-concept (Gottfredson, 1997). It is essentially a narrowed set of options based on how I actually see myself.

How Self-Concept Affects Career Decisions

We know that the adolescent years are when young people begin to make sense of who they are within the larger context of the society in which they live. Adolescents tend to have an evolving self-concept (or way in which they construct the world around them), and they are constantly seeking to make sense of who they are and where they belong in the world. For girls self-concept declines markedly from elementary school to middle school, and then again from middle school to high school. The adolescent years are when girls' self-concept and self-esteem are at their lowest points.

If girls' self-esteem is lowest during adolescence, and a great deal of career decision-making happens during adolescence, then how are girls' career decisions affected?

The following chart shows how the negative thoughts that girls have about themselves and their abilities, behaviors, aptitudes, and interests can have a significant impact on the decisions they make about their future. We need to work to instill in girls a strong sense of themselves as capable and competent. We need to provide girls with opportunities to develop skills and to realize that they are good at any number of things. We need to build them up during these tumultuous years so that they are able to consider the widest range of options for their future. Our understanding of the unique issues that affect girls' career development, specifically as it relates to self-concept, is important. With this fundamental background we can help girls engage in the career development process with increased awareness of how their thoughts and feelings about themselves can affect their ideas around career planning.

Girls' Self-Concept	Girls' Thoughts	Girls' Career Decision-Making
Self-concept, or the way I feel about myself, is at its lowest point for girls during adolescence.	I'm not really that good at anything.	Girls develop lowered career expectations.
Girls begin to question their abilities, intelligence, and competence.	I don't think I am smart enough for that career.	Girls impose limits on their options based on the fact that they don't perceive themselves as a good fit for a lot of careers.
Girls internalize societal messages about what girls can do or should be.	I don't see anyone who looks like me in that job. I don't think I can have a family and be successful in that career.	Girls choose less prestigious, lower-paying careers.

Planning for a Future That She Will Love

As girls begin to envision who they can be, we don't want their dreams to be negatively affected by low self-esteem or limited societal expectations. We want girls to envision themselves as successful, happy, and fulfilled in their future career. We need to provide them with the opportunity to explore their "possible selves"—or who they can be in the future.

When we encourage girls to explore what they hope, expect, or fear to become in the future, we motivate them to make intentional academic and occupational choices. Envisioning what we want to be in the future, and how we see ourselves in the future, can guide our academic and career decisions. This is the first step in career planning: becoming aware of choices and decisions (see Figure 10.2). We want girls to actually know what is out there so they have a chance to see beyond their current environment or perceived limitations and explore vast possibilities for their future.

Career decision-making is a developmental process. As girls mature, they pass through a series of developmental tasks that allows them to begin to form ideas about who they are and what they might be able to accomplish as adults. If we think of this process as occurring in stages, we can help identify where girls are in the process and how we can support them to think more intentionally about their role in crafting a future that they will love. Consider career planning as a series of stages that we pass through in an attempt to make a career decision. Use the career awareness and planning model in Figure 10.2 for reference (Hinkelman & Sears, 2009).

Figure 10.2 Career Awareness and Planning Model: Helping Girls Think About Their Career Plan

Source: Hinkelman & Sears, 2009.

Start with providing girls with the opportunity to learn about educational and career decisions. Where do they see themselves? Will they go to college? How much money will they make? Getting a sense of the possibilities that exist is the first step in planning for the future.

Next, we want girls to have the opportunity to learn about themselves. What do they like and dislike? What are they passionate about? Some questions to ask girls are the following:

1. What kinds of things or activities do you like to do?
2. What are your favorite subjects in school?
3. What subjects seem easy to you?
4. What are the subjects in which you do your best work?
5. What do you like to do for fun or as a hobby?
6. What are you passionate about?
7. What/who inspires you?

The third step is for girls to explore various occupational options. There are many resources now that can provide girls with information about a wide range of careers. One of the easiest and most accessible is an online resource called O*Net (The Occupational Information Network, www.onetonline.org). O*Net is a database that contains information on hundreds of different occupations. Individuals can explore various professions and examine the knowledge, skills, and abilities that are required for each occupation. Educational requirements, salary information, and anticipated demand for the profession are included as well.

Career Girls (careergirls.org) is a girl-specific tool for career exploration and exposure. This is a free to use, comprehensive, video-based career exploration tool with a massive collection of career guidance videos focused on diverse and accomplished women in hundreds of occupations throughout the world. Girls can search by industry or job and find high-quality videos and interviews with amazing women in careers of all kinds.

The fourth step is to make plans for the education and training required for the types of careers that seem interesting. We can help girls understand the importance of the academic and curricular deci-sions they make at various points throughout their education. Girls can inadvertently restrict future opportunities by the course patterns they choose in middle school. For example, girls who avoid advanced math courses minimize or eliminate their chances to pursue science, engineering, or technological occupations in the future unless they take remedial coursework. Encouraging girls to take the most rigor-ous courses that are available and then helping them to be successful in those courses is very important. Girls might think it is better to get an "A" in a general math class than to get a "B" in a higher-level course. But colleges report that it is better to take higher-level courses and earn slightly lower grades than to take easier courses and breeze through with all "As."

Some girls are now taking courses in middle school that count for high school credit and sometimes even college credit. This means that the traditional idea of the ninth-grade year being the year where things "start to count" is no longer true. Middle school is now when the college planning track begins, and it is important for girls and their parents to recognize this reality. Girls cannot explore or choose educational or occupational goals without rel-evant information and an understanding of the consequences of their curricular decisions. Mapping out courses well in advance of the next academic year is a wise and thoughtful decision. Starting this process in middle school will ensure that girls have the oppor-tunity to take the highest-level courses.

The final step is taking action. When girls register for their high school courses, enroll in postsecondary options while still in high school, sign up for a job shadow, or apply for internship experi-ence, they are taking action. Point this out to them, and continue to encourage their active participation!

What Can We Do?

So much more goes into career planning and decision-making than simply the presence of career role models or mentors. Yet this has been one of the primary strategies for increasing female representa-tion in a variety of careers. From business to government, to STEM and computers, girls are still underrepresented in these fields. However, ensuring that they have increased exposure to diverse opportunities as well as role models is merely the first step in the process. Piquing their interest does not necessarily lead to their pursuit of a particular subject or career. The career development process shows us that girls have to see themselves as a good fit for a particular career and also believe in their own ability to be successful in that role. They can have the interest and the exposure, but if they don't have the ability to envision themselves in that particular role or as capable of being successful in that job, they may very well take a pass.

Much of the career exploration and development curricula that are utilized in schools focus on the characteristics of different types of work and on individual interests, traits, and abilities. Unfortunately, these approaches to career development fail to account for the way interests, traits, and abilities are developed and shaped in individual children. If a girl's sense of self is changing, unstable, and easily influenced during adolescence, then social, environmental, and psychological factors must be considered as we attempt to promote career development.

Ensure that girls have access to a wide range of gender-neutral toys, experiences, and activities. We know that children learn through play and develop ideas as well as skills and competencies through their early exposures. Provide both boys and girls with toys that will allow them to develop the widest range of skills. Boys can learn to be nurturing, and girls can learn to build.

Broaden the horizons of young girls. Some of us may think that occupational stereotypes are no longer a problem and that girls have a much broader vision of what they can do. In some instances this is in fact the case. But many of the same stereotypical ideas about what occupations are like and what girls should or should not pursue cause many girls to undervalue their talents and skills and ignore nontraditional occupations. You can make a difference by helping girls learn more about themselves, assess their skills accurately, and explore a wider variety of occupational options. We need to recognize the social pressures that exist for girls and work to illuminate role models and successful women in a wide range of careers.

Conveying the message to girls that they can be successful in any type of career, including male-dominated careers, may inspire young women to consider occupational possibilities that they may have initially rejected.

Provide opportunities for career-related internships and job shadows. Internship programs can give girls the opportunity for actual work experience and the opportunity to try out a possible occupation. Internships, co-ops, and job shadows can give an authentic sense of what it might be like to work in a particular industry and allow girls to see how it might fit with their own skills, interests, and abilities.

Provide opportunities for intensive programs. Intensive summer programs can provide in-depth opportunities for career exploration and development. They give girls the chance to immerse themselves into a field or a subject and be around others who share their interests. Many organizations, colleges, and universities offer intensive summer programs for girls. Check with your local institutions of higher education, Boys and Girls Clubs, recreation centers, and youth organizations to see what type of summer programming they offer.

Connect girls with career mentors. Provide opportunities for girls to connect with career mentors—older, more experienced people who act as role models and advocates. Career mentoring can have academic, professional, or personal functions and can be developed through formal or informal networks. Career mentors can help model or validate career possibilities for young girls (Packard & Nguyen, 2003). Often, girls have fewer same-sex and same-ethnicity work models to observe than boys. Many girls have not been exposed to women in nontraditional occupations and thus fail to see themselves as possibly succeeding in those occupations. Providing girls with opportunities to meet with female mentors who look like them and listen to speakers from nontraditional occupations are strategies that you can use to help female students begin to view themselves as individuals who can be successful in various career arenas.

Confront the stereotype that girls are not good at math and science. We need to question why so many girls like science in the beginning of elementary school but have begun to lose that interest before middle school. Research supported by the National Science Foundation (2003) showed that in fourth grade 66% of girls and 68% of boys reported liking science. While boys' interest continues, girls begin to lose interest in science by the end of elementary school. Perhaps girls are socialized to see math and science as something only boys do. Research shows that teachers' and parents' support is critical to fostering girls' interest in science, engineering, and math. Making girls more aware of the science- and math-related careers that are available can influence their decisions about what courses to take in high school, laying the foundation for an STEM career.

Expose female students to successful career women in nontraditional occupations. Young girls continually endorse career aspirations that are stereotypically female because they do not have exposure to women who are in nontraditional careers. While girls might easily have exposure to women who occupy traditional careers, there is a lack of female role models throughout the educational system and in society as a whole. Direct and personal exposure to actual women who embody nontraditional occupations is imperative to the conceptualization of a wide variety of career possibilities for young women. It is additionally important that girls have the opportunity to see women who are of the same ethnicity as they in different career roles. Being able to picture oneself in a particular job makes the possibilities seem more realistic.

Conduct activities and develop programs for girls that focus on improving self-esteem and self-concept. With the recognition that self-concept is inextricably related to career development, we can devise individual and group activities that foster self-reflection. Through an examination of the types of stereotypes that exist in our culture for women and the way in which women are portrayed in the media, girls can look within themselves to clarify what is truly of value to them and compare that with the values that society holds. Activities can teach girls to recognize the ways in which media and society work to enhance girls' insecurities and perpetuate an unequal distribution of access to power. Group activities are ideal for adolescents because they give them a safe place to express their feelings and to explore their deep thoughts and beliefs. They are able to examine self-doubts and come to the realization that they are not alone in their thought process and that their peers share the same concerns. Girls find comfort in knowing that the insecurities and pressures that they experience are not unique, and they often readily accept such social support (Wigfield et al., 2002).

Challenge institutional and societal reinforcement of stereotypes. Promoting change in an unsupportive environment is difficult; however, maintaining the status quo can result in the lack of forward progress of students. Schools can be prime examples of the reality of gender stereotypes: women occupy the majority of teaching and secretarial positions, while men engage in the more powerful administrative positions of principals and superintendents. Young women need role models who demonstrate the belief that they are competent, capable, and entitled to pursue careers that may be inconsistent with those they see in their environments.

CEOs, Politicians, and Superintendents 11

But Where Are All the Female Leaders?

Leadership skills help girls to capitalize on their education, express their opinions and ideas, take action on issues of personal importance, make healthy decisions, and work toward future dreams and goals.

—CARE USA Girls' Leadership Development

Wandering through a bookstore and scrolling online to check out the books that focus on leadership and leadership development, I found book after book on how to succeed in business, how to get other people to follow you, how to lead for change, and how to develop effective leadership practices. There were books and workbooks on organizational culture, leadership in education, leadership assessment, and developing effective teams. There were increasingly more books that focused on women's leadership, but I could not find much of anything that focused on girls.

So I jumped into the professional literature. What kind of research has been done on girls' leadership development, and what have we learned about effective ways to foster leadership in girls? While there is a growing body of research that looks at women's leadership, there is surprisingly little actual research that focuses on girls. I came across popular culture articles and books, as well as a variety of organizational reports, but I was surprised to learn that there is not much out there that really looks at evidence-based strategies to foster leadership in girls. If girls are going to be our future leaders, shouldn't we be thinking about how we actually develop their leadership skills?

Even as women's performance, opportunities, and representation have increased over the past decade, there is still a massive disparity between what women are capable of and where they are positioned in our society (AAUW, 2019). Girls are earning higher grades than boys and attending college at higher rates, yet men are much more likely to occupy leadership roles. Something happens along the path to leadership that is causing women to lose professional ground (AAUW, 2016).

In the United States women represent fewer than 5% of Fortune 500 CEOs and less than 25% of the country's elected officials (Figure 11.1). Even in one of the most female-dominated industries like education, women constitute approximately 85% of K–12 teachers across the country, but when it comes to who is actually

Figure 11.1 Women's Representation as Fortune 500 CEOs, Elected Officials, and School Superintendents

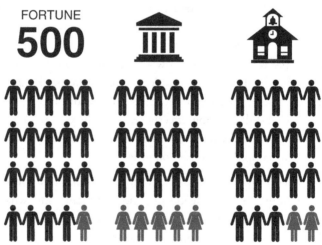

Figure 11.2 Why Girls Struggle With Leadership

1 IN 2 GIRLS ARE
AFRAID TO SPEAK
THEIR MIND
OR DISAGREE WITH OTHERS
BECAUSE THEY WANT TO
BE LIKED

1 IN 3 GIRLS
STAY AWAY FROM
LEADERSHIP BECAUSE
THEY DON'T WANT OTHERS
TO THINK THEY ARE
BOSSY

Source: The Girls' Index, 2017.

running the school districts, only around 15% of school superintendents nationally are women. This statistic drops to 1% for Black women's representation (AAUW, 2016).

One of the organizations that has taken the lead on much of the information and research that exist regarding leadership development in girls is Girl Scouts USA. They have conducted large-scale studies to better understand the way in which girls define leadership and how they perceive themselves as leaders. Interestingly, this 2008 research found that while 69% of girls see themselves as leaders right now only 39% of girls want to be leaders in the future. My research for The Girls' Index™ (Hinkelman, 2017) found that 61% of girls say that they like being in charge; however, 46% reported that they don't say what they are thinking or disagree with others because they want to be liked, and one in three reported that they are afraid to be a leader because they don't want others to think that they are bossy (Figure 11.2). One of the top reasons why girls don't want to be leaders is that they view leadership as incompatible with how they see themselves.

Views of Leadership

Most authors who write about leadership seem to agree that leadership, in general, consists of the ability to provide others with a sense of direction, a willingness and capacity to assist others in the improvement of their performance, and the ability to make up one's mind, delegate tasks, and maintain efficiency. When looking at the individual traits and characteristics that are necessary to achieve these outcomes, the research becomes a bit more ambiguous. Examining the individual characteristics and numerous models of leadership can make for a very confusing understanding of what leadership actually is—and who is best equipped to be a leader.

Our descriptions of leadership are often based on our experiences with and exposure to different types of leaders. Part of the challenge in addressing leadership development with girls and women is differentiating and isolating the actual traits and characteristics that are associated with leadership and then having girls and women see themselves in that description. Many of the concepts surrounding leadership tend to connect to traditional male models of leadership. Complete the following activity, and then look at the traits that you identified as traits of leadership; which traits would you say have been considered more "male" in nature, and which traits are more "female" oriented?

☆☆ ACTIVITY: WHAT MAKES A LEADER?

Examine the list of traits below, and write the ones in the box that you think describe effective leadership:

- Harsh
- Inspiring
- Self-assured
- Passive
- Emotional
- Caring
- Decisive
- Aggressive
- Dramatic
- Vulnerable
- Volatile

- Confident
- Kind
- Assertive
- Selfless
- Organized
- Good listener
- In control
- Creative
- Competitive
- Visionary
- Risk taking
- Collaborative
- Strong
- Makes others happy

Traits of Leadership

Generally, most people would say that girls and women are more often described as passive or emotional, and boys and men are more often described as self-assured or in control. Does your leadership box have more male or female traits? If you are like most people, including girls who were asked to identify traits of leadership, you are likely to have identified more stereotypically masculine characteristics than stereotypically feminine characteristics.

This stereotypical view of leadership contributes to the reality that girls can have a difficult time seeing themselves as leaders. When leadership is described using words and terms that I do not use to describe myself and I don't see any people who look like me in leadership positions, then it can be hard for me to see myself as a leader. While girls struggle to see themselves as leaders, they also have biases against other girls as leaders. Twenty-three percent of girls and 40% of boys prefer male political leaders over female leaders (Weissbourd, 2016). The perception that effective leadership is more aligned with boys and men and incongruent with girls and women continues to be held and actualized in the representation of leadership across sectors.

Let's take a look at some of the institutions where leaders have a great deal of influence, such as businesses, schools, organizations, and government. We can look to some of these prominent leadership positions in our local communities to determine if they are posts that are generally held by men or if we have female leaders in these positions who can serve as role models for our girls. Use the following activity to begin to identify who holds various leadership positions in your community.

⭐ ACTIVITY: LEADERS I KNOW

This is an activity you can complete yourself or have girls complete. It is an opportunity to identify the people who are in leadership positions in your school, organization, community, state, and country.

	Male	Female
1. The pastor/leader at my place of worship is	☐	☐
2. The governor of my state is	☐	☐
3. The president of my country is	☐	☐
4. The CEO of my company is	☐	☐
5. The superintendent of the school district in my community is	☐	☐
6. The president of the college that I attended is	☐	☐
7. The mayor of my city is	☐	☐

This type of activity can be a good starting place to talk with girls about who are the people who occupy powerful positions in their communities. Are there more men or women in these roles? Are there people of their own race and ethnicity in these positions? What do they believe it takes to be successful in different types of leadership roles? Why do they think there is generally higher representation of men than women in these roles?

We know that women are not simply denied top leadership opportunities at the culmination of their long and successful careers; rather, their opportunities disappear at various points along the journey (AAUW, 2016). While there are clearly institutional and systemic issues, biases, and stereotypes that affect women's access to and opportunities in leadership, there are also individual factors that contribute to girls' own leadership aspirations. As girls begin to pay attention to people in leadership positions and develop their own perceptions of what it means to be a leader, we need to focus on the concerns that girls have about their own expression of leadership as well as other girls' leadership. The Girl Scouts USA (2008) and Making Caring Common Project (Weissbourd, 2016) researchers found that girls have unease about becoming leaders and see some barriers to their own leadership development.

Girls' top concerns about leadership include

- being in charge all the time,
- getting a lot of attention,
- having a lot of power and authority, and
- having a lot of responsibility.

The barriers girls identified regarding their own leadership development include

- lack of confidence in their skills and competence,
- difficulty with public speaking or talking in front of others,
- potential for embarrassment or being laughed at, and
- not wanting to appear bossy, to make people mad, or to be disliked by others.

Girls' biases against other female leaders are due to

- competition between girls,
- their own insecurities and lack of self-esteem, and
- believing that other girls are emotional or dramatic.

We can easily see how girls could feel uncomfortable in taking on leadership roles if they think that they do not have the skills or capacity to be effective leaders and they also internalize their own stereotypes about women's fitness for leadership. The issues around low confidence and needing to be liked are major barriers to effectively standing up for oneself, let alone leading others. Couple this with girls' own perceptions and biases toward other girls, and the picture of how girls continue to struggle interpersonally in leadership begins to develop. This information can help us determine what we need to address with girls regarding their perceptions of leadership as well as their perceptions of themselves.

Expanding the Definition of a Leader

As girls develop a firmer understanding of leadership traits, skills, and behaviors, we want to enhance the congruity between these skills and their sense of themselves:

> I think when people think of leaders, they automatically think of strong, aggressive men because they are the ones that you see out there leading things. They are running the businesses, coaching the big sports teams, and basically running the country. I just don't think you would ever see a woman doing some of that stuff. Not because women don't want to but because everyone would try to stop her from doing it. I think women can do the same things that men can do, but I don't think they have the same opportunities. People still seem to think that there are certain things that men and women should do, and being in top leadership positions is not something that you see a lot of women being able to do. Unless you have grown up in a family where you were constantly told that you can be a leader and saw your mom or grandma taking leadership—if you were just sort of looking around at the world, you would automatically think that men are the ones who are the leaders and that women are the ones that support them.
>
> —Maggie, eleventh grade

We need to help girls realize that being a leader does not mean acting like a boy, being loud and aggressive, or controlling everyone around you. Girls need the opportunity to broadly conceptualize leadership and to begin to see themselves as having the potential to develop the traits and characteristics associated with various types of leadership. This means that we have to help them understand that being a leader can mean running a big company, gaining the most prestigious high-paying positions, or having influence over an entire city, state, or country; it can also mean much more than that.

There have been efforts over the years to expand the definition of leadership from being controlling and competitive to being more multifaceted, with an ability to inspire and to steer ahead. Organizations have recognized the value of different leadership styles and have flourished with strategies such as inclusion, cooperation, quality control, and an emphasis on collaboration (Catalyst, 2007). Some of these traits and characteristics, which have been thought to be traditionally female, are becoming more desirable among leaders. So the question is "Do female leaders more easily embody the communicative and pleasant roles? Do they excel more in the areas of interpersonal communication, relationships, and interest in other people?" Conversely, are traditional masculine leadership characteristics truly the most effective? Perhaps women do possess characteristics that are more direct and assertive; however, when they use these skills or strategies, they are often viewed as aggressive, moody, volatile, or bossy. Consider the following case study.

CASE STUDY

You are running late for work, and you have an important presentation coming up. Your boss has been on your back about this presentation for weeks and has told you what feels like 100 times that the "big dogs" from New York are going to be there. You are carrying your child into the day care, and he spits up on your suit jacket. You try your best to wipe it off but realize when you are back in your car that there is still a faint hint of white on your navy suit.

(Continued)

(Continued)

Your presentation is at 9:00 a.m., and you are supposed to meet with your boss and the entire team at 8:15 to review the final details. You're parking your car at 8:10 and know you are going to be late. Should you run to the bathroom to try to get the formula off of your coat or just go into the meeting and hope for the best?

You grab a wet paper towel on your way in and start dabbing your jacket. You apologize profusely for being late and try to quickly explain and laugh off the wardrobe issue that you are having. Some of the people in the room seem sympathetic. Your boss, clearly not amused, says, "I have repeatedly told you this is one of the most important meetings this company has ever had. The stakes are high, and everything needs to be perfect. Please go clean yourself up, and we will continue when you return."

You rush out to deal with your jacket, and when you return you find that the meeting is almost over. Your boss gives you a stern glance and asks you to stay back after the meeting, while the rest of the group is dismissed; your boss then says, "We need to get through this meeting, and then you and I need to meet this afternoon to get a few things straight. Go set up your presentation, and pick up your handouts. I will see you at the meeting."

You leave the room and think to yourself, "Geez . . . my boss is such a _____."

How did you fill in the blank? Did you picture the boss as a man or a woman? If you pictured your boss as a man, take a moment and reread the story picturing a female supervisor. If you pictured a woman, reread it with the boss as a male. Did you have a different reaction? Do you think the boss would respond differently if the parent were a man or a woman in this scenario? Would a mother or a father elicit more empathy and understanding from the boss?

This case study is designed to make us think about the different ways in which we expect leaders to act based on their gender. Let's picture the scenario with a different response from the boss:

Oh my, what a stressful morning you've had. I know that baby formula can be tough to get out of a suit. Last year, when Alyssa was a baby, I felt like I was coming to work with formula and baby food on my suit every day. Just take a minute, and try to get that clean before the meeting.

Do your thoughts or expectations about the gender of the boss change? Do your thoughts about the leadership capacities of the boss change?

Girls and women are in a dilemma. When they perform the behaviors that have been associated with effective leadership, they violate the conventions of appropriate female behavior and can be viewed as overly harsh or unfeminine (Catalyst, 2007). As one high school girl I interviewed said, "People get nervous if girls are too opinionated or direct. So if we stand up for ourselves or are too strong, they will call you a bitch." Conversely, when girls and women do not engage in the more traditional leadership behaviors, they are often viewed as poor leaders. To solve this problem, one of two things could happen:

1. Girls need to learn to develop increased comfort with some of the traditional traits and characteristics that have been associated with effective leadership.

2. The way we define and conceptualize leadership needs to change.

I believe that both of these things need to happen. Girls need to be comfortable speaking their mind, standing up for themselves, making a decision and taking responsibility for it, and taking the initiative to create change. We also need to expand the definition and understanding of leadership to incorporate different approaches and a wide variety of skill sets. Ambition is not an inherently masculine trait.

A New Model of Leadership

How can we construct a new model of leadership for girls? We need to focus on the actual skills, traits, and dispositions we want girls to develop that will assist them in effectively navigating their lives while helping them develop a leadership identity. As we do this, we also need to work to promote the understanding that leadership takes on different forms and requires a wide range of skills, attitudes, and behaviors. The narrow definitions of leadership have served to limit girls' participation because they do not see their own skills as leadership skills.

We can draw on the research of several different organizations that focus on girls' leadership development to bring together the components necessary for fostering girls' leadership. Girl Scouts USA (2008), CARE (2009), and the Ms. Foundation for Women (2002) have all publicized various works focusing on girls' leadership development. In the following I summarize and extend their findings and recommendations:

- *Passion:* "I know what I care about."

  Girls need opportunities to be exposed to many different people, places, issues, and ideas in order to determine what it is they are passionate about. A leader has to believe in what she is doing in order for others to believe in it as well.

- *Motivation:* "I have identified something that I care about, and I am willing to do something about it."

  Girls can feel passionately about an issue, but they must also develop the motivation to take action. This demonstrates that they care enough to actually do something about it.

- *Creativity:* "I know what I am good at."

  When girls identify a passion and find the motivation to create change, they must determine how they are going to create the change. What are their individual skills and gifts? How can they most effectively use their energies in the most productive and useful ways?

- *Assertiveness:* "I am willing to stand up for myself and the topic/idea/principle/project that I care about."

  Leaders must possess the ability to articulate their thoughts and make decisions. They should ask questions and be assertive because they believe that their opinions matter.

- *Decision-making:* "I know that the decisions that I make matter to me and to my community."

  Leaders recognize that they often need to make difficult decisions and that sometimes their decisions affect others. They recognize that they can create opportunities for themselves and that they are in control of their own decisions.

- *Self-confidence:* "I like who I am, and I value myself as a person. I can recognize my strengths, and I know the things that I do well."

  Leaders need to both possess and project confidence. They should recognize their internal value and worth and work to build up those around them.

- *Organization and follow-through:* "I can see the project through from start to finish. I organize myself to achieve my goals."

  Having the idea, motivation, and wherewithal to start an initiative is all for naught if it lacks organization and follow-through. Leaders will stay motivated and organized to ensure that their vision is achieved.

- *Vision/ability to motivate others:* "I can bring people together to use their own skills and talents to accomplish something."

  Leaders must develop the ability to involve others in their vision so that they are not alone in their journey. Empowering others to identify their strengths and the ways their skills can be used increases engagement and commitment.

Thinking about leadership in this way creates an opportunity for girls to see where they can fit into the model. They can assess their own attributes and determine how they can use their skills and abilities to make an impact. We also want girls to have a broad sense of what leadership looks like from the perspective of successful female leaders. What do they do, and how do they describe themselves?

Preparing Girls for Leadership

What do we want girls to accomplish by developing leadership skills? What do we want them to be doing differently after they participate in a leadership program? How can we prepare them for the challenges that they will face as they attempt to exercise their leadership capacities in different environments? These are the questions that I believe we need to explore as we consider building young female leaders.

Female Leaders Describe their Leadership Styles

While it is important to look at the traits that help girls become leaders, it is also important to study flourishing female leaders to understand the attributes they possess and activities they engage in that have helped them become successful leaders. Susan Madsen (2008) studied the leadership styles of women who are presidents of colleges and universities. These women described themselves in the following ways:

I am . . .		I . . .
A consensus builder	Ethical	Communicate well
A risk taker	Fair	Delegate
A strong communicator	Honest	Develop others
An analyzer	Nice	Do not micromanage
Business minded	Not afraid	Engage with others
Committed	Open to criticism	Give credit to others for successes
Collaborative	Open to learning from mistakes	Have a deep understanding of issues
Confident	Perceptive	Have a strong personality
Cooperative	Plain spoken	Have detailed knowledge
Decisive	Productive	Have a high standards
Demanding of self	Results focused	Have strength
Demanding of others	Supportive	Hire the best people
Focused	Team oriented	Involve others in decision-making
Inclusive	Service oriented	Listen well
Engaging	Visionary	

There are many community and school-based programs and initiatives that focus on leadership development for girls. However, a challenge of these types of programs is that they are most likely to attract girls who already see themselves as leaders, who already evidence leadership characteristics, or who have been identified by adults as emerging leaders. What about girls who don't have this advantage? Too often, only a select group of girls have access to leadership development activities, programs, and training. Girls are often targeted at young ages for being confident or outgoing and are selected for leadership positions in their school, troops, or youth groups, while other girls who are less outgoing or charismatic get left behind. It is important that we also reach girls who have great potential but not the self-awareness or necessary adult encouragement to readily seek out leadership development activities. In doing so we ensure that all girls have access to opportunities to enhance their skills and develop a leadership identity.

Additionally, we must be aware of the fact that the concept of leadership development does not resonate with and excite all girls. For girls who are living very intense lives and who are dealing with stressors such as living in violent homes or communities, attempting to get their basic needs met, dating or sexual violence, and the daily drama between and among girls, participating in a leadership program may be of secondary importance to managing the challenges of day-to-day life. While we recognize that developing leadership qualities would likely help girls navigate many of these challenges, we need to connect with and support them in the most relevant manner based on their circumstances.

This does not mean that we should forgo our efforts to engage girls in leadership development work; rather, it means that we need to embed leadership development activities into other programming that is addressing the current issues that resonate with girls. Often adults believe that leadership development is critical for youth; however, girls sometimes find that there are other issues they are dealing with that feel more relevant to their present-day lives than leadership.

What Can We Do?

Provide safe girl-only spaces for trying out new skills. Girls need the opportunity to have all-girl environments, where they can explore new and different ways of being and relating to others. Building a space that is emotionally safe, confidential, and empowering allows girls to explore their thoughts and ideas, challenge their thinking or beliefs, and try out new behaviors. It is much easier to try out something new and scary if you are in a setting where you will be supported and reinforced. If you have to worry about your emotional safety, or that you are going to be made fun of or criticized, you are less likely to want to try anything new or take a risk.

Connect girls with female leaders in your community. Strong female leaders can act as mentors and role models to girls and young women. Mentors can provide an authentic voice while giving honest feedback to girls. The truth is that leadership is not without its challenges, and many female leaders will tell you that they have had to sacrifice some things as they moved up the leadership ladder. Allowing girls to meet and talk with women from various backgrounds provides the opportunity for girls to become inspired—or not—by different experiences. I was working with a young women's leadership academy and was interviewing the participants after they had completed an 18-month program. Throughout the experience the young women had had the opportunity to interact with a variety of female leaders from different backgrounds and disciplines. Some of the leaders were high-powered executives who worked in very stressful but rewarding and influential jobs. The leaders talked about their rise to the top, their decision to have or not have children, and the ways in which they manage their business and their home life. They shared the challenges that they face as female executives in a male-dominated arena and the difficulty that they have managing their time and getting everything done. As I interviewed the young women participants after their exposure to the women leaders, it was interesting to see that some had been inspired and excited by their experience with these high-powered women. Others saw the difficult and demanding lifestyle and determined that they might not be a good fit for that type of leadership position. However, without the exposure they would not really have known what they think or feel regarding the various leadership options for women. Bringing guest speakers to your school or community organization or having girls interview or job shadow different types of women leaders are ways by which girls can expand their leadership understanding and exposure.

Teach girls that leadership skills are skills for success. They are not boys' skills or girls' skills. Despite the fact that some leadership characteristics and traits have been coded as traditionally masculine or traditionally feminine, there are attributes of leadership that all girls would benefit by possessing. For example, assertiveness is generally a characteristic associated with boys and men; however, it is a skill that is also necessary for effective and authentic communication—a key trait of leadership. Assertiveness does not mean aggressiveness or demanding to get one's own way; rather, it means ensuring that your voice and opinions are offered and heard. Being a good listener, demonstrating empathy, and creating an environment of mutual respect and collaboration are all traits of effective leadership. Yet these would also be characteristics that are more associated with a feminine approach to leadership. There are many skills associated with effective leadership, and whether they are connected to boys or girls should be irrelevant; rather, we should focus on the skills and outcomes that we want girls to develop as they begin to develop a leadership identity. The reality is that all these skills are necessary for success as a leader.

Allow girls to demonstrate leadership by giving them opportunities for meaningful participation. Girls need opportunities to demonstrate leadership both in and outside of the school setting. Parents, teachers, counselors, and administrators can intentionally provide opportunities for girls to develop their leadership skills while adding value to the school or home environment. For example, at home, give girls an opportunity to research and plan a family activity or trip. Invite girls to share their opinions and develop the skills to defend their perspectives. If your daughter does not think that a particular expectation or consequence that you have in place is fair, invite her to propose and present an alternative solution, and then together you can discuss the pros and cons. In schools, give girls opportunities to research and develop policies, spearhead extracurricular activities and initiatives, and help contribute in a positive manner to the school climate. One of the best examples I have seen of this is when a new charter school opened in my community. The school was still developing their policies on student behavior and school climate. A small group of high school girls were concerned that there was no student code or policy that adequately addressed sexual harassment. They brought their concerns to the administration and instead of the school leadership drafting a policy and presenting it to the students, they empowered the girls to take the initiative to research and develop a model sexual harassment policy for the school. The students spent weeks conducting surveys, running focus groups, and hosting brainstorming sessions, until they developed and proposed a policy complete with examples, expectations of student behavior, reporting procedures, and consequences. The girls were able to have a leadership role in a process that had a substantial and systemic impact on their school and their educational experience.

Remind girls that when they practice leadership behaviors, not everyone is going to like them or want to follow them—and that is okay. In general, girls feel great pressure to be nice, helpful, and caring. The helping aspects of leadership resonate with most girls more than any other facet of leadership. The challenge to this is that girls also report a concern about not being liked if they were a leader. Girls feel pressure to choose between relationships and leadership (Girl Scouts USA, 2008) and will work to ensure that the people around them are happy—sometimes at the expense of their own happiness. When girls stand up for themselves or participate in leadership activities, there is always the chance that their friends, family, and peers will not agree with them. Sometimes this fear is enough to keep girls from speaking up, making decisions, or expressing opinions that are different. We need to prepare girls for the reality that when they do speak up or assert their leadership, they may not be liked by everybody. This does not mean that they should stop these behaviors; rather it means that girls need to be emotionally ready for any negative fallout. Our job is to let them know that this is a possibility and a reality for all successful leaders and to equip them with the skills to effectively manage these situations and emotions.

Prepare girls for the challenges they may face on their leadership journey. Even if girls do everything right—develop a strong sense of confidence, have good self-awareness, hone their interpersonal skills, attend leadership seminars, take risks, and push themselves to take increased leadership opportunities—they still will face discrimination and challenges along their journey. As stated earlier, there are individual factors that we can develop and instill in girls that will equip them for success, but there are also long-standing inequities that persist that can impede their progress. We have a responsibility to address and dismantle the system that is unfairly biased, while we simultaneously equip individual girls to be effective and savvy in their ability to navigate the system. They need to know the reality of the landscape so that they can develop the skills to overcome the barriers and successfully conquer the complex system.

What Girls Want 12

An authentic connection with girls and an understanding of their experiences is something that everyone who works with or cares about girls seeks to accomplish. Hundreds of parents and teachers in workshops, focus groups, and interviews openly express their concern for the girls in their lives and their genuine desire to increase their communication with them and promote the girls' success. However, the more we approach our work with girls by telling them what *we* think they need, the less relevant we become to their lives. We as adults do have a great deal of insight into the needs of girls, yet we often fail to take the time to intently and adequately listen to the girls in our lives. We need to approach our relationships with girls from a position of seeking to understand. We want to understand their feelings and perspectives and connect with them so that we can keep the lines of communication open. We need to focus on building trust and empathy and we need to know, from girls, how best to accomplish this.

It has been interesting to realize that one of the most common ways that adults believe they can connect best to girls is unfortunately one of the top things that girls say drive them crazy. In an attempt to cultivate empathy and a sense that we have "walked in their shoes," we might often say, "When I was your age . . . " or "I know exactly how you feel; I had the same thing happen to me at your age." We feel that we are letting girls know that we truly understand what they are going through, that we have had a similar experience, and that we can fully comprehend their feelings. We want to be contemporary and relevant while we communicate a sense of understanding: "I have been there; I know how this feels."

Intellectually, this makes sense because most of us have been there and we do have some sense of how girls might be feeling. However, many teens have the perspective that no one can understand what they are feeling or going through—especially an adult. Their emotions feel confusing and complex, and they truly believe that their situation is so unique that they may be the first person to ever feel what they are feeling at this particular moment. So when we say, "I know how you feel," it can sound patronizing and even make us seem out of touch. It can be hard for girls to envision the adults in their lives having similar feelings and experiences because they see us as so far removed from the intense realities of their lives.

The phenomenon of believing that my emotions and experiences are completely unique to me is what human development researchers refer to as the *personal fable*. There is a genuine belief that no one else can possibly understand me—especially an adult (Vernon, 2009). This sense of isolation can play itself out in various ways in girls' lives and can distance them from their peers and from the caring adults in their lives. They feel that they have to figure it all out on their own because of their belief that no one else *truly* understands. However, when we put girls in a safe space together and provide them with the opportunity to discuss the things going on in their lives, they are always surprised to learn that the other girls are going through the same things that they are going through. While this seems like common and logical sense to us, to girls it truly feels revolutionary to find out that other girls are having similar experiences. They realize that other girls are having similar intense, confusing, and isolating thoughts, and they don't feel so alone. They feel a sense of belonging and understanding.

Our goal should not be to convince girls that we have been there and that we do understand; rather, we should seek to understand their current experience. Girls believe that their issues are far more serious than anything we could have experienced, and as such, our ability to effectively relate to them and their problems can seem impossible. Our role should not be to try to make them see our perspective or be convinced that we understand but to ensure that they know we are there to listen and to withhold judgment. Teens tend to view adults as being "way older" and far removed from their issues and can see parents' or teachers' experiences as irrelevant to their lives. While many of the issues addressed in this book have stood the test of time in regard to the problems that girls are dealing with, there are also many experiences and concerns that are, in fact, unique to today's girls and teens. Think about the intense issues girls are facing that involve technology and social media. Most of us did not have to deal with the same issues as teenagers. We can show interest without having to be the expert and, in doing so, can demonstrate effective listening skills with girls.

We Asked Girls, "How Can Adults Better Support You? What Do You Need From the Adults in Your Life?"

When we ask girls what they want from the adults in their lives, many of the comments are focused around issues of communication and trust. Overwhelmingly, girls feel that the adults in their lives do not trust them and that they do not have effective ways to communicate in a positive and constructive manner with parents, teachers, and other adults in their lives. Adults feel quite the same: "I have no idea how to talk to these girls." They are frustrated by their inability to "get to" girls, and they feel that girls are "impossible to talk to."

Clearly, communication has broken down; however, there are strategies to help ease the situation, and I believe that it is adults' responsibility to figure out new ways of communicating with and relating to teen girls. Girls say that they would rather talk to their peers or to girls who are older than them than to adults. When we asked them why they don't want to talk to adults, they told us that adults don't get them, they don't understand, and that they don't really care. The reality is that many adults care very deeply about the girls in their lives; however, they lack the skills to adequately communicate this care and concern and then are unable to connect effectively with the girls.

We asked the girls, "If the adults in your life could better support you, or if you could tell the adults in your life anything that you wanted about how best to support you, what would you tell them?" Not surprisingly, the things that the girls said were amazingly consistent. Girls of all ages, races, and backgrounds had similar ideas about how the adults in their lives could best support and encourage them. I selected several of the most recurring themes to share with you in this chapter.

"Listen to What We Have to Say. Consider How We Feel, and Just Listen Instead of Jumping to Conclusions."

Girls do not feel listened to. They feel that adults do not spend the time to listen to what they're actually saying, and when they do, girls feel that adults think their problems and feelings are stupid or childish. Girls talk about sharing certain concerns or feelings with adults, and then, instead of the adults affirming their feelings or the situation, they jumped to a conclusion and began to offer advice or tell the girl that how she handled the situation was wrong and that she needs to do it differently.

Often, we just want people to listen to what we have to say. We are not always looking for advice; we're not always looking for their opinion; we're just looking to be heard and to feel that we are understood. The same thing applies for girls; they just want to know that we are listening to them and that we are trying to understand the situation, as difficult as that might be for us.

Listen to understand. Don't listen to respond. This is perhaps one of the hardest concepts for any of us to comprehend. We become so accustomed to listening to what other people are telling us that instead of truly trying to understand what they are saying and comprehend the actual feeling and meaning, we constantly try to think of what our response should be. We are thinking of what should come out of our mouth next instead of taking the time to hear what is being said. How fantastic it would feel if we told someone a problem that we were dealing with and they simply said, "Wow, that is so hard. . . . I am so sorry that you are going through this." Unfortunately, we rarely respond in this manner. Rather, we try to think of a good response, or we get caught up in offering advice and suggestions. Girls need an adult who will just listen without judgment and without offering unsolicited advice. Just because someone is sharing a problem or challenge with us does not mean that they are looking for an intervention or a solution or for us to solve their problem. They may just want to get something off of their chest and feel listened to and understood. Tina, a fifth grader, said, "Don't tell me that my feelings are stupid. I can't help how I feel." Even as adults we know that we need to be heard, valued, validated, and understood. We often just want someone to tell us that we are okay and that our feelings are okay. Girls want the same thing. They just want us to listen, to care, and to let them know that what they are feeling or thinking is okay.

"Stop Yelling, and Talk More to Me. Yelling at Me Isn't Going to Make Things Better."

Girls perceive that the adults in their lives are constantly yelling at them. They say they get yelled at by their teachers and by their parents and that when the yelling starts, they simply "tune out" the person who is yelling. Adults say that they don't like to yell and that they wish they didn't have to yell. Many have stated that they do not yell until they have "calmly asked several times for something to happen." Girls, however, feel that they are constantly being yelled at. Obviously, there is a disconnect here because the perceptions of parents and girls are very different.

I know what happens to me when somebody yells at me. I get very adrenalized and yell back louder, or I retreat and completely tune out the other person. Obviously, neither of these strategies is effective in enhancing communication or accomplishing much of anything. As one seventh-grade girl shared, "Talk to me in a calm voice, and I will understand you." We all want to be treated with dignity and respect. Yelling at one another makes us feel defensive, guarded, belittled, and demeaned. We need to calm ourselves down before we can expect to have a useful conversation. We can role model healthy and effective communication by interrupting the yelling exchange and saying, "Let's take a break from this conversation for a few hours and come back to it later when we are both cooled off."

"Don't Freak Out When I Tell You Things. When You Do, It Makes Me Wish I Never Told You."

Girls sometimes want to share information with adults, but they will gauge what they share based on the reaction of the adults. If I know that you are going to start yelling at me or criticizing me if I tell you something, I am going to think twice before I tell you. We tell girls to share with us when they have difficult experiences, are upset by their peers, have had something bad happen to them, or are angry or frustrated. Yet when they tell us some of these difficult things, our own internal sense of protection kicks in. We get angry when there is injustice and protective when there is harm. Because we care so deeply for our girls, it can be difficult for us to keep our composure when we believe that our child or student has been taking advantage of, hurt, or mistreated.

Girls learn at young ages to observe the adults around them and to ensure that they don't do anything that will distress them. This can mean that girls will restrict their own emotional responses if they sense that adults will get angry or sad. They don't want to be the cause of our distress, so they will hold back their feelings, only share limited information, or not tell us anything at all. As girls learn to read the emotions of the people around them, they also learn how to manage those emotions. Girls do not want to upset the people they care about, and so it is often easier for them to keep things to themselves, rather than deal with the negative reactions of the adults that they may talk to.

For example, I was talking to an eleventh-grade girl, Shawna, who skipped school with one of her friends to meet up with some college guys. It was a Friday afternoon, and the girls drove down to the university campus to meet up with the boys and their friends. The girls had been drinking some alcohol, and through the course of the day Shawna and her friend got separated. When Shawna finally found her friend several hours later, she seemed out of it and was crying. As they drove home, Shawna's friend told her that two of the guys had made her do stuff sexually that she didn't want to do. She said that she didn't know what to do or who she could talk to. I asked Shawna if she had talked to her parents or anybody at school about the situation. She laughed and said,

> You're kidding, right? If I told anyone at school, I'd get in trouble for skipping school. And if I even try to talk to my mom or dad about this, I can only imagine what I would hear. I bet they would care less about the fact that my friend was taken advantage of and more about the fact that I skipped school and was drinking. There is no way in the world that I would even think about telling them anything that happened.

While this is an extreme example, other girls have shared similar experiences of intense responses from adults surrounding the difficult situations that they faced. A seventh grader told me about a situation where she was being bullied on the bus every day by a group of ninth-grade girls. She said that the girls would make her leave the seat she was sitting in and go to another seat. When she would move to a different seat, then they would laugh and make her move seats again. She told me that this happened every day and that she didn't know what to do about it. She decided to tell her mom about what was happening. She said,

> Then my mom went crazy. She was so mad at the ninth-grade girls and started to say things like, "Who do they think they are telling people where they can and can't sit on the school bus? Do they own the school bus? I don't think so!" Then my mom said that she was going to come to the bus stop with me tomorrow and get on the bus and "give those girls a piece of her mind." I begged her not to do that; I can't imagine what would happen if she actually did that. It would be the worst thing ever, and I would never live that down. I know that I will think twice before I tell her anything like that again.

We are responsible for our own emotions and responses. As adults we have an increased ability to control our emotions and more sophisticated coping skills for managing anger or conflict. When girls feel like they have to censor themselves so they can regulate our emotions, we are not providing them a safe place to share their thoughts or experiences, nor are we providing them with good role modeling for how they can handle tough situations.

"You Just Telling Me Not to Do Something Is Going to Make Me Want to Do It More."

Adolescence is a time when girls seek to develop their own individual identities while they push the limits of adult authority. Girls seek to be independent but recognize that they also need and want caring adults in their lives. Girls can be curious and inquisitive and may want to try out new experiences and push the limits. They want to explore new things and new relationships, and they want to be relevant and accepted in their social circles. Have you ever heard something like "But Janelle's parents are letting her go; I don't get what the big deal is. No one else's parents care. This is so not fair"?

Adults have a tremendous need to protect the girls in their lives and often try to restrict and limit their behaviors for their own well-being and safety. Unfortunately, girls can internalize these limits as perceived challenges: "If you are not going to let me do something, I am going to figure out a way to actually do it." We are often drawn toward things that we perceive to be "off limits" and sometimes think, "If you tell me that I can't have it or can't do it, then I want to have it or do it even more." Developmentally, teenagers are right in that space. Pushing boundaries and limits is part of the adolescent experience.

Ninth grader Madison shared with me an experience about wanting to put blue-colored streaks in her hair. She said that her entire field hockey team was going to put semipermanent blue dye streaks in their hair for their upcoming championship game. When Madison talked to her mother about it, she said her mom "totally freaked out." Her mom said, "Absolutely not. You will not dye your hair. That's absolutely ridiculous." Madison asked her mom why she thought it was so stupid, and her mom said, "You have beautiful hair; don't you dare do anything to ruin that." Madison told me,

It was like she was totally missing the point. To tell the truth, up until that point I didn't really want to do it. I thought it looked kind of stupid, and I was secretly afraid that the blue would stay in my hair longer than I wanted it to. But as soon as my mom told me that I wasn't allowed to do it, I decided that I absolutely had to do it. So I figured out a way to stay at my friend's house that weekend so that we could both dye our hair together. My mom almost lost her mind when I came home that weekend. I thought it was really funny.

This is a more lighthearted example of how setting arbitrary limits can provoke an adolescent to push the boundaries and test the limits of authority. If the reaction of Madison's mother had been more moderate and they had an opportunity to talk out the situation, perhaps the response would have been different. What if Madison's mom had said, "Wow . . . blue hair! . . . Tell me how the girls came up with this plan"? At that point Madison wasn't really sold on the idea of dyeing her hair blue and probably would've said, "I'm not really sure about it. I think it looks kind of silly, but everybody else seems to be doing it." How different the reaction, and the ensuing response, may have been if this conversation had happened.

"Accept Us for Who We Are, and Don't Pressure Us to Be Different."

Girls tell me that they feel intense pressure from teachers, parents, and their peers. The pressure can be related to how they look, what they're good at, who their friends are, and how they perform academically. Girls feel like they are often compared with others and that they don't always measure up.

"Don't compare me to my sister or compare me to what you were doing at my age. Just compare me to me." Girls want to be valued and appreciated for who they individually are, not who they are in relation to other people. Girls don't want to feel like they have to live up to the achievements of their siblings or their parents. They want to be successful and accomplished for themselves and not always feel like they have something to prove to others. "I just want them to think that I am good enough like I am. I don't want everyone to think that I have to change or be something different to be okay in their eyes."

Helping girls identify their own unique strengths, abilities, and skills can help them realize that their own special talents are important. If everything that a girl accomplishes is viewed in comparison with the achievements of her siblings, her classmates, or her teammates, then she may constantly be trying to keep up with or compete with someone else. This message tells her that she, herself, is just not good enough but, rather, she has to be better than everyone else to be okay in our eyes:

> I feel so much pressure to be perfect. I have to get perfect grades, do perfect in sports, and even look perfect. I have to get into a good college, and I need to get an athletic or academic scholarship to be able to pay for it. I feel like if I mess one thing up that I am letting everyone down and disappointing my parents or my teachers. I hear my parents talk to other parents, and I realize that they are so proud of me, . . . but that makes me feel even more pressure. I have to do well so that my parents aren't embarrassed of me! There is nothing worse than hearing someone say that they are disappointed in you. I can deal with them being mad at me, but disappointed in me is totally different.
>
> —Jaylee, eleventh grade

Girls internalize the expectations that are communicated to them, and while we want to hold high expectations for girls, we need to be mindful of the ways girls may experience pressure. As adults it is easy to look at the lives of middle or high school students and yearn for those carefree days! As we look back, we think that we didn't have to worry about a thing—no mortgage or health insurance to worry about, no kids to take care of, no bills to pay. So what would teens actually have to worry about? In their minds, plenty!

The stress that teens feel is real. Their lives are full of things that legitimately stress them out. As Jaylee stated above, she feels that she is dealing with a lot of big issues and decisions. Comparing her issues with our adult issues only serves to minimize her experiences and her feelings. Lindsee, an eighth grader, said,

I was telling my dad that I was so stressed out trying to get good grades so that I could get into a good high school. He totally laughed at me and said that there was no way I could be stressed out. He said that I needed to wait until I had a job and a house and a family and then I would know what stress feels like.

How different Lindsee would have felt if her dad had said, "Honey, tell me what is stressing you out."

"Don't Be Up in Our Business All the Time. We Need Some Privacy and You Need to Trust Us More."

Girls desperately feel a need for privacy that generally begins around puberty and gets more intense as they progress through early and middle adolescence. Girls are trying to make sense of what is happening to their bodies while they are trying to navigate relationships with friends. They want to figure things out on their own and may be unlikely to feel that adults have much to offer in the way of guidance around these issues. Girls report having parents and teachers who are always "in their business" and are always trying to get information about where they are, who they're with, and what they're doing.

While adults recognize that this is part of monitoring teens and ensuring that they are doing the right things, girls see it as restrictive and intrusive:

> Sometimes I feel like adults always think that we're up to no good. That everything that we are doing is wrong or sneaky and that we're always doing something to get into trouble. Sometimes we just need time with other people our age, and we don't want adults to be around. There are lots of things that we can't talk about with our parents or our teachers, so we just need time to talk to our friends about some things.

> I have a friend whose mother is, like, totally in her business all the time. It's like she can't even get a text without her mom asking who is texting her. Her mom goes online and looks at all the phone numbers that she texts and keeps major tabs on her social media. She's not allowed to have a lock on her

bedroom door, and her mom just comes in and goes through her stuff whenever she wants. Every time I'm over there her mom always asks me all kinds of questions about our friends, and I sometimes feel nervous about talking to her. I know that my friend doesn't tell her mom very much anymore. She feels like everything that she talks about she's going to get in trouble for, so she figures she'll just leave lots of details out. Like last week we were going to hang out and meet up with some friends, but she told her mom that it was just going to be the two of us. I think sometimes it's easier to just leave information out than have to deal with getting in trouble. I guess it would be different if we were actually doing something to get in trouble but we're not. I just don't get why parents don't trust teenagers at all. It's not even like we've done anything to make them not trust us; they just don't, and it doesn't seem like there's anything that we can do about it.

It can be hard for adults to trust teenagers, particularly because adults were all teenagers once and know what they did during their teenage years. Some parents have said to me, "I know that I couldn't talk to my mom and dad growing up, and I don't want the same thing to happen for my daughter." Unfortunately, it seems that most teenage girls don't feel like their parents trust them and don't think that they can talk to them about serious issues, particularly as they get to the middle school years. Talking openly about issues of trust and how trust and respect are gained and lost is an important conversation that, unfortunately, does not happen with great frequency. Helping girls understand how they can demonstrate that they are trustworthy and respectful and treating them with the appropriate levels of trust and respect are important for maintaining an open and communicative relationship. When they perceive that the default position is that they are not trusted and not respected, then girls will retreat from the relationship and view it as more adversarial than supportive.

Girls Want to Be Taken Seriously

Too often adults think that girls' concerns and problems are immature and juvenile; however, to girls the issues that they're dealing with are serious and stressful. As we try to understand how girls are processing their experiences, we have to take into consideration their chronological and developmental levels. The adolescent brain is still developing, and girls' cognitive complexity is limited. Sometimes when we hear the issues that girls say are affecting their lives and the issues that they believe to be important, it is hard for us, as adults, to see them as legitimate concerns.

We easily question how girls can get so upset about things that seem silly or inconsequential. There are a couple reasons for this: (1) Adolescents are not able to process information and experiences the same way as adults can, and (2) adolescents have not had the experiences or frame of reference that adults have to manage emotional situations.

When girls are upset about friendships, dating, or school and we minimize their concerns, it reinforces to them that we don't understand their reality. Girls want their concerns to be taken seriously. When we listen to them express their concerns, we have to remember that we are looking at the situation from *our* point of view. This view probably includes many more years, many more friendships and relationships, and much more life experience. Our view also includes a fully developed brain and a much more sophisticated and cognitively complex way of thinking and reasoning. Part of how girls are making sense of their situation is based on their youthful biology—or their inability to think in abstract ways—as well as their experience and frame of reference. When we hear things that sound silly, unbelievable, or just plain immature, we have to remember that girls see the situation as serious and meaningful. Despite what we might be feeling or thinking on the inside, we must communicate care and concern to girls to show that we are seeking to understand their reality and what is happening to them at that moment.

All these identified themes lead to a breakdown in communication between adolescents and adults, and as we know, communication is crucial in any relationship, especially when trying to help the girls in our lives. As discussed in the previous chapters on girls' relationships with other girls, many girls do not come back to their relationships with their parents until much later in life, if at all. They simply find other individuals who seem to have an open mind about their experiences and who listen to them without judgment when they share their problems. Girls are not looking for friendships with the adults in their lives. They don't want their parents or their teachers to be their "best friends," but they do want these people to understand, believe, and respect them.

It is important to understand that it is okay if our daughters don't tell us everything that is going on in their lives at this very moment. Chances are that when they are ready, they will tell us what they need us to know about the tough situations in their lives, but we need to give them the space to do so. We demonstrate our understanding and respect for girls by taking the time to listen to what they're saying, connect with them in meaningful ways, and support them through their difficult challenges. When we give girls the ideal balance of space, privacy, trust, and respect, they tend to give the same balance back to us.

What Girls Need 13

Girls Need to Be the Experts on Their Own Lives

When we allow girls to be the experts on their own lives, we work to intentionally place them in a position of *knowing*. This means that when we talk to girls, we allow them to describe their experiences, their thoughts, and their perspectives to us, rather than telling them what these perspectives should be. In counseling we call this taking a "one-down" position. It means that we purposefully and intentionally approach the relationship or the conversation from a position of *not knowing* and give up some power to allow the other person to perceive that they have some control in the relationship (Vernon, 2009).

When adults and teenagers interact, there is always an inherent power differential. In almost every situation an adult has more power than a teenager. I am not talking about physical power but, rather, age and societal and interpersonal factors that can play into the dynamics of a relationship. There are many relationships that have an inherent power differential: teacher-student, principal-teacher, boss-employee, and parent-child. If we want to create environments and opportunities for others to feel safe and valued, we need to play an active role in mitigating that power differential.

This can start simply by deciding where we sit when we are talking to young girls. Do we stand over their desks while we ask them to explain themselves, or do we sit down next to them in a chair or at a desk of the same height? Do we sit behind our giant and intimidating desk in our big leather executive chair, or do we plop down on the floor and ensure that we are at the same relative height as the student? Physical proximity and physical placement have a lot to do with how people perceive power dynamics and authority. So part of taking this one-down position is placing yourself alongside the girl you're talking to. When we do this, we communicate to the girl that we are here alongside her and we are coming to the conversation from a place of equality rather than superiority.

Another aspect of taking a one-down position is to come to the conversation from a "not knowing" position. This means that we allow the girl to be the expert on her life and describe it to us. We seek to understand her reality by asking her to teach us about it. We might say things such as "Help me understand how this argument with your friend really feels" or "I don't really know much about field hockey; maybe you can teach me more about it" or "I don't think I have a good sense of how to use Snapchat; can you show me how to set it up?" Taking a one-down position is an intentional communication strategy that shifts the power dynamic in a relationship and provides the teenager the opportunity to be the expert on their life and perhaps even the expert in the conversation. It is an effective strategy for beginning to build rapport and provides a sense of safety and comfort to the girl.

Girls Need Adults to Communicate Openly

I was talking with a mother who is very concerned about the changing dynamics of her relationship with her 13-year-old daughter. She says that they've always had an open and communicative relationship; however, lately things feel like they're changing. She says she has a hard time talking to her daughter, and every time she asks questions, her daughter gives simple "yes" or "no" responses and then won't say any more. I asked her to share with me a little bit about some of the questions that she asks her daughter. The mom said,

> Every day when she comes home from school I ask her if she had a good day. My daughter will simply say, "Yeah, it was fine," and that will be the end of the conversation. I feel like I'm just not getting the same kind of conversation that I used to get even last year. Another example would be when my daughter comes home from a softball game and I know that they have won the game. I'll ask her, "Hey honey, how did the game go?" Depending on her mood, she'll say, "It was good" or "It was fine," and then that feels like the end of the conversation.

Often, closed questions such as these can lead to closed responses. For example, "Did you have a good day today?" can elicit a response that is either "yes" or "no." If we rephrase that question and instead say, "Tell me about your day," we create the opportunity to have a very different conversation. Granted the response could be "What do you want to know?" But it is more likely that this simple change in communication will open the lines of discussion further. If "Did you have a good game?" was changed to "Tell me all about the game," we provide a different opening to have a different kind of conversation.

Using open-ended questions is an effective communication strategy with teenagers and adults alike. It demonstrates that we are interested in what the other person has to say, and it gives them the option to decide what is important and what they want to share with us. Even a simple "Tell me about yourself" can elicit a disclosure from the person's own space. It allows them to decide what is important, what they want to tell us, and how they will share that with us. It can change the dynamic from a question-answer session to a more open, engaging, and rich conversation.

Girls Need Opportunities to Improve Their Confidence, Self-Esteem, and Self-Efficacy

In a survey I conducted with teachers I asked them what they thought girls need to be successful. Without fail the number one response that teachers gave was that girls need more self-confidence. When we asked girls the same question, they gave the exact same response. Self-esteem and self-confidence are related to almost every dimension of our lives. Self-concept is connected to our academic achievement, our career development, our friendships and relationships, and our leadership development. If we have a strong sense of ourselves, know what we are good at, and have confidence in our abilities, then we are more likely to try new things, take risks, and put ourselves out there in a way that we may not if we were constantly doubting or questioning ourselves. Girls who have more confidence make better decisions in nearly every aspect of their lives.

A strong sense of self is not something that we are all born with; rather, it develops based on our learnings and our interactions with others and our environment. If we have opportunities to explore and develop our skills on a consistent basis, we will be able to identify and develop the dimensions of ourselves that are strong and efficacious (Baldwin & Hoffman, 2002).

We want girls to have a positive *self-concept*, or *self-esteem*. These terms are generally interchangeable. They refer to the way we feel about ourselves and the regard we have for ourselves. Self-esteem develops through our childhood years and unfortunately drops during our adolescent years. The drop in self-esteem is greater for girls than for boys, and for many girls their self-esteem does not rebound after they progress through adolescence. We need to focus on how we help maintain young girls' confidence and how we rebuild the confidence of teens and young adults.

Another important term that is related to the way we feel about ourselves is *self-efficacy*. Self-efficacy is different from self-esteem or self-concept in that it is related to my perception of myself as competent in different areas. Whereas self-concept is related to how I feel about who I am, self-efficacy is related to what I *think* I can *do*. It is my sense of myself as capable and my perception of my ability to do something well.

Our goal should be to enhance both the self-esteem and the self-efficacy of girls, and we do this by providing girls opportunities where they experience themselves being successful, where they can build their confidence and their belief in themselves as capable, so that they become more willing to try new things in the future.

We do not build self-esteem in girls by telling them that they are smart and pretty. Compliments do not build confidence. Despite what we see in a lot of girls' self-esteem programming, merely telling girls how great they are does not affect the way they actually experience themselves. Building a stronger sense of self means that we believe that our value is internally derived. We have to actually feel it for ourselves to believe it about ourselves.

When I talk about enhancing girls' self-esteem, I often ask, "If I am not there every day to tell you that you are smart and beautiful and competent, do you experience yourself that way?" Our sense of ourselves has to come from our internal experience, not from another's perception of us. While girls are certainly subject to external pressures and influences, there is much that we can do to build their internal strength and fortitude. A middle school teacher shared the following story with me:

> I have a student, Lauren, in my eighth-grade class who is very shy but very smart. She gets great grades and is truly a self-regulated learner, but I feel like she lacks self-confidence. I notice that every time we do small-group activities as a class, she is never the leader or the spokesperson for her group, although I am fairly confident that she has done the bulk of the work for her group. It is almost like she gets lost in the class because she's not sure of herself. I think she has so much potential, but I feel like her lack of confidence could hold her back. I have a great relationship with her, and so I wanted my classroom to be a safe place for her to "break out of her shell." I started out by ensuring that I intentionally called on her when I knew she had the correct answer to a question. For example, after an exam the students get their tests back, and we review them as a class. Lauren generally does well on the exams, so I took note of her tests and what her strongest answers were; then in the review I made sure that she was called on to share at least one or two answers. She never volunteers on her own but is okay when she is

called on. This gave her the opportunity to share in front of the class and gave me the opportunity to publicly praise her accomplishments. I noticed that after a couple weeks of doing this, she began to raise her hand to volunteer when she had the correct answer. I must admit I was really excited when I began to see these small changes in her confidence! We moved on from there to speaking in front of the class and eventually to taking the lead in a small-group project. She rose to the occasion each time. It was like each time she realized that she could do it, she got more confident in her ability to actually do it.

We have to provide girls with opportunities to do things well. The "things" can be almost anything: communicating with friends, public speaking, making a campfire, shooting a basketball, changing a tire, standing up for themselves, writing code, cutting the grass, doing the dishes, completing a math equation, writing a poem, saying "no" to someone, competing in a science fair, or trying out for the choir. The numerous opportunities that we provide girls to allow them to develop a new set of skills and competencies are how we build their self-esteem, self-concept, and self-efficacy. Every opportunity that they engage in is an opportunity to build a set of skills.

Girls need to experience themselves as being good at a lot of things, but unfortunately, many of them do not. Next time you are with a girl, ask her to name five things that she is good at. You will be surprised to see that some girls can give you a list of many things they are good at while some have trouble coming up with just one. Girls need to find value in themselves that is not related to how they look but rather to who they are and what they're good at.

Girls Need Exposure to Realistic and Positive Female Role Models

"Girls just don't have anyone who they can look up to these days." I hear this from many adults who complain that there are no good role models for girls. In part, I can see how this is true. Girls see confusing images of women. On the one hand, there are more strong female characters on TV, in movies, and on social media than ever before and even female athletes who have become household names. On the other, there are lots of women who conflate sexuality with influence and make a confusing case for female power. One father told me,

> I can't stand reality television. There's nothing positive on TV these days for my daughter to watch. All I see are shows that glorify things like teenage pregnancy, partying and hooking up, and cat fighting. I think it can make girls feel like there is something wrong with them if they don't have some kind of crazy problem. These are not the kind of influences that I want to expose my daughter to, but it seems like that is all that is out there right now. Where are the strong role models and the positive influences? When do girls get to see images of people's lives that aren't so horrible or dramatic? Where are the women that we want our girls to grow up to be like? I just am not seeing that anywhere.

He's right; we need more strong, diverse female role models in all spaces. Not just in the media but everywhere. We need to expand our thinking of what a role model actually is. Role models do not need to be famous people, athletes, actresses, or movie stars. Role models can be regular people who do things well and who we admire. Our family members, teachers, coaches, and mentors can be role models. Arguably, exposure to these "real-life" role models has a more substantial impact on a girl's ability to see herself in a particular role than exposure to media stars or famous people, who are seemingly out of her reach.

Also, girls need role models who look like them. They need to be exposed to women who may have had a similar background or experience and who is someone they can relate to. Girls need to see people in a wide variety of jobs and careers. They need to see real women who get along with one another and support one other. They need to meet actual ladies who are athletes, community activists, businesswomen, or entrepreneurs. We need to broaden girls' horizons around what women *can* do and what women *actually* do. We want to give girls exposure to more of everything. More options, more occupations, more subjects, more culture, and overall more opportunity.

Where will we find these role models? Role models are women in our everyday lives. They are our colleagues, neighbors, friends, and associates. They are the people who have qualities and attributes that we want to emulate. A role model can be the neighbor girl next door who just got accepted into medical school. These women may not be perfect, but they have characteristics that are worthwhile and valuable for our girls to experience. In our research we asked girls to identify who their role models are and tell us why they selected a particular person. The girls' responses ranged from famous musicians to actresses, to teachers, to family members. Interestingly, more than any other response, the girls identified their mothers or another female family member as their primary role model. Girls see traits in these women that they want to develop for themselves, such as strength, the ability to multitask, caring, self-sufficiency, and reliability. We all know lots of women who have these kinds of characteristics.

Girls Need Specific Praise and Constructive Reinforcement

Girls need positive reinforcement and encouragement. They need to feel that someone is supporting them and cares about them. Reinforcement for girls has often taken the shape of complimenting girls on their clothes, hair, or physique. In general, girls receive more compliments about how they look than about what they do. As we work to shift this reality and focus our attention on the things that girls actually *do* well, we must ensure that our praise and reinforcement have the greatest impact.

Adults are eager to build up girls' self-confidence and self-esteem by providing them with positive reinforcement for being good, looking nice, and treating other people with respect. This type of praise—ongoing and general—does not actually have the impact on children that we would hope. When we reinforce kids for just "being great," we don't actually prepare them to do anything better. We actually prepare them instead to expect to receive ongoing praise for being great. Simply stated, ongoing general praise and consistent messages about how great or wonderful you are do little for improving how you feel about yourself. Instead, you become accustomed to everyone telling you how wonderful you are, and when you don't have that, you get upset (Bronson & Merryman, 2009).

When it comes to building self-esteem in an individual, what is most important is a person's internal sense of themselves. If our reinforcement comes from others' perceptions of our being "good enough," what happens when we don't have that on a consistent basis?

We need to praise girls for their *effort* versus praising them for being smart. Kids who think they are just generally smart often will not put out as much effort as kids who believe that their effort is connected to their achievement. Kids who become used to receiving praise learn to seek praise from adults and will actually take on fewer challenges because they are afraid to fail, afraid that they won't receive praise, or afraid that they won't be labeled as "smart" (Bronson & Merryman, 2009).

This is not to suggest, by any means, that girls should not be praised and reinforced for the things that they do. Rather, we want to ensure that we are providing them with *quality* compliments and praise. Praise needs to be specific and sincere and should provide the reinforcement that will have the greatest impact on a girl's perception, performance, and persistence.

Girls Need Us to Believe Them When They Tell Us Things That We May Not Want to Believe

Sometimes girls have a difficult time sharing things with adults because they are afraid that they won't be believed. Particularly if the issue is related to another adult, girls assume that we will always take the side of the other adult. Their experience also supports this idea. Often when teenagers complain about a parent, teacher, or coach, the response back to them from other adults is generally "Well, what did you do wrong to deserve that?" When girls feel like something is not fair or that they've been mistreated, and they share their concerns with us, we must be mindful of how we respond.

I was working with a tenth-grade girl, Emily, who shared with me her experience of sexual inappropriateness on the part of her brother's friend. She talked about him making comments about her body and also trying to touch her breasts and buttocks when he was hanging out with her brother. She said that this went on for several weeks and she kept telling him to stop. She told her brother also that this happened, and he just laughed it off and said, "Shut up! You probably like it." She finally decided to tell her parents what was happening, and their response was "Emily, we've known him for such a long time and have never seen him do anything like that before. He's such a nice kid, and he comes from such a good family. Why don't you just try keeping your distance if you don't like the attention?"

Emily was devastated after talking with her parents. She felt like she was not believed, and her parents made her feel that she was lying about the situation. Why would she lie about something so serious? Unfortunately, when it comes to issues of sexual boundary crossings and child sexual abuse, children are likely to tell several adults before somebody actually believes their story. Girls need to know that we believe them and that we will protect them.

Girls Need Us to Take Their Concerns Seriously and Not Minimize Their Experiences

As mentioned before, girls feel extremely frustrated and dismayed when adults do not take them seriously. Often, girls feel that their voices are unimportant, their opinions are devalued, and their contributions go unnoticed. We want to instill in girls at an early age that what they have to contribute is valuable and that we are interested in who they are and what they think. We want girls to know that we understand that their lives are intense and we respect their feelings. We may not be able to fully understand their feelings, but we have to respect how they feel.

Harper shared with me about feeling like nobody really understood what was going on for her:

> I have been really good friends with this one girl for about three years. When we started high school, she became very

different. She started to hang out with a different group of kids, and it seemed to me that our friendship was not as important to her as it used to be. We slowly started drifting apart, except that I kept trying to keep our friendship going. I would make plans to invite her to do things, I would get tickets for concerts and movies, and I would generally just look for opportunities for us to hang out. She would say things like "Oh okay, that's cool; let's do that." But then she wouldn't show up when it was time to go somewhere. I actually had to go to a concert by myself because she ditched me. This sort of stuff went on for about six months, and every time it happened my feelings would get really hurt. I kept a lot of it from my parents because I figured that everything would get smoothed out soon enough and I didn't want them to hold a grudge against her. But the day that she embarrassed me at school was like the hardest day ever. She totally called me out in front of a whole group of students and then laughed at me in front of, like, the whole cafeteria. I was talking to my mom about what happened, and she said to me, "I've been watching what's been happening with her for months, and I don't even know why you try to be friends with her. She's obviously not a very good friend, so why don't you just stop trying. You'll make new friends. You should just cut things off now before she keeps hurting you." You know, I get what my mom is saying, but it just didn't feel good to hear it from her. It made me feel like she had no idea what I was feeling and no sense of how much I was hurting. I just wanted her to understand that everything sucks, and I don't need her to fix it; I just need her to get it.

Adults can minimize lots of things in girls' lives, from relationships to school pressures, to puberty and periods. It is a really big deal when you are in the fourth, fifth, or sixth grade if you've gotten your period, or if you're the only one who *hasn't* gotten her period. Adults approach girls with a casual discomfort and air of humor and make comments about them "becoming a woman." Let's face it; no girl wants to hear that comment. We need to be sensitive to the fact that puberty is a really big deal. What your body looks like, what your hair looks like, and what your face looks like are all changing. We, as adults, have a hard time remembering the intensity of that experience. Instead of laughing it off when girls get their periods or have questions or concerns about what's happening to them, we need to provide them with support and good information.

Riley, a sixth-grade girl, narrated her experience talking to her mother about the fact that she had not yet gotten her period:

> I remember talking to my mom after I got home from a sleepover at my friend's house. There were three other girls there, and all of them had gotten their period last year except me. I wondered if something was wrong with me because they were all in the same grade as me and I was the only one left. I remember asking my mom a question about it, and she said, "You should be glad you haven't gotten your period yet; it's such a pain; you're going to hate it anyway." I think I wasn't just concerned about getting my period, but my friends also have boobs and look way more grown-up than I do. I feel like I look like a baby next to my friends, but I couldn't really tell my mom that. I felt stupid for even bringing it up.

Girls Need Help in Learning How to Establish Healthy Boundaries

There are many aspects of a girl's life where she needs to learn how to set boundaries and communicate those boundaries to others. We want girls to have control over their experiences, bodies, relationships, academics, and careers. We want girls to believe that they have the right and the ability to stand up for themselves, their values, and their bodies if they don't agree with something or feel that they are being taken advantage of.

One of the hardest things about defining boundaries and communicating them means that you're telling somebody else, "No," or telling them something that they don't want to hear. This can be very difficult for girls and adults alike. Establishing boundaries means that you are setting guidelines around how you are willing to be treated by others and what access you allow other people in the world to have to you. Healthy boundaries mean that we ourselves get to decide what is okay with us and what is not. We put some insulation between us and the world in order to keep ourselves safe.

Defining boundaries can be difficult for girls, and in many ways girls lack adequate role models of healthy and appropriate boundaries from the adults in their lives. I am thinking about the impact of social media and how that has created blurred boundaries for many of us. In earlier times what we were thinking, wearing, and eating, and even where we were, was our personal information that perhaps only a few people knew. Now everyone in our "friend" or "follower" network has a lot of information about what we are doing at any given time. How do we tell girls to set boundaries around information that they share with others when, as adults, we are not doing a very good job of that ourselves?

Girls also need to learn how to establish boundaries around their body and dating. Girls need conversations about what is okay and what is not okay with them when it comes to dating. Girls need opportunities to practice verbalizing their boundaries before they find themselves in situations where they need to impose these limits.

Girls Need Hope for the Future

Finally, girls need hope for their future and to know that we believe in them. We want to help girls see beyond their current circumstances or situation, no matter how difficult, and envision a rich and fulfilling life for themselves. We know that girls' experiences can be very different and their lives can be full of difficulty and chaos, but girls are very resilient and possess the internal fortitude to rise above the situations they find themselves in to ultimately construct a life that they love.

Girls need to know that they can be anything they want to be, but we have to support them to achieve these goals and prepare them for what they might face on their journey to realize their aspirations. We want girls to have access to the widest range of possibilities and options for their lives. We want girls to love being girls, not because they can wear dresses and get their hair done but, rather, because being a girl means that they can be anything they want to be, do anything they want to do, and go anywhere they want to go. We want them to understand that being a girl does not mean that you're limited in any way but, rather, that you are full of possibilities. Our role is to help girls see their own potential and to help them see the strengths in themselves that they have difficulty identifying. We want girls to find value in themselves so they can add value to the world.

References

American Association of University Women Educational Foundation. (2011). *Crossing the line: Sexual harassment at school.* https://www.aauw.org/app/uploads/2020/03/Crossing-the-Line-Sexual-Harassment-at-School.pdf

American Association of University Women Educational Foundation. (2016). *Barriers and bias: The status of women in leadership.* https://www.aauw.org/resources/research/barrier-bias/

American Association of University Women Educational Foundation. (2019). *The simple truth about the gender pay gap.* https://www.aauw.org/resources/research/simple-truth/

Anderson, M., & Jiang, J. (2018). *Teens, social media and technology 2018.* Pew Research Center.

Armitage, C. (2012). Evidence that self-affirmation reduces body dissatisfaction by basing self-esteem on domains other than body weight and shape. *Journal of Child Psychology and Psychiatry, 53*(1), 81–88. https://doi.org/10.1111/j.1469-7610.2011.02442.x

Baldwin, S. A., & Hoffmann, J. P. (2002). The dynamics of self-esteem: A growth-curve analysis. *Journal of Youth Adolescence, 31*(2), 101–113. https://doi.org/10.1023/A:1014065825598

Basile, K., Smith, S., Breiding, M., Black, M., & Mahendra, R. (2014). *Sexual violence surveillance: Uniform definitions and recommended data elements* (Version 2.0). Centers for Disease Control and Prevention, National Center for Injury Prevention and Control.

Bernard, B. (1993). Fostering resiliency in kids. *Educational Leadership, 51*(3), 44–48.

Bronson, P., & Merryman, A. (2009). *NurtureShock: New thinking about children.* Hachette Book Group.

Brown, L. M. (1998). *Raising their voices: The politics of girls' anger.* Harvard University Press.

Brown, L. M. (2003). *Girlfighting: Betrayal and rejection among girls.* New York University Press.

CARE. (2009). *"The Power to Lead: A leadership model for adolescent girls.* https://care.org/wp-content/uploads/2020/05/GE-2009-PW_ Leadership.pdf

Catalyst. (2007, July 15). *The double-bind dilemma for women in leadership: Damned if you do, doomed if you don't.* https://www .catalyst.org/research/infographic-the-double-bind-dilemma- for-women-in-leadership/

Centers for Disease Control and Prevention. (2012, June 8). *Youth risk behavior surveillance: United States 2011* (Surveillance Summaries). https://www.cdc.gov/mmwr/preview/mmwrhtml/ ss6104a1.htm

Centers for Disease Control and Prevention. (2015). *Intimate partner violence surveillance: Uniform definitions and recommended data elements.* https://www.cdc.gov/violenceprevention/pdf/ipv/ intimatepartnerviolence.pdf?mod=article_inline

Chesler, P. (2009). *Women's inhumanity to women.* Lawrence Hill Books.

Child Welfare Information Gateway. (2012). *Sexual abuse indicators* [online]. U.S. Department of Health and Human Services, Administration for Children and Families.

Crick, N. R., & Grotpeter, J. K. (2005). Relational aggression, gender, and social-psychological adjustment. In M. Gauvain & M. Cole (Eds.), *Readings on the development of children* (4th ed.). Worth.

Crowley, B. Z., Datta, P., Stohlman, S., Cornell, D., & Konold, T. (2019). Authoritative school climate and sexual harassment: A cross-sectional multilevel analysis of student self-reports. *School Psychology, 34*(5), 469–478. https://doi.org/10.1037/spq0000303

Curran, T., & Hill, A. (2019). Perfectionism is increasing over time: A meta-analysis of birth cohort differences from 1989 to 2016. *Psychological Bulletin, 145*(4), 410–429. http://dx.doi .org/10.1037/bul0000138

Damour, L. (2019). *Under pressure: Confronting the epidemic of stress and anxiety in girls.* Ballentine Books.

D'Antona, R., Kevorkian, M., & Russom, A. (2010). Sexting, texting, cyberbullying and keeping youth safe online. *Journal of Social Sciences, 6*(4), 521–526. https://doi.org/10.3844/jssp.2010.523.528

Davies, J. (2017, March). Female Instagram users get 5× more likes than men. *Digital Marketing Magazine.* https://digitalmarketingmagazine.co.uk/social-media-marketing/female-instagram-users-get-5x-more-likes-than-men/4209

Davis-Keane, P. E. (2005). The influence of parent education and family income on child achievement: The indirect role of parental expectations and the home environment. *Journal of Family Psychology, 19*(2), 294–304. https://doi.org/10.1037/0893-3200.19.2.294

Dichter, M. E., Cederbaum, J. A., & Teitelman, A. M. (2010). The gendering of violence in intimate relationships: How violence makes sex less safe for girls. In M. Chesney-Lind & N. Jones (Eds.), *Fighting for girls: New perspectives on gender and violence* (pp. 83–106). SUNY Press.

Dweck, C. S. (2006). *Mindset: The new psychology of success.* Random House.

Eliot, L. (2009). *Pink brain, blue brain: How small differences grow into troublesome gaps—and what we can do about it.* Houghton Mifflin Harcourt.

Englander, E. (2015). Coerced sexting and revenge porn among teens. *Bullying, Teen Aggression & Social Media, 1*(2), 19–21.

Ford, H. H., Schindler, C. B., & Medway, F. J. (2001). School professionals' attributions of blame for child sexual abuse. *Journal of School Psychology, 39*(1), 25–44. https://doi.org/10.1016/S0022-4405(00)00058-3

Gartner, R. E., & Sterzing, P. R. (2016). Gender microaggressions as a gateway to sexual harassment and sexual assault. *Affilia, 31*(4), 491–503. https://doi.org/10.1177/0886109916654732

Gilligan, C. (1982). *In a different voice: Psychological theory and women's development.* Harvard University Press.

Girl Scouts USA. (2008). *Change it up! What girls say about redefining leadership.* Girl Scout Research Institute.

Gottfredson, L. (1997). Assessing gender-based circumscription of occupational aspirations. *Journal of Career Assessment, 5*(4), 419–441. https://doi.org/10.1177/106907279700500404

Gottfredson, L. (2002). Gottfredson's theory of circumscription, compromise, and self-creation. In D. Brown (Ed.), *Career choice and development* (4th ed., pp. 85–148). Jossey-Bass.

Grotpeter, J. K., & Crick, N. R. (1996). Relational aggression, overt aggression, and friendship. *Child Development, 67*(5), 2328–2338. https://doi.org/10.2307/1131626

Haimovitz, K., & Dweck, C. (2016). Parents' views of failure predict children's fixed and growth intelligence mindsets. *Psychological Science, 27*(6), 859–869. https://doi.org/10.1177/0956797616639727

Hewitt, P., & Flett, G. (2004). *Multidimensional Perfectionism Scale (MPS): Technical manual.* Multi-Health Systems.

Hewitt, P., Flett, G., & Mikail, S. (2017). *Perfectionism: A relational approach to conceptualization, assessment, and treatment.* Guilford Press.

Hinkelman, L. (2017). *The Girls' Index: New insights into the complex world of today's girls.* Ruling Our Experiences.

Hinkelman, L., & Bruno, M. (2008). The identification and reporting of child sexual abuse: The role of elementary school professionals. *Elementary School Journal, 108*(5), 376–391. https://doi.org/10.1086/589468

Hinkelman, L., & Sears, S. (2009). *SASS-E Girlz: Giving girls the skills, attitudes, smarts, and science for engineering* (SASS-E Girlz Lesson Plan Package). Society of Women Engineers.

Kaukinen, C., Gover, A. R., & Hartman, J. L. (2011). College women's experiences of dating violence in casual and exclusive relationships. *American Journal of Criminal Justice, 37*(2), 146–162. https://doi.org/10.1007/s12103-011-9113-7

Knobloch-Westerwick, S., & Crane, J. (2012). A losing battle: Effects of prolonged exposure to thin ideal images on dieting and body satisfaction. *Communication Research, 39*(1), 79–102. https://doi.org/10.1177/0093650211400596

Kutob, R. M., Senf, J. H., Crago, M., & Shisslak, C. M. (2010). Concurrent and longitudinal predictors of self-esteem in elementary and middle school girls. *Journal of School Health*, *80*(5), 240–248. https://doi.org/10.1111/j.1746-1561.2010.00496.x

Larsson, I., & Svedin, C. (2002). Sexual experiences in childhood: Young adults' recollections. *Archives of Sexual Behavior*, *31*(3), 263–273. https://doi.org/10.1023/A:1015252903931

Leaper, C., & Brown, C. (2008). Perceived experiences with sexism among adolescent girls. *Child Development*, *79*(3), 685–704. https://doi.org/10.1111/j.1467-8624.2008.01151.x

Leaper, C., Farkas, T., & Brown, C. S. (2012). Adolescent girls' experiences and gender-related beliefs in relation to their motivation in math/science and English. *Journal of Youth and Adolescence*, *41*(3), 269–282. https://doi.org/10.1007/s10964-011-9693-z

Lenhart, A., Smith, A., & Anderson, M. (2015). *Teens, technology and romantic relationships.* Pew Research Center.

Lipkins, S., Levy, J., & Jerabkova, B. (2010). *Sexting . . . is it all about power?* Real Psychology. https://www.realpsychology.com/sextingis-it-all-about-power

Lippman, J., & Campbell, S. (2014). Damned if you do, damned if you don't . . . if you're a girl: Relational and normative contexts of adolescent sexting in the United States. *Journal of Children and Media*, *8*(4), 371–386. https://doi.org/10.1080/17482798.2014.923009

Madsen, S. (2008). *On becoming a woman leader: Learning from the experiences of university presidents.* Jossey-Bass.

McAlinden, A. M. (2006). "Setting 'em up": Personal, familial and institutional grooming in the sexual abuse of children. *Social Legal Studies*, *15*(3), 339–362. https://doi.org/10.1177/0964663906066613

Merrell, K. M., Buchanan, R., & Tran, O. K. (2006). Relational aggression in children and adolescents: A review with implications for school settings. *Psychology in the Schools*, *43*(3), 345–360. https://doi.org/10.1002/pits.20145

Morrison-Breedy, D., & Grove, L. (2018). Adolescent girls' experiences with sexual pressure, coercion, and victimization: #MeToo. *Worldviews in Evidence-Based Nursing*, *15*(3), 225–229. https://doi.org/10.1111/wvn.12293

Ms. Foundation for Women. (2002). *The new girls' movement: Charting the path.* The Collaborative Fund for Healthy Girls/Healthy Women Project.

Nadal, K. L. (2014). A guide to responding to microaggressions. *CUNY Forum, 2*(1), 71–76.

National Science Foundation. (2003, August 20). *New formulas for America's workforce: Girls in science and engineering.* https://www.nsf.gov/pubs/2003/nsf03207/nsf03207.pdf

Nelson, A., & Brown, C. (2019). Too pretty for homework: Sexualized gender stereotypes predict academic attitudes for gender-typical early adolescent girls. *Journal of Early Adolescence, 39*(4), 603–617. https://doi.org/10.1177/0272431618776132

Office for Civil Rights, U.S. Department of Education. (2010, October 26). *Dear colleague letter.* Office of the Assistant Secretary. https://www2.ed.gov/about/offices/list/ocr/letters/colleague-201010_pg6.html

Orienstein, P. (2012). *Cinderella ate my daughter: Dispatches from the front lines of the new girlie-girl culture.* Harper Paperbacks.

Packard, B. W., & Nguyen, D. (2003). Science career-related possible selves of adolescent girls: A longitudinal study. *Journal of Career Development, 29*(4), 251–263. https://doi.org/10.1177/089484530302900403

Patchin, J. W., & Hinduja, S. (2012). *Cyberbullying prevention and response: Expert perspectives.* Routledge. https://doi.org/10.4324/9780203818312

Raby, R., & Pomerantz, S. (2013). Playing it down/playing it up: Girls' strategic negotiations of academic success. *British Journal of Sociology of Education, 36*(4), 1–19. https://doi.org/10.1080/01425692.2013.836056

Raskausas, J., & Stoltz, A. D. (2004). Identifying and intervening in relational aggression. *Journal of School Nursing, 20*(4), 209–215. https://doi.org/10.1177/10598405040200040501

Remillard, A., & Lamb, S. (2005). Adolescent girls' coping with relational aggression. *Sex Roles, 53*(3–4), 221–229. https://doi.org/10.1007/s11199-005-5680-8

Salomon, I., & Brown, C. S. (2019). The selfie generation: Examining the relationship between social media use and early adolescent body image. *Journal of Early Adolescence, 39*(4), 539–560. https://doi.org/10.1177/0272431618770809

Simmons, R. (2009). *The curse of the good girl: Raising authentic girls with courage and confidence.* Penguin Press.

Skelton, C., Francis, B., & Read, B. (2010). "Brains before 'beauty'?" High achieving girls, school, and gender identities. *Educational Studies, 36*(2), 185–194. https://doi.org/10.1080/03055690903162366

Smith, M., Saklofske, D., Stoeber, J., & Sherry, S. (2016). The Big Three Perfectionism Scale: A new measure of perfectionism. *Assessment, 34*(7), 670–687. https://doi.org/10.1177/0734282916651539

Smith, P. H., White, J. W., & Holland, L. J. (2003). A longitudinal perspective on dating violence among adolescent and college-age women. *American Journal of Public Health, 93*(7), 1104–1109. https://doi.org/10.2105/AJPH.93.7.1104

Spencer, R., Walsh, J., Liang, B., Mousseau, A., & Lund, T. (2018). Having it all? A qualitative examination of affluent adolescent girls' perceptions of stress and their quests for success. *Journal of Adolescent Research, 33*(1), 3–33. https://doi.org/10.1177/0743558416670990

Stone, E., Spears Brown, C., & Jewell, J. (2015). The sexualized girl: A within-gender stereotype among elementary school children. *Child Development, 86*(5) 1604–1622. https://doi.org/10.1111/cdev.12405

Twenge, J. M., Martin, G. N., & Campbell, W. K. (2018). Decreases in psychological well-being among American adolescents after 2012 and links to screen time during the rise of smartphone technology. *Emotion, 18*(6), 765–780. https://doi.org/10.1037/emo0000403

U.S. Department of Justice. (2000, July). *Sexual assault of young children as reported to law enforcement: Victim, incident, and offender characteristics.* https://www.bjs.gov/content/pub/pdf/saycrle.pdf

Verhaeghe, P. (2014). *What about me? The struggle for identity in a market-based society.* Scribe.

Veronneau, M., & Dishion, T. J. (2011). Middle school friendships and academic achievement in early adolescence: A longitudinal analysis. *Journal of Early Adolescence, 31*(1), 99–124. https://doi.org/10.1177/0272431610384485

Vernon, A. (2009). *Counseling children and adolescents* (4th ed.). Love.

Weissbourd, R. (2016). *Leaning out: Teen girls and leadership bias* (Making Caring Common Project). Harvard Graduate School of Education.

Weissbourd, R., Anderson, T., Cashin, A., & McIntyre, J. (2017, May). *The talk: How adults can promote young people's healthy relationships and prevent misogyny and sexual harassment* (Making Caring Common Project). Harvard Graduate School of Education. https://mcc.gse.harvard.edu/thetalk.

Werner, N. E., & Grant, S. (2009). Mothers' cognitions about relational aggression: Associations with discipline responses, children's normative beliefs, and peer competence. *Social Development, 18*, 77–98. https://doi.org/10.1111/j.1467-9507.2008.00482.x

Wigfield, A., Battle, A., Keller, L. B., & Eccles, J. S. (2002). Sex differences in motivation, self-concept, career aspiration, and career choice: Implications for cognitive development. In A. V. McGillicuddy-De Lisi & R. De Lisi (Eds.), *Biology, society, and behavior: The development of sex differences in cognition* (pp. 93–124). Ablex.

Young, E. L., Boye, A. E., & Nelson, D. A. (2006). Relational aggression: Understanding, identifying, and responding in schools. *Psychology in the Schools, 43*(3), 297–312. https://doi.org/10.1002/pits.20148

Index

A SAGE Publishing Company

Helping educators make the greatest impact

CORWIN HAS ONE MISSION: to enhance education through intentional professional learning.

We build long-term relationships with our authors, educators, clients, and associations who partner with us to develop and continuously improve the best evidence-based practices that establish and support lifelong learning.

Solutions YOU WANT | Experts YOU TRUST | Results YOU NEED

EVENTS

>>> **INSTITUTES**

Corwin Institutes provide large regional events where educators collaborate with peers and learn from industry experts. Prepare to be recharged and motivated!

corwin.com/institutes

ON-SITE PD

>>> **ON-SITE PROFESSIONAL LEARNING**

Corwin on-site PD is delivered through high-energy keynotes, practical workshops, and custom coaching services designed to support knowledge development and implementation.

corwin.com/pd

>>> **PROFESSIONAL DEVELOPMENT RESOURCE CENTER**

The PD Resource Center provides school and district PD facilitators with the tools and resources needed to deliver effective PD.

corwin.com/pdrc

ONLINE

>>> **ADVANCE**

Designed for K–12 teachers, Advance offers a range of online learning options that can qualify for graduate-level credit and apply toward license renewal.

corwin.com/advance

Contact a PD Advisor at (800) 831-6640 or visit www.corwin.com for more information